David Lodge and the Tradition of the Modern Novel

DAVID LODGE

and the Tradition of the Modern Novel

J. RUSSELL PERKIN

McGill-Queen's University Press
Montreal & Kingston • London • Ithaca

ISBN 978-0-7735-4319-5 (cloth)
ISBN 978-0-7735-4320-1 (paper)
ISBN 978-0-7735-9179-0 (ePDF)
ISBN 978-0-7735-9180-6 (ePUB)

Legal deposit second quarter 2014
Bibliothèque nationale du Québec

Printed in Canada on acid-free paper that is 100% ancient forest free (100% post-consumer recycled), processed chlorine free

This book has been published with the help of a grant from the Canadian Federation for the Humanities and Social Sciences, through the Awards to Scholarly Publications Program, using funds provided by the Social Sciences and Humanities Research Council of Canada.

McGill-Queen's University Press acknowledges the support of the Canada Council for the Arts for our publishing program. We also acknowledge the financial support of the Government of Canada through the Canada Book Fund for our publishing activities.

Library and Archives Canada Cataloguing in Publication

Perkin, J. Russell (James Russell), author
David Lodge : and the tradition of the modern novel / J. Russell Perkin.

Includes bibliographical references and index.
Issued in print and electronic formats.
ISBN 978-0-7735-4319-5 (bound). – ISBN 978-0-7735-4320-1 (pbk.)
ISBN 978-0-7735-9179-0 (ePDF). – ISBN 978-0-7735-9180-6 (ePUB)

1. Lodge, David, 1935– – Criticism and interpretation. I. Title.

PR6062.036Z65 2014 823'.914 C2013-907091-5
C2013-907092-3

This book was designed and typeset by studio oneonone in Sabon 10.2/13

Frontispiece: Courtesy of Daniele Roberts

To Deborah

Contents

Acknowledgments

I would like to begin by expressing my thanks to David Lodge for writing the marvellously varied novels that are the subject of this book and for writing the criticism that so helpfully maps the territory of modern fiction. I am also grateful to him for kindly granting me permission to obtain a copy of his MA thesis on the Catholic novel.

I was introduced to Lodge's work by David Baron, in whose undergraduate classes on modern literature at Acadia University I first read many of the authors discussed in this book. It is a pleasure to be able to acknowledge David's fine teaching. I am also indebted to the many students whom I in my turn have taught in classes on the novel, on modern literature, and on literature and the Catholic tradition; their enthusiastic reaction to Lodge's fiction reinforces my sense of its importance and value.

For conversations about modern literature and for general encouragement, I am indebted to Stephen Cloutier, Michael DiSanto, Margaret Anne Doody, and David Heckerl. I am particularly grateful to David Heckerl for sharing his knowledge and understanding of the liberal tradition. Zachary Leader provided me with a valuable bibliographical reference. My father, James Perkin, took a supportive interest in this book from the beginning, and saved me from several errors of historical fact. I am also very grateful to him for giving me his collection of the novels of Graham Greene. I remember these books as occupying a significant place on the bookshelf while I was growing up, and it is perhaps to them that I can trace the origin of my interest in modern British literature.

I wish to acknowledge the role of Saint Mary's University in supporting this book. I received several research grants from the Faculty of Graduate Studies and Research, which facilitated travel and the hiring of two energetic research assistants, Tony Amoud in the initial stages of my investigation and Emily Pitts during the concluding phase. And as always, I am indebted to the excellent librarians and library staff of the Patrick Power Library.

The readers for McGill-Queen's University Press made some suggestions that were very helpful to me in clarifying my argument. Mark Abley has been all that a writer could ask for in an editor.

This book results from a suggestion made by my wife, Deborah Kennedy, and it has benefitted greatly from her advice and encouragement, and from the example of her devotion to the life of letters. The dedication is an acknowledgement of this, and of so much more.

Warburg, reprinted by permission of The Random House Group Limited. *Paradise News*, published by Secker and Warburg, © 1992 David Lodge, reprinted by permission of The Random House Group Limited and Viking Penguin, a division of Penguin Group (USA) LLC. *The Picturegoers*, published by MacGibbon and Kee, reprinted by permission of The Random House Group Limited. *Small World*, published by Secker and Warburg, © 1984 David Lodge, reprinted by permission of The Random House Group Limited and Viking Penguin, a division of Penguin Group (USA) LLC. *Therapy*, published by Secker and Warburg, © 1995 David Lodge, reprinted by permission of The Random House Group Limited and Viking Penguin, a division of Penguin Group (USA) LLC. *Thinks...*, published by Secker and Warburg, © 2001 David Lodge, reprinted by permission of The Random House Group Limited and Viking Penguin, a division of Penguin Group (USA) LLC. *Write On*, published by Secker and Warburg, reprinted by permission of The Random House Group Limited. *The Year of Henry James*, published by Harvill Secker, reprinted by permission of The Random House Group Limited and David Lodge. "MCMXIV" and "This Be The Verse" from *Collected Poems* by Philip Larkin, © 1988, 2003 Estate of Philip Larkin, reprinted by permission of Faber and Faber Ltd. and Farrar, Straus and Giroux, LLC.

David Lodge and the Tradition of the Modern Novel

Multiple Lodge
~James Joyce, *Finnegans Wake*

Really, universally, relations stop nowhere, and the exquisite problem of the artist is eternally but to draw, by a geometry of his own, the circle within which they shall happily *appear* to do so.
~Henry James, Preface to *Roderick Hudson*

If critics need a canon, novelists need a tradition.
~David Lodge, "The Novel Now: Theories and Practices"

1

The Liberalism of David Lodge

> I would regard myself as a liberal, and in some ways a rather secular kind of liberal in spite of the fact that I'm a Catholic – I'm not the kind who wishes to persuade other people to accept his Catholic beliefs.
>
> ~David Lodge, interview with John Haffenden

When David Lodge published his fourteenth novel, *A Man of Parts*, in the spring of 2011, he had been part of the British literary scene for just over fifty years. He is known above all for his academic novels, which brought him to international prominence in the 1980s. During that decade he was equally prominent as a literary theorist who mediated between continental theory and the more empirically oriented English approach to criticism. Lodge can also be regarded as a Catholic novelist, working in a twentieth-century tradition that includes Evelyn Waugh, Graham Greene, and Muriel Spark. A third aspect of his fictional oeuvre is his identity as a comic novelist, for he is an heir of Henry Fielding, H.G. Wells, and Kingsley Amis, highlighting as they do the comedy of sexuality and of social class. Lodge is a writer who continues to develop and surprise, and from the early 1990s he has followed another of his mentors, Henry James, by writing a number of works focussing on the ironies and anxieties of the lives of authors. Among these works are two historical novels, which are part of a recent renaissance of this literary subgenre. As both a respected and popular author, David Lodge is worthy of critical attention in his own right; his career is moreover an excellent vehicle for the investigation of many of the trends, themes, and issues involved in post-1945 British fiction.

Lodge's work is frequently mentioned not only in academic circles, where he is a favourite point of reference, but in literary and other forms of journalism.[1] He often writes in the British press and in the

New York Review of Books, and he regularly appears at literary festivals. It is a further sign of his popularity that some of his characters and phrases have floated free of their context to become part of the general currency of contemporary culture, for example his pair of opposed professors of English, the brashly American Morris Zapp and the very British Philip Swallow.[2] In the world of the literary imagination, the map of England includes the city of Rummidge, the setting for several of Lodge's novels. Rummidge, he explains in the author's note that precedes *Small World*, "is not Birmingham, though it owes something to popular prejudices about that city" (n.p.). Academics often refer to the party game "Humiliation," invented by Philip Swallow in *Changing Places* (135–7); in this game, the participants earn points by revealing the major literary works that they have *not* read. Lodge has given his own special resonance to the common phrases "changing places" and "small world," while Mark Lawson has noted the way that David Lodge is now inextricably associated with the British Museum in the popular imagination, thanks to his comic novel *The British Museum Is Falling Down* ("Introduction," v).

Despite his popularity, or perhaps in part because of it, Lodge has not received as much attention from academic literary critics as have some of his contemporaries, a deficit I hope this book will help to correct. He may not be taken as seriously as some other writers owing to the comic dimension of many of his novels, and also to the nature of their comedy, which is gentle rather than dark. Lodge was prophetic of this response to his own fiction when he wrote in an early critical study of Graham Greene, "It is difficult not to see behind a good deal of the hostile comment on Greene a certain academic suspicion of the popularly successful writer" (*Graham Greene*, 3). There are also some other factors which might have an influence on literary judgment. Lodge has never won the Man Booker Prize, an award that looms large in the literary world, although both *Small World* and *Nice Work* were nominated for it. He has won other prizes, including the Whitbread Book of the Year award in 1980 for *How Far Can You Go?*[3] *Small World* and *Nice Work* were adapted into successful television miniseries, but none of Lodge's books has to date been made into a motion picture, thereby establishing itself as his defining work in the way that, for example, *The Remains of the Day* has come to define Kazuo Ishiguro or *Possession* A.S. Byatt. Both of these novels, like Ian McEwan's *Atonement*, were made into successful films; this is not necessarily, of course, any reflection of literary merit, but film adaptation has nevertheless come to play a role in the construction of a writer's reputation. In the world of contemporary fiction, value is a volatile commodity, not yet tested by the passage of the century that Samuel Johnson, following Horace, regarded as the period necessary to establish literary merit (Preface, 321).

My impression is that Lodge is regarded more highly by fellow writers than by academic critics. He has reviewed many leading contemporary authors, such as Muriel Spark, J.M. Coetzee, and Julian Barnes, in prestigious dailies or reviews such as the *New York Review of Books*, while being reviewed in equally visible places by writers such as John Banville, Christopher Hitchens, Joyce Carol Oates, and Hilary Mantel. Anthony Burgess said in the course of a review of *Nice Work* in 1988 that it "confirms David Lodge's right to be taken very seriously indeed as one of the best novelists of his generation" ("Coketown in the 80s"). To take the testimony of another major literary figure, Jerzy Jarniewicz reports that Czeslaw Milosz exempted Lodge from his criticism of the "nihilism" of Western literature, characterizing Lodge's work as "frivolous, but at the same time morally serious" ("Interview," 48). The poet and critic Craig Raine has a very high opinion of Lodge's work, and he describes *How Far Can You Go?* as "one of the great post-war novels" (qtd. in Wroe, "Seriously Funny").

The primary goal of this critical study is to elucidate what I see as the central underlying and unifying feature of Lodge's oeuvre, the dialogue of his novels with the tradition of British fiction, in ways that are often highly self-conscious. Lodge's transactions with the literary tradition, and his recurrent struggles against strong precursors, make him a writer who could be described more than most as having an intertextual imagination. He writes about a recognizable world in a manner that owes much to classic realism, and at the same time is very aware of the role of literary language in mediating reality, and he represents the world through a texture of different voices.

Lodge was born in 1935, just too late to have been part of the "angry generation" of the 1950s, epitomized by the figure of Kingsley Amis, about whom he has written very perceptively. On the other hand, Lodge's age as well as his partial allegiance to the neo-realist aesthetic of the 1950s has marked him off from the generation of writers who came to prominence in the 1980s, such as Julian Barnes, Ian McEwan, Graham Swift, and Salman Rushdie. An interesting figure for comparison is Margaret Drabble, his near contemporary, and she will form a useful point of reference at various points in this study. Drabble was born a mere four years after Lodge, though she became popular with the reading public earlier than he did, and they are sometimes bracketed together as examples of "middlebrow" writers, too popular to be really serious.[4]

As an academic critic and literary theorist who has written many reviews and other forms of journalism, Lodge has had a long immersion in and involvement with the tradition of fiction from Fielding and Richardson in the 1740s to the present, and he has engaged with it not only in his criticism and journalism but in his fiction. Thus it seems to me that he is most appropriately regarded as a novelist-critic, a type of writer with a distinguished lineage. From Fielding's prefaces and prefatory chapters through Thackeray's parodies and authorial asides to the essays and prefaces of Henry James, there is a powerful tradition of British novelist-critics, writers of fiction whose critical utterances have shaped the way that we read both their own fiction and the works of others, and who have contributed significantly to the Anglo-American tradition of narratology. James's prefaces were systematized by Percy Lubbock in *The Craft of Fiction* (1921), and both James and Lubbock are presences in E.M. Forster's *Aspects of the Novel* (1927), one of the central texts in the tradition I am describing. I would argue that Lodge should be seen as another major figure in this tradition, and that this is the best context in which to do justice to his achievement. By virtue of his interest in narrative poetics and in the language of fiction, Lodge is a successor to James, a writer of great interest to him and the subject of my fifth chapter. By virtue of his liberal temperament and his dialogical imagination, Lodge has numerous affinities with Forster, on whom he has also written, and to whom he pays homage in *Nice Work*. Viewed in this way, I think Lodge's achievement seems more substantial than it does if he is regarded more narrowly simply as a novelist.

While the aims and methodology of this book are primarily explanatory and interpretive, there is a further evaluative argument, which for the most part will be left implicit, for I hope that the book provides good reasons for accepting the verdict of Milosz, Raine, and Burgess that in addition to being a very popular novelist, David Lodge is a major figure within the horizon of British literature of the post-1945 period. Finally, beyond the elucidation of Lodge's fiction, and its relationship with the tradition of the modern novel, this study aims to make a contribution to the literary history of the post-war period.

Lodge is profoundly enmeshed in the texture of twentieth-century British literature as a critic, a teacher, a literary journalist, a writer for television and theatre, and most of all as a novelist who has published novels in six successive decades, so an examination of his fiction and its connection with other writers is of necessity an examination of a whole literary-historical period.

In the political, literary, and religious spheres, David Lodge is best characterized by the word "liberal." He dislikes extremes and avoids ideological conflict; by temperament he seems to be skeptical and conciliatory, always able to see and to articulate positions other than his own. As a Roman Catholic, he grew up in a self-conscious minority within English society, but unlike many English Catholic intellectuals he has avoided triumphalist polemics, adhering to a liberal position within the church and eventually coming to describe himself as an "agnostic Catholic" (Bergonzi, "Conversation," 203). It may be helpful to develop an account of Lodge's liberalism by looking at various aspects of his identity in turn, so I will focus on his social origin and upbringing as they affect his work, his religious affiliation, and his role as a professional literary critic, before giving a brief overview of his career as a novelist. The sources for what follows include a number of interviews and profiles in the press, some of Lodge's own essays, especially those in *Write On* (1986), which is the most personally revealing of his books, and the various introductions and afterwords that he has written for new editions of his novels. Two interviews that give a noteworthy insight into Lodge are the conversation with John Haffenden included in the valuable collection *Novelists in Interview* (1985) and the two-part interview by the Polish writer and translator Jerzy Jarniewicz in collaboration with Craig Raine that was published in *Areté* in 2001.

Bernard Bergonzi noted in *Reading the Thirties* that the prominent writers of the 1930s had a remarkably homogeneous educational formation: in most cases they attended public schools followed by Oxford or Cambridge (10–11). The writers of the 1950s and early 1960s, on the other hand, typically attended grammar schools and then a provincial university (or if they did not attend a provincial university, they may have ended up working at one, like Philip Larkin and Kingsley Amis). In many ways, as he himself recognizes, Lodge was a characteristic figure of his generation. He grew up in the South London suburb of Brockley, attended a Roman Catholic grammar school, and then

University College London. In one interview, he comments that he did not want to go to Oxford or Cambridge because his impression of those universities was formed by the novels of Evelyn Waugh: "I knew it was all getting debagged in the quad by drunken raving aristocrats" (Llewellyn, "Bad Reviews"). After graduating with a first-class BA and spending two years in the army, Lodge then earned an MA from the University of London and proceeded to a position at the University of Birmingham, where he advanced through the academic ranks from a temporary lectureship to the chair of modern literature, earning a doctorate along the way for his influential critical study, *Language of Fiction* (1966).

In some ways, though, Lodge's career was different from that of the typical scholarship boy. His father, William Lodge, was a professional musician, who during the 1930s had played dance music in a nightclub frequented by Evelyn Waugh, and who later showed Lodge's writing "to people like Kenneth Tynan," the well-known theatre critic of the 1950s (Haffenden, "Interview," 148). In the essay "Waugh's Comic Wasteland," Lodge writes that "I was, I think, fifteen when my father put into my hands a tattered Penguin edition of *Decline and Fall*" (*Consciousness*, 161). Having a father who was a musician, and who additionally had a connection to the world of literature, must have been a significant influence on Lodge as a boy, and his father's gift reinforced the encouragement of the schoolmaster who introduced him to modern authors such as James Joyce and Graham Greene. Lodge goes on to note in the Waugh essay that "By Christmas 1950, when I was a month short of sixteen, I was sufficiently hooked to request as a seasonal present from my mother copies of *Vile Bodies*, *Black Mischief*, and *Scoop* in the Chapman and Hall Uniform Edition – books which I still possess and frequently reread with undiminished pleasure" (162). Furthermore, Lodge's Catholicism remained a significant part of his identity, and seems to have been a positive source of self-definition within the largely secular world of University College. Given that the two most prominent novelists of his youth, Waugh and Greene, were converts to Roman Catholicism, Lodge's religion provided a means of identification with them, even though as a cradle Catholic he had a very different experience of the faith. In that respect he has more in common with another writer who grew up in a Catholic community and attended a Catholic grammar school, the literary critic Terry Eagleton, although Lodge did not displace Catholic theology into Marxist dialectics as Eagleton did. Eagleton will be another point of reference in various places in this study.

Lodge had an aunt who worked for the American army in Germany and another aunt who lived in Belgium, and visiting them gave him an experience unusual for someone of his background during a period when, due to post-war austerity in general and currency restrictions in particular, it was difficult for the ordinary British person to travel in Europe. It perhaps contributed to his liberal outlook to observe life in foreign countries at an age when most of his schoolmates would have been restricted in their travels, and an early trip to Heidelberg to visit his aunt gave him a new perspective on the recent war and introduced him to one of the great themes of his fiction, the relationship between the cultures of Britain and the United States. Lodge's essays as well as his fiction attest to his affection for and admiration of American culture and Americans, in a kind of reversal of Henry James's celebrated "international theme," and this is something that sets him apart from many British writers of the twentieth century.

In "Memories of a Catholic Childhood," first published in *The Tablet* in 1976, Lodge writes that "Home was a small modern semi in a drab nineteenth-century London suburb, mainly lower-middle-class and working-class in social composition" (*Write On*, 28). This kind of background featured prominently in the most acclaimed and controversial writing of the post-war generation. I am thinking of the work of novelists such as John Braine and Stan Barstow, the poetry of the Movement, and the drama that flourished in the wake of *Look Back in Anger* (1956). I will discuss Lodge in the context of the literature of the 1950s in chapter 4. His first two novels are written in the neo-realist mode of that decade.

David Lodge remained at Birmingham University until his early retirement to pursue full-time authorship in 1987. The changes in the British university system during the Thatcher years were clearly a factor in his decision to leave teaching, along with the success of his novels in the 1980s. In a characteristically even-handed manner, Lodge's fiction indicates some of the reasons why Margaret Thatcher was so popular with the electorate at the same time that it depicts the adversities and challenges of life in Britain during the time that she was prime minister. He is a keen observer of politics, and *Nice Work*, *Therapy*, and *Thinks...* all offer insight into English life in the era from Thatcher's election to the rise of New Labour. Lodge has attracted some hostility from the Marxist left because his criticism and his fiction present a consistently liberal position: he certainly did not turn to the right in the manner of Kingsley Amis and other writers who emerged in the 1950s, but neither is he any kind of Marxist. He is not a political novelist as that term is conventionally understood, and Terry Eagleton has charged him with failing "to understand the point of the political, other than as handy material for satire" ("Living as Little"). But in fact Lodge has always been able to represent political issues at the level of the experience of the ordinary person, with a clear sense of the class system and the way that it functions.

While Lodge's pragmatic impatience with both ideology and nostalgia has affinities with the approach of New Labour under Tony Blair, his endorsement of state-funded higher education is more like that of "old Labour." In *Out of the Shelter* we see Timothy Young, in the early 1950s, make a life-changing decision to apply to university in spite of the discouragement of his parents; the end of the novel gives a brief glimpse of the beneficial consequences of this decision. Lodge's accounts of his own university education and his early days as a lecturer are almost wholly favourable, and describe a dynamic, challenging environment full of intellectual ferment. However, by the time we get to *Nice Work*, set in 1986, Lodge is presenting the university as an institution under attack. He is careful to show the flaws and inequities that characterize the day-to-day life of an actual, as opposed to an ideal university. At the same time, when a character describes universities as "the cathedrals of the modern age" (*Nice Work*, 241), I don't think Lodge is being entirely ironic; he retains some vestige of the utopian vision of state education which facilitated his own formative years.[5]

One way in which Lodge's personal history may have determined his social attitudes is in his response to the external signs denoting distinctions of social class. He has never been enthralled by the trappings of the upper-class lifestyle that for many self-made British people are the symbols of success. The characters in his novels tend to be members of the professional class, often of lower-middle-class backgrounds, and they are usually involved in education, the media, or the arts, although he also frequently represents the medical profession and has made an effort to include figures from industry and finance in some of his novels. Characters who have attended public school are rarely treated sympathetically in David Lodge novels, and Oxford and Cambridge are presented without any mystique. His is an urban and suburban imagination, without the nostalgic and powerful attachment to land and country houses that figures so prominently in English literature. Perhaps his early reading of Waugh helped to cure him of any attraction to such a life. Lodge had the opportunity to take a position in Cambridge in the 1960s, but elected to remain in Birmingham (Turner, "Words Never Fail Him").

Roman Catholics have tended to be politically liberal in England, due to their exclusion from public life for so long after the Elizabethan settlement, but until after the second Vatican Council (1962–65) theological liberalism was stringently policed. In the late nineteenth century, various Catholic thinkers, especially in France, but also a few in England, sought to rearticulate Catholic teaching in the light of recent scientific thought, biblical scholarship, and philosophical thinking. Their efforts were condemned as the heresy of Modernism by Pope Pius X in 1907, with the result that the church for the next half-century opposed itself to the modern world.[6] The church's presentation of the faith was renewed as a result of the second Vatican Council, convened by Pope John XXIII, and a period of ferment and dramatic change ensued, to be curtailed during the papacy of John Paul II.

Lodge's relationship to the church is complex. Unlike many cradle Catholic writers and intellectuals, he continued to practice his faith; on the other hand, apart from a very early and minor publication he has never been an apologist for it, but rather an honest recorder of the contradictions and difficulties of Catholic life. He was educated in religious schools and grew up attending the parish church, though in "Memories of a Catholic Childhood" (1976), Lodge describes how he rarely had a sense of belonging to a spiritual community due to being the only child of a "mixed marriage," for his father was not a Roman Catholic, unlike his mother, who was of Irish ancestry. Unlike many boys his age, he did not learn to serve at mass, and as a result "never felt really familiar and at ease with the liturgy," but rather regarded himself as "something of an outsider in the Church" (*Write On*, 30, 29). He describes his religious instruction at school as "very poor"; in the sixth form it was based on an American textbook called *The Question Box*, "which consisted of objections to the Catholic faith (many of which had never occurred to me before) followed by vigorous and dogmatic refutations" (30).

Given this background, it is ironic that Roman Catholicism turned out to be part of Lodge's self-definition at University College London.

Just as he had remained an outsider within the church as a boy, so at a secular university Catholicism gave him an identity that set him apart. This was reinforced by his choice of subject for his MA thesis, "Catholic Fiction since the Oxford Movement: Its Literary Form and Religious Content" (1959). As Lodge explains in one of his most personal essays, "My Joyce," the existence of a distinguished tradition of Catholic literature and thought in English, reinforced by various French writers, "made Catholic belief seem a potential asset rather than an encumbrance to the aspirant writer, its uncompromising supernaturalism an invigorating challenge to the liberal, secular, materialistic values of modern Western society" (*Write On*, 60). Existentialism was a dominant intellectual mode at this time, and the "Outsider" pose was fashionable in the wake of Colin Wilson's existential-critical treatise of that name (1956).

Lodge's first significant publication was a Catholic pamphlet of sixty-four pages entitled *About Catholic Authors* (1957). It was one of a series obviously designed to be sold in churches, and like all such works, it unquestioningly endorses Catholic teaching and the authority of the church. That said, it is incisively written and the future novelist is apparent in the pamphlet's fictional framework, for it consists of a series of letters from a priest to a young Catholic who is doing his National Service. Lodge's first published novel, *The Picturegoers* (1960), was reviewed as a new contribution to the genre of the Catholic novel. Catholicism plays an important role in many of his subsequent novels, though it is less significant in the campus trilogy, especially the first and third volumes, and in the novels of the new millennium. *How Far Can You Go?* (1980) records the changes in belief in a group of middle-class English Catholics over a period of about twenty-five years, and by intruding himself into the novel, Lodge connects his characters' stories to the development of his own religious views. Though Catholicism has been at the core of his fictional vision, he has never been one for making converts, as he told John Haffenden in the passage I used as an epigraph to this chapter; he also wrote in an essay on "The Catholic Church and Cultural Life" that history suggests that writers and intellectuals are better off "in a pluralist secular state than in one in which the Church played a dominant or militant cultural role" (*Write On*, 37).

Lodge told Bernard Bergonzi that while he has abandoned much of the Catholic world view that he grew up with, "he insists that religious language is not empty of meaning" (Bergonzi, "Conversation," 203). Lodge first identified himself with a liberal position in the church by the comic and satirical way that he treated the Catholic teaching on contraception in *The British Museum Is Falling Down* (1965). The novel appeared at a time when many Catholics were hoping that the church would declare that its traditional opposition to birth control did not extend to the contraceptive pill, but these hopes were disappointed by the reaffirmation of the traditional teaching by Pope Paul VI in the 1968 encyclical *Humanae Vitae*. In *How Far Can You Go?*, looking back on this phase of church history, Lodge explains how *Humanae Vitae* was the watershed event that gave many Catholics the confidence to defy the authority of the church, hastening its accommodation to the modern world. At the end of his essay on "The Catholic Church and Cultural Life" (1980), Lodge maintains that he does not regret the loss of a distinctively Catholic, as opposed to Christian, voice in British cultural life. He says that the church is now "a much more decent, humane, open-minded Christian community than it once was, but it is also rather blander, duller, and more amorphous. As a result of the upheaval of Vatican II, we have now a pluralistic kind of Church, which resembles Anglicanism much more than would have seemed possible twenty or thirty years ago" (*Write On*, 37). The Catholic world that Lodge explored in his academic research and described in his early fiction has been absorbed into the wider culture, and although it provided Lodge with an important aspect of his identity, his fiction also reveals a straightforward grasp of its shortcomings, much as James Joyce's *Dubliners* and *A Portrait of the Artist as a Young Man* do early in the twentieth century. But characteristically, Lodge also represents the weaknesses and contradictions of his own liberal position in *How Far Can You Go?* And in both that novel and in *Paradise News* (1991), he represents the Catholic charismatic movement in a manner that implies some sympathy.

A third facet of David Lodge's liberalism manifests itself in his literary criticism. He was a student during the period of the ascendancy of F.R. Leavis, whose dominant position in British culture in the mid-twentieth century has now been largely forgotten after the turn to theory that has occupied literary studies for the last forty years or so. To understand Leavis's influence one must see it as having several distinct aspects, each of which has been picked up by successors who have ignored the other aspects almost entirely. There was a strong ethical component, evident in the stress on "maturity" and "moral seriousness" in Leavis's evaluation of writers. In *The Great Tradition* (1948) and *D.H. Lawrence, Novelist* (1955) it is clear that a kind of displaced Puritan moral earnestness is one of the reasons that George Eliot, Henry James (excluding the novels of his final phase), and D.H. Lawrence are regarded so highly. At the same time, like I.A. Richards, Leavis pioneered a careful, rigorous scrutiny of "the words on the page." This emphasis on close reading, which was part of the teaching method that Leavis practiced at Cambridge, gives him affinities with the American New Critics. However, Leavis's criticism was supported by an analysis of British cultural history that was developed more fully in the work of some of his collaborators and notably in *Fiction and the Reading Public* (1932) by his wife Q.D. Leavis. This more sociological side of Leavis was an influence on Richard Hoggart's *The Uses of Literacy* (1957) and on the work of the British school of cultural studies as it developed under Hoggart's direction at the University of Birmingham. Leavis was never really a formalist, for he had very clear ethical and cultural goals for literary criticism, even if he rarely articulated these at length. At the same time, he and his collaborators in the journal *Scrutiny* were hostile to more overtly articulated forms of ideological criticism, especially to Marxist criticism and to criticism associated with the revival of orthodox Christianity inspired by figures like C.S. Lewis and T.S. Eliot.

One of the strongest testimonies to the influence of Leavis is the way that the Marxist critic Terry Eagleton went on arguing with it long after many others had ceased to worry about it. In fact, Eagleton's most influential book, *Literary Theory: An Introduction* (1983), is as much a quarrel with Leavis as it is a guide to contemporary literary theory. Leavis casts a long shadow in the history of modern British culture, both through the prestige of his own works – with their clear, but non-Marxist, program of social engagement, which sought to save authentic cultural traditions from the barbarousness of advertising, popular culture, and sloppy thinking – and through the mediated form of the leftist-Leavisite position of Raymond Williams. There was something messianic in Leavis's idea of criticism, as it was based on the assumption that the ills of modern society could be combatted by an intense and serious attention to the best literary texts.

As a critic formed by a Catholic education, Lodge did not share Leavis's instinctual sympathy with the Puritan tradition. On the other hand, he read James Joyce with a sense of immediate identification. As he advances his own formalist position in his first major critical book, *Language of Fiction*, Lodge frequently differs from Leavis. His principal complaint is that Leavis slips in ethical categories in the guise of formal judgements: "the objection to putting terms like 'moral intensity' or 'reverent openness before life' at the very centre of critical judgment, is that they are not really *literary* concepts, but ethical ones" (*Language* 67; italics Lodge's). In some revealing asides in later books and comments in interviews, Lodge expresses his disagreement with Leavis less respectfully and more directly. An essay in *After Bakhtin* contrasts the "star-system" of the American academy with the atmosphere in the British system, and Lodge observes in passing that F.R. Leavis is the only British critic he can think of who had a following, but "his image was antithetical to that of the film-star – it was the image of the saint. Leavis's authority and charisma depended crucially on his *not* having been given the conventional honours and rewards of academic distinction, and he paraded the slights he suffered from the Cambridge English Faculty like the stigmata all his life" (177; italics Lodge's). Lodge's bluntest comments about Leavis are contained in the interview with Jerzy Jarniewicz: "I have always felt very antagonistic towards Leavis. I don't actually think he was liberal. I think he was very intolerant. Basically he was a Puritan … The Leavis group was essentially a kind of secularised Protestant ethos – and I was Catholic. So I felt very alienated from it … There is a terrible earnestness and seriousness about Leavis. There is not much openness to comedy in Leavis. The keynote of his criticism was 'maturity.' And I think the fact that Leavis did not really think *Ulysses* was a great work says it all, as far as I am concerned" (48). This comment is especially significant in that it reveals that liberalism is the core value of Lodge's literary criticism, which is why he has so much time for E.M. Forster and Virginia Woolf, and why though he is acutely aware of issues of class he distances himself from Marxist critics. Similarly, while Lodge has a keen awareness of cultural difference from his extensive travelling and is no apologist for British imperialism, he does not indulge in flights of rhetorical outrage about empire.

Lodge is of part-Irish ancestry, and has an intimate personal knowledge of the Irish community in England. But this, and his love of America, must be balanced against what most observers see as his impeccable Englishness. Lodge has written very little criticism about poetry but references to poems occur frequently in his novels, and in *Deaf Sentence* the retired linguist Desmond Bates "still read poetry for pleasure, which couldn't be said for many people, including some who taught courses on it" (30). Significantly, the poets who turn up most often in his work, and who are clearly personal favourites, are the Irishman W.B. Yeats and that most English of poets, Philip Larkin. Lodge told Jerzy Jarniewicz, "I think Larkin is a wonderful poet. Very hard to explain that to people who don't read English. It is so English – the tone, the quality, the texture. Larkin got it absolutely right. Nobody's done it better" ("Interview," 52–3). On the other hand, he clearly dissociates himself from Larkin's insularity: "there is a part of me which is very different from him" (52). It is wholly characteristic of Lodge that his taste in poets should reflect a liberalism that is catholic as well as Roman Catholic.

In his early criticism, under the influence of one of his University College teachers, Winifred Nowottny, Lodge explored the application of linguistics and stylistics to literary criticism. He has described Nowottny as "a very charismatic teacher who had a big influence upon me critically" (Haffenden, "Interview," 148). As early as his MA thesis, Lodge was analyzing the role of key recurring words in Graham Greene's fiction, while in *Language of Fiction* he sought to provide the groundwork for a formalist poetics of fiction. What was missing, he later realized, was an analysis of the larger elements of narrative, such as point of view and voice, which are elements that can be translated into other languages. This led Lodge first into structuralism, and then into the poetics of fiction of Mikhail Bakhtin. But after Lodge left academe his criticism became less overtly theoretical, written instead from the perspective of the working novelist. He comments in the preface to *Consciousness and the Novel* (2002) that Bakhtin had satisfactorily answered the theoretical questions he had been working on, and that the post-structuralist turn away from the literary to the ideological, combined with his retirement, meant that he had more or less stopped reading literary theory (*Consciousness*, x). Although Lodge was a key figure in explicating continental theory, even producing a textbook of literary theory, one can detect a sense of relief at leaving behind a career that had become less and less rewarding due to the pressures of funding cuts and increased emphasis on scholarly productivity.[7] Furthermore, he characterizes much contemporary criticism and theory, viewed from the perspective of one no longer professionally involved with the university, as not worth the effort required to keep up with it: "A vast amount of it is not, like the work of Bakhtin, a contribution to human knowledge, but the demonstration of a professional mastery by translating known facts into more and more arcane metalanguages" (*After Bakhtin*, 8). Here, Lodge's characteristic ability to see both sides of an issue leads him to question much of what goes on today in literary studies, though without, it should be noted, indulging in the rhetoric of apocalyptic decline that tends to be found in those who make such critiques. In the 1984 afterword to a new edition of *Language of Fiction*, it is striking that Lodge emphasizes that his opposition to the post-structuralist critic Catherine Belsey's assertions about the death of the author "stems not from theoretical conviction, but from practice – the practice of writing fiction" ("Afterword to Second Edition," 300).

Finally, in relation to Lodge's liberalism, one should add that there is a personal source, as it seems to be the natural product of a temperament that he himself describes as "tentative, sceptical, ironic" (Haffenden, "Interview," 152). In the same interview, he says of his habit of putting different ideological positions into dialogue in his novels, "I hope it comes across ... more as honest doubt than as evasiveness" (152). What he is seeking, then, is dialogue among several positions, each of which he sees as having some claim to validity. A good example of this habit of mind is the way that he presents the arguments of both Vic Wilcox, the managing director of an engineering firm, and Robyn Penrose, a feminist academic, in *Nice Work*. Each of them is forced to concede the validity of points made by the other, and both change and grow as a result. It is significant that Lodge invokes Tennyson's celebrated phrase "honest doubt" to describe the effect he hopes to produce in his fiction; in its original context, Tennyson was referring to the position of the intellectually honest religious believer, who will not make a blind leap of faith: "There lives more faith in honest doubt, / Believe me, than in half the creeds" (*In Memoriam*, Poem 96, lines 11–12). Lodge's personal tentativeness of commitment was reinforced, if not produced, by the experiences of being a child during the Second World War and growing up during the period of post-war austerity. In the afterword to his Bildungsroman, *Out of the Shelter*, he says of the effect of the war on his generation: "Its anxieties and privations made us temperamentally cautious, unassertive, grateful for small mercies and modest in our ambitions" (276).

For Lodge, in an important passage in his book *The Novelist at the Crossroads* (1971), there is a clear link between liberalism and the realistic mode of fiction. It is instructive to compare him with his friend and fellow campus novelist Malcolm Bradbury in this respect. In spite of his personal commitment to liberalism, Bradbury's novels are preoccupied with identifying its limitations. James Walker, the British protagonist of Bradbury's *Stepping Westward* (1965), is told by an American academic, "Someone once defined liberals as people who embrace their destroyers" (254). Lodge's comic fiction, like the novels of Anthony Trollope, affirms a "conservative liberal" position, and perhaps in both cases the strength of that position comes from a religious commitment that underlies it, in spite of the way that both novelists pervasively question convictions and are suspicious of creeds and ideologies.[8] The title essay of *The Novelist at the Crossroads* was first published in 1969, and is a kind of manifesto of Lodge's fictional practice up to and including *Out of the Shelter*. In it, he writes that "If the case for realism has any ideological content it is that of liberalism. The aesthetics of compromise go naturally with the ideology of compromise, and it is no coincidence that both are under pressure at the present time" (33). Responding to those who argue that "reality" is so horrific and absurd that the conventions of classic realism are inadequate to deal with it, Lodge responds that "most of us continue to live most of our lives on the assumption that the reality which realism imitates actually exists. History may be, in a philosophical sense, a fiction, but it does not feel like that when we miss a train or somebody starts a war" (33). He has returned to this question in some subsequent essays, and he is still preoccupied with the debate about fiction, history, and realistic representation in *A Man of Parts*, as will be discussed in chapter 6.

Terry Eagleton has complained in a review of Lodge's *Nice Work* that the post-structuralist-Marxist-feminist academic Robyn Penrose is really a liberal underneath, and that it is disingenuous of Lodge not to represent her as being true to her espoused convictions ("Silences," 99). However, Lodge is fully aware of what he is doing, because at a crucial moment in the text Robyn herself is forced to recognize that she can only defend the humanities against Vic Wilcox's criticism by falling back on liberal humanist arguments (*Nice Work*, 218). This is a key part of the book's argument, and *Nice Work* most resembles E.M. Forster's *Howards End*, a novel it alludes to, in its refusal to come down on one side or the other. Lodge represents the positive side of post-structuralist literary theory when he contrasts Robyn's intellectual energy with the cynical old guard of the University of Rummidge English Department, who are stuck in an ossified form of liberal humanism. We see Robyn successfully teaching Victorian literature from a theoretically informed perspective, and illuminating not only the literary texts but the semiotic world that we all inhabit, as in the memorable passage where she deconstructs cigarette advertisements to an incredulous Vic Wilcox, who nevertheless eventually takes the point (*Nice Work*, 220–8). There is something very admirable about Lodge's liberalism: it is far more self-aware than his critics allow, and always open to considering new developments. There is a great integrity in the seriousness with which he investigates and interacts with writers, thinkers, and systems of thought differing radically from his own position, as in Lodge's characterization of the cognitive scientist Ralph Messenger in *Thinks...* (2001), or his engagement with the works and life of H.G. Wells.

The usual ways to discuss Lodge's work are either a chronological survey, or a division by type of novel, classifying his oeuvre into Catholic novels, campus novels, and social novels. However, in this study, I have decided to look at Lodge in relation to a series of modern writers who can be considered as major influences.[9] I was led to this approach by the realization that Lodge is a highly intertextual writer, and that his literary criticism and literary journalism illuminate his novels in significant ways. He has himself often discussed literary influence in his criticism, both in relation to his own work and to the work of other writers. Like Graham Greene, and like Henry James, Lodge often comments on his own work, and he has identified a number of important influences. Though I do not think one should follow these suggestions uncritically, many of them are illuminating. Each of the writers that I have chosen provides a particular vantage point, a unique lens or window through which we can view Lodge's work. My hope is that these multiple perspectives on Lodge will combine to enlarge our critical understanding of his work, especially his fiction but also his criticism, and that I will thereby facilitate a clearer understanding of Lodge's place on the crowded map of post-1945 British literature. There will be a disproportionate emphasis on the earlier novels, not because I think they are the best, but because they are the most revealing in terms of literary influences. In each of the early novels, Lodge engages with several of the major precursors who are the focus of this book, and therefore the early novels will figure in more than one chapter.

When Lodge introduces Robyn Penrose to the reader in *Nice Work*, he begins appropriately enough by presenting her principal ideas, as she might articulate them, interspersed with somewhat ironical narrative commentary. Like Roland Barthes, Robyn believes that "Every text is a product of intertextuality, a tissue of allusions to and citations of other texts" (40). As a literary critic and theorist of the novel, Lodge is both aware of this tenet of post-structuralism and also extremely knowledgeable about the history of the novel, so that his novels are to a high degree intertextual. He observed at the beginning of an address to a conference on the state of the novel: "if critics need a canon, novelists need a tradition. You cannot begin to write novels without having read at least one, and probably hundreds; without defining yourself in relationships of apprenticeship, discipleship, rivalry, antagonism with precursors and peers" ("The Novel Now," 126). Similarly, Lodge says that his reading of James Joyce, "the greatest innovator in modern prose fiction," has inevitably shaped the fiction that he has written himself: "There is a kind of influence that modern criticism calls 'intertextuality,' and it is inescapable" (*Write On*, 57).

Of course, it is not just modern novelists who have influenced Lodge. He writes very much in the spirit of Henry Fielding, who is a precursor both as the originating English comic novelist, and as a novelist-critic, whose comments in his prefaces and authorial asides are vital to the theorizing of the novel in the eighteenth century. Lodge always tends to the Fieldingesque comic pole, rather than to the Richardsonian interiority that is the other major tradition in English fiction, and he sometimes aspires as well to the documentary realism of Defoe. Among the classic novelists whom he has discussed in critical essays, edited, or alluded to in significant ways in his fiction, there are a number of writers from the Leavisite canon: Jane Austen, George Eliot, Henry James (without Leavis's reservations about the late novels), and to a lesser extent Joseph Conrad. A particularly important novel for Lodge is Austen's *Emma*, which he edited for the Oxford University Press World's Classics series. Lodge admires Austen's control of narrative voice and point of view, and he writes that "There is, to my knowledge, no precedent for such a novel before *Emma* – that is, a novel in which the authorial narrator mediates virtually all the action through the consciousness of an unreliable focalizing character. The effect is not only a wonderful multiplication of ironies and reversals but also an intensification of what Henry James called the sense of felt life" (*After Bakhtin*, 128).[10] Dickens is another novelist with whom Lodge has significant affinities: again he has written about him in various places, and he also adapted *Martin Chuzzlewit* for an acclaimed television miniseries. One can detect hints of Dickensian influence in Lodge's representation of London, or in his transatlantic comedy. Nevertheless, I do not think that Lodge responds to these earlier writers with the same intensity, or the same anxiety, to use Harold Bloom's term, as he does to a personal canon of modern writers – both modernists and antimodernists – with a strong Catholic content, as well as a strong flavour of liberalism. Even in the passage about Jane Austen that I have just quoted, Lodge reinforces his praise for Austen's fictional achievement by a reference to Henry James. Lodge's modern canon includes Henry James, H.G. Wells, James Joyce, Virginia Woolf, E.M. Forster, Evelyn Waugh, Graham Greene, Kingsley Amis, and Muriel Spark. Some of these writers were denigrated by Leavis, who notoriously described Amis as "a pornographer" when he was elected to a fellowship in Cambridge.[11]

D.H. Lawrence is the major excision that Lodge makes from the Leavis canon. Lodge does not dismiss his importance: he wrote an article for the *Guardian* in 1985 on the occasion of the centenary of Lawrence's birth ("Heretic of the Heart"), and several of his critical books include an essay on Lawrence.[12] Nevertheless, the briskly matter-of-fact judgments that Lodge makes about Lawrence show that he was never under the Leavisite spell, and in fact the centenary essay attracted some letters to the *Guardian* complaining that it was unfair or inaccurate. Lodge begins the article rather ironically, noting that many critics have considered Lawrence the greatest twentieth-century English novelist, and he acknowledges that this is true if "English" is interpreted in the narrowest way possible, "excluding Irishmen, naturalized Americans and the odd expatriate Pole" (*Write On*, 188). But the passage most troubling to Leavisites was undoubtedly the declaration that Leavis "ignored or underplayed some of the less obviously healthy elements in Lawrence's thought and fiction, such as his readiness to sacrifice individual human lives to Life with a capital 'L' ... his sexism, and his messianic, apocalyptic mysticism, that sometimes drew him towards fascist ideological positions, and on occasion to the edge of madness" (*Write On*, 190–1).

From Lodge's "personal canon" of modern writers, I have selected four major influences who will each be the focus of a chapter: Graham Greene, James Joyce, Kingsley Amis, and Henry James. Each of these figures represents a very different social and cultural world, as well as a very different kind of literary sensibility. My last chapter will be concerned with H.G. Wells and the poetics of fiction, because although perhaps not such a major influence as the other four, Wells is the subject of Lodge's most recent novel, *A Man of Parts*. Furthermore, Wells was involved in a controversy with James about the art of the novel that is central to Lodge's developing and changing thought on that topic. It was not difficult to select the four writers who are the main focus of this book: after re-reading the whole corpus of Lodge's fiction with the question of influence in mind, and also going back to his criticism, Greene, Joyce, Amis, and James emerged as almost self-evident choices. Though there are other writers who have certainly had a major influence at various points, these four seem to me consistently important in a way that puts them in a distinct category. In discussing Lodge in relation to the modern novel, I am aware of the problematic nature of the terms "English" and "British," and of the facts that James Joyce is an Irish writer, and Henry James an American writer. Nevertheless, both are inescapably, however problematically, also part of modern British literature, and chapter 3 will discuss not only Lodge and Joyce, but more generally the relationship between the ideas of Englishness and Irishness in Lodge's fiction. Similarly, chapter 5 will include some attention to Henry James's international theme as it has manifested itself in Lodge's life, by looking at his relationship to the United States and the way that it has shaped his work.

I begin with Graham Greene, because he seems to me the crucial influence of Lodge's adolescence, and he provided the central example for Lodge's identity as a Catholic novelist. Lodge has written about Greene from his MA thesis and first Catholic pamphlet to an essay in his most recent critical book, *The Year of Henry James* (2006), and some subsequent forewords and reviews. James Joyce was another author whom Lodge discovered in adolescence, and he is a Catholic author in terms of upbringing and subject matter if not of actual religious belief; he exemplifies Lodge's attachment to high modernism, as well as his cosmopolitan dimension and interest in things Irish. Furthermore, Joyce clearly seems to be Lodge's favourite author. Kingsley Amis is a writer with whom Lodge feels a significant personal affinity, and who was beginning to publish while Lodge was a student. It is a nice coincidence that Amis gave Lodge's first novel a very favourable review. Amis is important both on his own terms and as a representative of the realist writers of the 1950s generation, who critically scrutinized the literary tradition, seeking to find a way of giving linguistic representation to the social dislocations that were taking place following the end of the Second World War. Lodge begins a review of Zachary Leader's massive biography of Amis by asking whether the subject is worthy of such a vast effort: "Whether you immediately answer 'Yes' or need to be convinced will depend very much on your age and nationality. For English readers and writers born in the 1930s (like myself) or a little before or after, Kingsley Amis was a key figure in postwar British culture, whose importance and influence cannot be measured simply by the intrinsic merit of his books" ("'Bad Behavior'"). Lastly, Henry James is a writer Lodge came to appreciate a bit later than the others, but who figures prominently in his first critical book, and is thereafter consistently important until Lodge's preoccupation with him culminated in *Author, Author*, a novel with James as the principal character, and *The Year of Henry James*, a book whose long title essay tells the fraught story of that novel's composition, publication, and early reception. The works from James's extensive oeuvre that are most important to Lodge seem to be *The Ambassadors*, exemplifying James's international theme and his late style, and the stories about literary life, such as "The Aspern Papers" and "The Middle Years." Following the discussion of Lodge in relation to these four writers, the last chapter will review the dialectic between realism and formalism in some of Lodge's essays on the theory of the novel as a genre, and will examine the place of H.G. Wells's fiction in Lodge's criticism. This will prepare the ground for a discussion of *A Man of Parts* against the background of *Author, Author*, in an effort to define the present state of Lodge's thinking about the novel and its relation to history.

I have not forgotten that Lodge is very open to and aware of American literature, and writers such as Kurt Vonnegut, J.D. Salinger, Norman Mailer, and Vladimir Nabokov have certainly contributed to his fictional voice. However, in a lecture on Nabokov, Lodge said that he came to that novelist's work too late to be influenced by him: "The formative literary influences of my apprenticeship years were Graham Greene, Evelyn Waugh and James Joyce" (*Practice*, 152). I think that this statement is accurate as far as Nabokov goes, and it would also apply to the other American writers I have mentioned. Their influence is not as fundamental as that of the writers whom I discuss in detail. Lodge's comment raises another, and an obvious question, namely why Evelyn Waugh does not merit a chapter of his own in this book. He was a significant youthful literary interest of Lodge's; he was a successful Catholic writer, a comic and satirical novelist, and someone with whom Lodge had a sort of personal connection through his father. Nevertheless, I still maintain that Waugh is not a major influence. He was not a writer against whom Lodge had to struggle to define himself, as he did with Greene and Joyce, nor was he the kind of writer from whom Lodge could learn key elements of his own literary manner, as were Amis and James. The primary reason for this is a social one, though it also manifests itself in literary terms as a fundamental difference in tone and voice. Lodge is a much more benevolent writer than Waugh, with a comic view of the world that is unlike the angry anarchist satire found in Waugh's most characteristic works. It is clear that for Lodge, Waugh's novels presented an exotic world that had very little in common with the world of suburban post-war south London where he lived. He writes that "I suppose I found these books fascinating precisely because they opened my eyes to the existence of a milieu wholly different from my own – adult, glamorous, hedonistic, and quintessentially 'prewar'" (*Consciousness*, 162). Lodge wrote about Waugh in his MA thesis, and in a number of other subsequent works, including a short book in 1971 in the Columbia Essays on Modern Writers series (*Evelyn Waugh*). But there are not many traces of Waugh in Lodge's fiction; the major one is the character Percy Higgins in *Ginger, You're Barmy*, who is a kind of parody of one of Waugh's "old Catholic" gentry characters. A useful contrast might be to look at the fiction of A.N. Wilson, a novelist who clearly has been influenced greatly, and some might say irrecoverably, by Waugh. It is possible that Waugh determined Lodge's life in one important way, by providing an outrageous picture of life at Oxford and Cambridge that confirmed Lodge in his choice of the University of London.

The feminist reader has no doubt already noted the absence of women in my list of major literary influences on David Lodge. The women writers who are most important to him include Jane Austen,

Virginia Woolf, and Muriel Spark. If one wished to pursue further the question of Lodge and women writers, one could also look at the portrayal of fictional women novelists in his first play *The Writing Game* and in the novels *Small World* and *Thinks...*, as well as the historical figures of Constance Fenimore Woolson in *Author, Author* and Rebecca West in *A Man of Parts*. His relationship with Spark is the most rewarding to explore. Like Graham Greene and Evelyn Waugh, she was a convert to Roman Catholicism, and in fact she received valuable assistance and encouragement from both of those writers.[13] Though significantly older than Lodge (she was born in 1918), Spark did not publish her first novel until 1957. As a critic, Lodge has been generous to her, promoting her reputation in more than a dozen reviews and articles, most of the earlier ones in the *Tablet*, with the more recent pieces in such prominent papers as the *Guardian* and *New York Review of Books*.[14] In the earliest of these reviews, published in 1960, Lodge described *The Bachelors* as "a wise and witty performance, informed with Catholic moral values which are the more telling for being unobtrusive" ("Various Vocations," 1176). The following year he reviewed *The Prime of Miss Jean Brodie*, but he came to consider that review so inadequate that he characterized his extended article on the novel as "a personal act of amends" (*Novelist at the Crossroads*, 124).[15] Reviewing *The Abbess of Crewe* in 1974, he wrote that "She continues to amaze by her originality and daring as a writer" ("Prime Spark"). Lodge praises Spark as a unique voice and as someone ahead of her time, "a postmodernist writer before that term was known to literary criticism" ("Rereading"). In a review of Spark's collected short stories in the *New York Times*, Lodge gives the clearest statement of his overall assessment of her importance, declaring that "I consider Mrs. Spark to be the most gifted and innovative British novelist of her generation, one of the very few who can claim to have extended and altered the possibilities of the form for other practitioners" ("Marvels").

But in spite of his admiration for her, I do not consider Spark to be a major influence on Lodge in the way that Greene was; she was not a precursor whose influence both shaped his imagination and needed to be resisted for his own voice to emerge. Rather, she was a contemporary exploring the same questions of fictional form and style in response to the realities of post-war Britain, and therefore someone from whom Lodge could learn in a way that was not marked by anxiety. It is always her daring and originality that he emphasizes and pays tribute to. Lodge took what he needed from her, but at the same time accommodated himself much more to the various literary traditions represented by the influences that I have identified. It is possible that Spark helped to free him from the conventions of the realist fiction of the 1950s, in order to explore other narrative possibilities in works such as *Small World*, for in *The Ballad of Peckham Rye* (1960), Spark parodies many of those conventions, such as the representation of lower-middle-class family life and courtship. The disruptive figure of the Scotsman Dougal Douglas is blatantly presented as a kind of agent of the devil, a diabolical figure whose influence disrupts the rituals of south London, whether in the home, the dance-hall, or the workplace.

Another feature of Spark's fiction is the way that she often, in a short novel such as *The Prime of Miss Jean Brodie*, shifts the perspective abruptly from one to another of a fairly large cast of characters, and at the same time moves back and forth in time rather than allowing the story to unfold in a conventional chronological order. Both *Small World* and *How Far Can You Go?* make effective use of a large cast of characters and of shifts of point of view, and the latter employs audacious time shifts in the manner of *Jean Brodie*, although with a rather different kind of narrative voice. In his essay "The Uses and Abuses of Omniscience," Lodge relates Spark's flaunting of authorial omniscience in *The Prime of Miss Jean Brodie* to the theological concept of divine omniscience, though he adds that in Spark "this providence remains ultimately mysterious and incomprehensible because the world is a fallen one and not even the novelist can claim to understand it fully" (*Crossroads*, 122). Lodge also refers to Graham Greene's essay on François Mauriac, in which Greene links Mauriac's Catholicism to his preference for a traditional narrative voice: "The exclusion of the author can go too far. Even the author, poor devil, has a right to exist, and M. Mauriac reaffirms that right" (Greene, *Collected Essays*, 117). Of course, when an author reaffirms the right to exist in the wake of the criticism of Henry James and the practice of the great modernists, the resulting authorial intrusions have a quite different effect from when they occur in a Victorian novel, and Lodge makes good use of that effect in several of his works, most notably *How Far Can You Go?*

A final instance of possible influence is the economy of effect in Spark's novels. A great deal is always suggested about characters through a few small telling details. For example, in *Jean Brodie* the members of the Brodie set are first characterized by a single detail that they are "famous for," and then we learn a few things about their family background. Where one lives in Edinburgh, what one's father does for a living, where one worships on Sunday – each of these details is of great significance in the novel, and they add up to a represented social world that is remarkably solid for such a brief work. Lodge is also capable of suggesting a great deal through a few details, particularly in the novels where he most seems to have learned from Spark. For example, like her Lodge is always good at characterization through clothing, something he draws attention to in *How Far Can You Go?* when he analyzes his own previous description of the characters he has recently introduced to the reader: "Adrian, bespectacled (=limited vision), in belted gaberdine raincoat (=instinctual repression, authoritarian determination), not to be confused with Ruth's glasses and frumpish schoolgirl's raincoat, signifying unawakened sexuality and indifference to self-display" (14). But even as this example suggests, Lodge takes only what he needs from Spark, and puts it to service in a very different kind of novel. His benevolent vision lacks the hard cruel edge that one finds in Spark as in Waugh. When Mary Macgregor runs "hither and thither" to her death in a burning hotel in *The Prime of Miss Jean Brodie* (28), the dominant suggestion is that this is the logical conclusion of the stupidity that she manifested as a little girl, and that caused the other girls, with the tacit encouragement of Miss Brodie, to victimize her. Spark's world is a harsh place where everyone in different degrees manifests aspects of original sin; in Lodge's world, on the other hand, most of the characters are fundamentally decent, however flawed, and many of them are capable of transformation into something different and often better than what they were.

There has not been a great deal of criticism written about David Lodge. There are a large number of book reviews, journalistic profiles, and interviews, a number of which will be cited in this book.[16] Within the academic world, Lodge has been discussed as a literary theorist and critic of the novel. His contributions to literary theory have sometimes been attacked, like those of Jonathan Culler, for "domesticating" literary theory, as though there were something wrong with attempting to elucidate and explain difficult and often confusing ideas. There are several different kinds of discussion of Lodge's fiction. To begin with, there are various introductory guides, among them books by Bernard Bergonzi, Bruce K. Martin, and Merritt Moseley. These are all worth reading; Bergonzi's is the briefest contribution, somewhat limited by the format imposed by the "Writers and Their Work" series of which it is a part, but written by an outstanding critic with a sympathetic understanding of Lodge's background and work. Moseley's book is a useful introduction to Lodge's fiction up to the end of the 1980s, though it is not widely available. Bruce Martin's Twayne study includes Lodge's novels of the 1990s, and contains some valuable analysis and primary research. Some critics discuss Lodge as a Catholic novelist; the most recent examples include Marian E. Crowe's three chapters on Lodge in her *Aiming at Heaven, Getting the Earth* (2007), Daniel Lenoski's chapter in *Between Human and Divine* (2010), and a brief section in the final chapter of Richard Griffiths's *The Pen and the Cross* (2010).[17] There has been a lot of commentary on *Author, Author* in relation to other recent novels about Henry James, and this will be cited in chapter 5. Lodge has been discussed as a campus novelist, notably by Elaine Showalter in *Faculty Towers*. There are a number of monographs on him by European scholars, who seem to take him more seriously than do critics in the English-speaking world.[18] In *The Dialogic Novels of Malcolm Bradbury and David Lodge* (1989), Robert Morace argues that Bakhtin's concept of dialogism explains much in the work of these two novelists, and his book is an invaluable contribution to the critical discussion of Lodge, though one that needs to be supplemented as Lodge has published another seven novels since it appeared.

David Lodge has written fourteen novels, along with three plays, one of which he turned into a novella, and a few short stories. His first novel, *The Picturegoers* (1960), was largely written during his time in the army, and is about Catholicism, popular culture, and family life. It was reviewed very positively, immediately establishing Lodge as a promising young writer. *Ginger, You're Barmy* followed two years later, and is a rare fictional account of an experience shared by the majority of young men in Britain in the 1950s, peacetime National Service; again there are strong Catholic themes. *The British Museum Is Falling Down* (1965) is Lodge's first campus novel, although there are hints of that genre in the two earlier works. It treats Catholicism in a comic and sometimes satirical manner, and its metafictional passages reveal a new interest in narrative experiment.

The 1970s began with what Lodge hoped would be a breakthrough novel, *Out of the Shelter*, but it has never received the recognition that it deserves. Lodge changed publishers to Macmillan for *Out of the Shelter*, and the novel was plagued by bad luck during the production process. The first edition contains many errors that persist from a disastrous experience with an early version of typesetting software. Publicity was not helped by the fact that the rules concerning eligibility for the Booker Prize changed during 1970, and a number of books published during that year, including *Out of the Shelter*, were not considered for the prize.[19] It is the only one of his novels that he revised for the Penguin reissue, where he was able to restore numerous passages that had been cut when Macmillan insisted he reduce its length by a quarter. Lodge told John Haffenden that the relative failure of *Out of the Shelter* caused a crisis of self-doubt, adding that "I don't think I really made it as a writer until *Changing Places* in 1975, when I was 40" ("Interview," 150). With *Changing Places*, Lodge commenced what would become his "campus trilogy"; it is one of his most popular novels and it firmly established his reputation as a witty academic novelist and a keen observer of international differences. In 1980, he published what I consider one of his finest works, the Catholic novel *How Far Can You Go?* This novel is a moving chronicle of social change, both in England as a whole and within the Catholic church, and it is insightful about culture, sexuality and marriage, politics, and friendship. *How Far* was succeeded by the other two novels in the campus trilogy, although it should be said that each of these three books is quite different from the others. *Small World* (1984) is a freewheeling romance, and a celebration of energy and desire, while *Nice Work* (1988) is an example of the condition of England novel, with a dour realism that is appropriate for an exploration of the consequences of Thatcherism in both the university and British industry. The 1990s brought a return to Catholic themes, and also a continuation of *Small World*'s preoccupation with international travel, in two novels, *Paradise News* (1991) and *Therapy* (1995). Both of these could also be described as mid-life novels. I think that *Paradise News* has not been sufficiently appreciated, while *Therapy* seems to me another of Lodge's major achievements, and it is in some ways a summation of all the fiction he had written up to that point. It has interesting complexities of narrative voice, in part connected to Lodge's use of Kierkegaard, and it incorporates Catholic themes, while returning, from the perspective of the 1990s, to the south London terrain of *The Picturegoers* and to the 1950s. Other elements, such as the setting in the entertainment industry and the pervasive concern with writing as a form of therapy, look forward to the novels that Lodge published in the new millennium.

After *Therapy*, Lodge's fiction took some surprising turns. First he published *Home Truths* (1999), a novella based on his play about celebrity journalism, and a work that must give journalists preparing to interview Lodge a serious pause for reflection. That was followed in 2001 by *Thinks...*, a novel about the nature of consciousness, setting the humanities against cognitive science in a manner that updated the dichotomy identified by C.P. Snow in his Rede lecture of 1959 as the "two cultures." Three years later came another surprise, a historical novel about Henry James. *Author, Author* continues the exploration of the life of the writer that is found in different ways in many of Lodge's later works. *Deaf Sentence* (2007) returns to the familiar ground of the campus, but in a darker mode, as Desmond Bates has retired from his teaching position in linguistics, and is dealing with issues of illness, both mental and physical, along with aging and death. Lodge began the second decade of the new millennium with another historical novel. From the celibate champion of the art of the novel in *Author, Author*, he turns in *A Man of Parts* (2011) to the philandering anti-aesthete H.G. Wells, whose novels overlap with his journalism and political activity. Lodge gives considerable attention to Wells's involvement in the Fabian Society, and *A Man of Parts* explores the connections between private and public life, and between the concerns of Wells's time and those of our own.

In discussing Lodge's fiction and the question of influence, I have often found inspiration in Lodge's own critical prose. He is a highly self-conscious writer, and in the manner of his mentors Greene and James he has surrounded his fiction with an array of prefaces, afterwords, interviews, and essays. By providing carefully shaped accounts of aspects of his life and by commenting on his novels in relation to his life and to other writers, Lodge authoritatively claims to control the terms on which he is read. This makes it sometimes difficult to discuss him in a way that he has not already anticipated, unless one embraces the terms of a competing ideology such as Marxism to combat Lodge's liberalism. This self-commentary, for a novelist who is such an influential critic, may be Lodge's shrewdest strategy for asserting the strength of his own fiction. I have certainly followed many of his hints in this book; but I have disregarded others. For example, I do not agree with Lodge about the extent of Waugh's influence on his work, and I have a somewhat different view of the influence of Joyce from the one he articulates. Ultimately, of course, in terms of Harold Bloom's theory of the anxiety of influence, it is up to the next generation of writers to determine the strength of Lodge's achievement, by manifesting the anxiety of influence in relation to his body of work.

My own reading of Lodge began with his criticism, and like many other readers I came to his novels via the campus trilogy in the 1980s. I then kept up with his new fiction while reading the earlier novels as they were re-issued by Penguin. At the same time, as a university teacher of English, I found Lodge's criticism indispensable as a guide to teaching courses on the novel, and his essays and his novel *How Far Can You Go?* have been central to a course I teach on the Catholic tradition in modern English literature. More recently, *Author, Author* and some of Lodge's criticism inspired a course on "the afterlife of Henry James." As I absorbed Lodge's work, I realized that one of the reasons I responded so strongly to it was that his personal canon included many of the books that were important to me, and this realization led to the present book.

To conclude this chapter, I will say something about the critical methodology that I have employed in this study of Lodge. First and foremost, my endeavour has been to emulate Lodge's own criticism as far as possible. He is that rare critic whose books of critical essays are marketed to the general reading public, as well as to an academic readership. I have sought to write about Lodge in a way that takes full account of literary scholarship, and of various theoretical approaches in literary criticism, and that is at the same time useful as practical criticism of his novels and as literary history of the period from 1950 to the present. I would like to think that any devoted reader of Lodge would be comfortable with this book, as well as academic specialists in modern British literature.

In formulating my approach to literary influence, I have drawn on the work of Harold Bloom, especially his books *The Anxiety of Influence* (1973) and *A Map of Misreading* (1975). Lodge refers to Bloom a number of times in his work, and he uses Bloom's ideas to discuss Graham Greene's fiction in "Graham Greene and the Anxiety of Influence." In the textbook *Modern Criticism and Theory*, Lodge describes Bloom as "very much his own man, one of the most idiosyncratic critics writing today" (240). Using terminology from classical literature and theology, Bloom offers an essentially psychoanalytic account of the operation of literary influence, which is seen as a contest in which the young writer must adopt one or more of a variety of strategies to deal with the otherwise crippling effect of a strong precursor. The classic example in Bloom is the way that the major poets in the Romantic tradition resist the overwhelming influence of John Milton. They are also struggling against a sense of belatedness, that is, against the burden that the achievements of the past impose on a writer who has a strong sense of the preceding tradition. Yet paradoxically it is the poets of the present who create and maintain that tradition, by electing as major writers those who are the strong precursors against whom they must struggle.

Bloom's theory is especially useful for considering the way that writers of the second half of the twentieth century deal with the great and innovative masterpieces of the modernist movement. Bloom's analysis is also helpful for analyzing Lodge's relationship to Graham Greene, just as it is for analyzing Greene's struggle against the influence of Joseph Conrad. I draw on Bloom at various points through this book, though I have not sought to employ his theory systematically. I have occasionally used the specific terms of his "revisionary ratios," but for the most part I have not found them applicable to the strategies that Lodge employs for dealing with his precursors.[20] Bloom's books are for the most part concerned with describing relationships among a handful of major poets, and his theory can only be applied to the kind of literary history I am interested in writing in the broadest terms. It needs to be supplemented by attention to issues of social class, national and religious identity, and the history of literary production and reception. In the history of the modern novel at least, these factors are inextricably linked with the more specifically literary issues in a way that Bloom's approach is inadequate to analyze.

There is a less conflictual model of literary influence in which younger writers emulate, borrow from, and are mentored by older writers. This notion of influence has ancient origins and is exemplified in the neoclassicism of Ben Jonson. The way that Lodge learned in matters of style and voice from Kingsley Amis and Henry James, and in matters of concision, handling of time, and use of detail from Muriel Spark, is in keeping with this older notion of influence, though it must be said that when Lodge took on James directly in *Author, Author*, the result was more of a contest than he probably bargained for.

Several other theorists have helped me to think about the relationship between literary history and the social issues that Bloom's model tends to slight. The work of Hans Robert Jauss is an important background presence in this book. Jauss seems to me, in *Toward an Aesthetic of Reception*, to have provided a highly flexible and attractive model for the historical study of literature, as his notion of the "horizon of expectations," within which any work is produced and read, incorporates both specifically literary and wider social and cultural elements, and suggests ways that these two interpenetrate.[21] His theory of literary history is a highly productive account of the relationship between the literary history of styles, genres, and forms of narration and the larger history of the social and political institutions and values within which culture is embedded. In describing the socio-cultural contexts of literature, Marxist critics such as Fredric Jameson and Terry Eagleton have also influenced my thinking. Their emphasis on class and class struggle is often clarifying, and structuralist Marxism is a powerful model for looking at the social factors implied by the formal properties of a literary work. Lastly, another important model has been the criticism of Bernard Bergonzi, a critic associated with Lodge due to their shared Catholic background and their common interest in modern British literature. Bergonzi's *Reading the Thirties* strikes me as an exemplary work of literary history. His criticism is in its assumptions and style largely within the empirical British mode, but it combines formalist analysis with literary and socio-cultural history in a manner that draws on continental theorists, even if it does not emulate them by using elaborate categories and an abstruse vocabulary. Bergonzi's work illustrates the flexibility and analytical force of the British liberal and empirical tradition of criticism in the way that it can incorporate insights from other theorists without losing its own identity.

To summarize, my aim in this book is to study David Lodge's literary relationships with some significant figures in the tradition of modern literature in English, and to do so in the context of the various social and literary horizons that constitute the history of post-1945 British literature. My approach draws on the various theorists whom I have mentioned, and seeks to recognize both the wider historical context in which literature is written and read, and the way that literature has its own intrinsic qualities and particular history. I have chosen five major writers as different lenses through which to view Lodge's work, with the aim of producing, by means of this multiple perspective, a wide-ranging overview of his literary achievement. I hope that this will assist Lodge's readers to a greater understanding and appreciation of his fiction, and of its place in the fascinating literary history of the last five decades of British literature.

2

Lodging in Greeneland

There is a splinter of ice in the heart of a writer. I watched and listened. This was something which one day I might need.
~Graham Greene, *A Sort of Life*

In 2004, David Lodge gave a lecture at the annual Graham Greene Festival in Berkhamsted on the topic of "Graham Greene and the Anxiety of Influence."[1] He analyzed the way that Greene's literary imagination was formed by his childhood reading, notably by the portrayal of evil and treachery in Marjorie Bowen's historical romance *The Viper of Milan* (1906). Greene records in "The Lost Childhood" (1947) that "when – perhaps I was fourteen by that time – I took Miss Marjorie Bowen's *The Viper of Milan* from the library shelf, the future for better or worse really struck. From that moment I began to write" (*Collected Essays*, 17).[2] In addition to Bowen and other popular adventure fiction, Lodge discussed Greene's relationship to modernism, to Joseph Conrad, and to Henry James. What Lodge did not mention in his insightful lecture is that the same anxiety of influence that he traced in Greene's relationship to these various precursors characterizes Lodge's own relationship, as a novelist, to Greene himself. This can be documented from Lodge's critical essays and the prefaces and afterwords to his novels as well as from the novels themselves.

Like Greene, Lodge has provided, over the years, a fragmentary account of his own life in interviews, in several autobiographical essays, and in comments scattered through his criticism. Like Greene, too, he has commented at some length on his own fiction, although unlike Greene he has not published an autobiographical memoir as yet. Beginning with Lodge's own account of Greene's influence on him, I will proceed to an analysis of several of his novels in order to demonstrate not only the specific manifestations of that influence but also the various fictional strategies through which Lodge establishes his distinctive voice and imaginative world. The manifestation of literary influence in Lodge's work can be clarified by reference to some of the revisionary ratios of Harold Bloom's *The Anxiety of Influence*.

Lodge was thirteen in 1948, the year that the success of *The Heart of the Matter* established Greene as the pre-eminent novelist in England. Since Greene was widely perceived, in spite of his own protests, as a "Catholic novelist," it is not surprising that Lodge focussed on him as a significant preceptor. He has described this influence in several places. In a long review essay first published in the *New York Review of Books* in 1995, Lodge confesses that "The work of Graham Greene was more closely entwined with my own pursuit of a literary career than that of any other contemporary writer" (*Practice*, 70). As a literary influence, Greene showed Lodge how to make fiction out of the dilemmas and conflicts engendered by adherence to Roman Catholicism, though Lodge has generally avoided the modernist vision of extremity that characterizes Greene's fiction.[3] Furthermore, reading Greene "suggested that it was possible to be all the things that an artistically inclined adolescent dreamed of being – rebellious, bohemian, shocking to the bourgeoisie – while writing within a framework of Catholic faith and practice" (*Practice*, 71). Greene is discussed briefly in Lodge's first publication, *About Catholic Authors* (15), and he figures prominently at the end of his long master's thesis on the Catholic novel. He has been a regular point of reference throughout Lodge's critical writings and in his fiction; in 2005 Lodge wrote the foreword to a new edition of two little-known film treatments by Greene that were published by the Hesperus Press under the title *No Man's Land*. In 2011 he wrote the foreword to *Dangerous Edges of Graham Greene*, a collection of essays first presented as lectures at the Graham Greene Festival.

Lodge and Greene knew each other personally, and Lodge records some reminiscences of their friendship in *The Practice of Writing*. Their first contact took place when Lodge sent Greene a copy of *The British Museum Is Falling Down*, and Greene wrote back "I have enjoyed it immensely. It's very funny and very important at the present time" (qtd. in *Practice*, 73). Greene gave Lodge permission to use this quotation on the dust jacket of the American edition of *The British Museum*.[4] Lodge comments, "Needless to say, this was a priceless endorsement as far as I was concerned" (*Practice*, 73). Lodge also describes an interview he conducted with Greene for the British Council, which took place in a setting straight out of a Greene novel. He recalls how the producer "led us along a damp, dirty, and cluttered passage to the crummiest and most cramped recording studio I have ever been in. The table on which the microphones stood was covered with dirty brown baize, scorched with cigarette burns and apparently slashed with razor blades" (*Practice*, 75). On another occasion, Lodge and his wife visited Greene's flat in Antibes. A few days later he was writing some notes on their conversation when one of the sudden whirlwinds characteristic of the south of France strewed Lodge's papers across the landscape (77–8). Lodge sums up their friendship by saying "I have only warm memories of Graham Greene, which the revelations of his biographers have done nothing to shake, though they have perhaps mitigated any regret that I didn't know him better" (78). That comment may reveal something about Greene's influence on Lodge as well, suggesting that Lodge needed to cultivate a wary independence in order to define his own voice against that of the writer he admired so much.[5]

Since Harold Bloom's theory of influence is primarily elaborated by commentary on English and American poetry from Shakespeare and Milton to the present day, Lodge's account of Graham Greene's literary influences and his modes of overcoming them is a valuable adaptation of that theory for the discussion of prose fiction. Lodge does not use the variety of idiosyncratic terms that Bloom developed in *The Anxiety of Influence*, but rather incorporates the main assumptions underlying Bloom's approach into his own distinctive critical voice. Lodge's criticism in general is informed by both structuralism and post-structuralism, but retains affinities with the plain style of the critics who dominated the 1950s. It is enlivened by flashes of wit and personal reference, and always reveals his uncanny instinct for the most telling example. His is an understated critical voice in which less is emphatically more. The virtues of Lodge's criticism are abundantly displayed in "Graham Greene and the Anxiety of Influence." The essay shows how, as a young novelist in the 1930s, Greene swerved from the dominant models of modernism by grafting modernist literary techniques onto such popular forms as the detective novel or the espionage thriller.[6] Joseph Conrad proved to be such a powerful influence that Greene had to stop reading him, and he also repudiated the two novels that he wrote when most under the spell of late Conrad: *The Name of Action* (1930) and *Rumour at Nightfall* (1931) have never been reprinted since their first editions. With Henry James, on the other hand, Greene engaged in a strong misreading in several critical essays, turning James into an honorary Catholic novelist to whom he attributes "a sense of evil religious in its intensity" (Greene, *Collected Essays*, 23). Greene writes about *A Portrait of a Lady* in terms more applicable to one of his own novels, observing that "what deeply interested [James], what was indeed his ruling passion, was the idea of treachery, the 'Judas complex'" (*Collected Essays*, 60). Harold Bloom has commented that "I have read no stranger criticism of Henry James than that ventured by Graham Greene, who has contrived to persuade himself that James was essentially a *religious novelist*" (Introduction, 2; italics Bloom's).

As a critic and as a novelist, Lodge has approached Graham Greene from a variety of perspectives. These reveal both Lodge's great admiration for his precursor and his need to define a distinctive voice of his own, just as Greene had to do in relation to Conrad. In his earliest attempt at writing fiction, dating from his undergraduate years, Lodge seems by his own account to have been wholly under the sway of Greene. *The Devil, The World and the Flesh* was never published, but Lodge gives a brief account of it in his introduction to the 1993 Penguin reprint of *The Picturegoers*, describing it as an "embarrassing mixture of religious melodrama and sexual fantasy" (xii). He explains that the novel was the story of a Catholic schoolboy who has a relationship with the daughter of a teacher at his grammar school. She becomes pregnant, refuses an abortion, and dies, leaving the protagonist "to be consoled by her more high-minded sister, who has recently returned home after trying her vocation as a nun" (xii). Echoes of Greene's *The End of the Affair* are evident from this summary of the plot. Lodge drew on this unpublished work for a few elements of *The Picturegoers*, which tells the story of a number of characters in a south London suburb called Brickley who are linked by their attendance at the Palladium cinema on Saturday night and in some cases by their attendance at mass on Sunday morning at the church of Our Lady of Perpetual Succour. Lodge documents the importance of movies in the lives of all these characters, while commenting on it somewhat ironically through the voice of one of them, a student of English literature called Mark Underwood. Because his mother was a Roman Catholic, Mark had an early Catholic education, but his parents do not attend church and he has not practiced his religion for a long time.

There is a strong interest in documenting popular culture in *The Picturegoers*, not only movies but also advertising and rock and roll music. In this aspect of the novel, Lodge was influenced by Richard Hoggart's influential study of working-class culture, *The Uses of Literacy* (1957).[7] Hoggart broke new ground by applying the methods of literary analysis to the working-class culture of industrial Yorkshire, where he grew up. There are also some significant Joycean elements in *The Picturegoers*, which will be discussed in chapter 3, while Greene's presence can be seen in its preoccupation with the interaction of religious belief and sexuality. The Teddy boy Harry, with his flick knife and violent misogynist fantasies, is clearly indebted to the character Pinkie in Greene's novel *Brighton Rock* (1938), as Lodge acknowledges in an interview with Lidia Vianu, while the attempt to dramatize the opposition between a genuine religiosity and the dull routine of the weekly mass is fully in the tradition of the modern Catholic novel. In his essay on Evelyn Waugh in the Columbia Essays on Modern Writers series, Lodge defines the Catholic novel as one which "is characteristically concerned with the operation of God's grace in the world, with a conflict between secular and divine values in which the latter are usually allowed an ironic and unexpected triumph" (*Evelyn Waugh*, 30).[8] In the 1993 introduction to *The Picturegoers*, Lodge describes the experience of re-reading his novel after the passage of many years. He was surprised by the extent to which it deals with religion, and especially by the way that it focusses on the conversion experience that leads Mark Underwood back to the church. Lodge attributes this not to any comparable religious experience of his own, but to his reading of Catholic fiction, and adds, "Looking back at that aspect of *The Picturegoers* from my present demythologized, provisional, and in many ways agnostic theological perspective, it seems like the work of another person" (ix). Greene's influence can be detected in Lodge's presentation of the artistic rebel Mark, whose conversion is linked to the prayers of Clare Mallory, the oldest daughter in the house where he boards. Clare, like the "high-minded sister" in *The Devil, The World and the Flesh*, has returned from a convent where she has unsuccessfully tested her vocation to be a nun. She rationalizes her attraction to Mark by telling herself that she is an agent of God's grace, with the task of bringing him back to the church. After he agrees to attend mass with her the next day, she prays, "Please God, You must do something to help. When the priest elevates the Host at Mass, You could appear to Mark. You've done it before" (98).[9] The atmosphere of Mark's conversion calls to mind *The End of the Affair*, and Clare's prayers echo those of Sarah Miles as she pleads with God for Bendrix's life after he is apparently killed in the blast from the V1 flying bomb: "Give him a chance. Let him have his happiness. Do this and I'll believe" (Greene, *End*, 76).

In her bargaining with God, Sarah says that she will give up her lover forever, if only he can live. In Lodge's novel there is not such an explicit bargain, but Clare's prayers ironically produce a similar effect: Mark is not only converted but discovers a religious vocation that means he must break up with her and lead a celibate life, when all that she wanted was for him to become a Catholic and marry her. Lodge's resolution of the plot hints that his real allegiance is to the ordinary people of Brickley rather than to the supernatural melodrama of Mark's story. In a concluding scene Clare assists at the humble Catholic wedding of another couple, Bridget and Len. Although she is suffering from the end of her relationship with Mark she will clearly recover, and already she is finding some solace in an act of charity, as she arranges accommodation for the newlyweds. If Mark remains in the baroque world of a novel by Graham Greene, Clare inhabits the more quotidian reality characteristic of Lodge's fiction. Lodge never saw Catholicism as romantic or exotic. While converts were often drawn to the historical and cultural tradition of the church, Lodge sardonically notes in one of his essays that the upper-class convert's view "had relatively little to do with, say, Rosary and Benediction on a Sunday evening at the parish church of an industrial suburb, followed by a meeting of the Legion of Mary and a whist drive organized by the Union of Catholic Mothers" (*Write On*, 33). Thus *The Picturegoers*, in a move characteristic of the fiction of the 1950s, resituates the Catholic novel on a lower-middle-class, suburban terrain.

The most obvious debt to Greene in *The Picturegoers* is Lodge's use of several striking similes, imitating Greene's characteristic habit of yoking the abstract and the concrete, sometimes in a way that reverses their normal relationship. A famous example, quoted by Lodge in his booklet on Greene, occurs in *The Power and the Glory*, where the unnamed "whisky priest" who is the main character "drank the brandy down like damnation" (169).[10] In the same novel, Greene describes how the priest "could feel his prayers weigh him down like undigested food" (151). In *The Picturegoers*, Mr Mallory reflects on an unpleasant young man who left a Catholic seminary: "The fellow carried his failure before him like a monstrance" (114), while Mark Underwood's regaining of faith is described with the simile "belief leapt in his mind like a child in the womb" (111). Lodge acknowledges Richard Hoggart as the critic who drew his attention to Greene's practice of reversing the usual figurative relationship of abstract and concrete, and he observes that "Greene might say with Mauriac, 'I am a metaphysician who works in the concrete'" (*Graham Greene*, 23).[11] In *The Modes of Modern Writing* (1977), Lodge notes that Greene's practice is characteristic of writing from the 1930s in general, part of a revival of the metonymic practices of realism in that decade in response to the more metaphorical writing of the modernists.[12] Also typical of the period is Greene's use of synecdochic detail to evoke a scene and symbolize an abstraction at the same time (*Modes*, 191).

By imitating Greene's style, Lodge was at once advertising his derivation from Greene as a Catholic writer, concerned with mediating the world of grace and the material world, and signalling a tension between his use of symbolic modernist techniques derived from James Joyce and his realistic desire to document the way of life of a particular social group. This legacy was recognized by Kingsley Amis who, in the course of a positive review of *The Picturegoers* in the *Observer*, referred to the presence of "two or three lapses into pea-Greene simile" ("Insolent Chariots"). It is worth pointing out that Amis had an ambivalent view of Greene, whose name he parodied as "Grim-Grin" (*I Like It Here*, 45), and whose style he parodies in a passage in *Lucky Jim* (185). On the other hand, in the late 1940s Amis wrote a book on Greene, though it was never published and the manuscript does not seem to have survived.[13] On the occasion of Greene's death, Amis was quoted as saying "He will be missed all over the world. Until today, he was our greatest living novelist" ("Literary Titan").

In the course of an essay on the Catholic novel, Bernard Bergonzi quotes a passage from *The Picturegoers* describing the religious objects that decorate the kitchen of the Mallory household: "The kitchen into which he was ushered confirmed his suspicions about Mrs Mallory's religious background: the evidence of the plastic holy water stoup askew on the wall, the withered holy Palm, stuck behind a picture of the Sacred Heart which resembled an illustration in a medical textbook, and the statue of St Patrick enthroned upon the dresser, was conclusive" (44). Bergonzi comments on this passage that "As one who grew up in something like the milieu described in *The Picturegoers* I find such descriptions disturbingly accurate. It has rarely been caught in English fiction, for the upper-middle-class converts who wrote Catholic novels had little contact with it, and the closest parallels are in Joyce's domestic interiors" ("Decline and Fall," 180). However, there is a sympathetic precision of observation, a density of realistic detail without the imposition of symbolic levels of meaning, that distinguishes Lodge from Joyce here, and that is more akin to the comic realist novels of H.G. Wells.[14] I suspect that *The Uses of Literacy* was an influence on this aspect of *The Picturegoers*, for Hoggart describes working-class life and cultural practices without judgment and with a novelist's eye for specific details, as he lists, for example, the holiday souvenirs, the contents of shop windows, or the children's toys and candies of his childhood in Leeds. Lodge focusses on communal activities, and the way that they structure the work week and bring his characters together; in this way his novel follows Hoggart's description of the typical routine of a working-class community. While *The Picturegoers* is an impressive first novel for a very young writer, the way it is narrated raises some problems for the reader. Although the narrative moves back and forth among a variety of points of view, the central perspective is that of Mark Underwood and the central action is his journey towards faith. The parallels with Joyce's *Portrait* suggest that the reader should endorse Mark's discovery of a religious vocation, even if it is treated with some irony, just as we are supposed to accept Stephen Dedalus's literary vocation, even if at times he seems a humourless and priggish young man. The problem in Lodge's novel is that there is a dissonance between the Catholic drama of loss and gain of faith and the affectionate realism of the portrayal of the Mallory family. In terms of influence, one might say that there is a dissonance between the influence of Graham Greene and that of Richard Hoggart.

Lodge's second novel, *Ginger, You're Barmy* focusses on the experience of National Service, and it has affinities with numerous other novels about military life. Lodge organizes the plot of *Ginger* around the friendship of two young servicemen. The Roman Catholic Mike Brady has failed his university finals and is idealistic and irresponsible, while the narrator of the novel, Jonathan Browne, is a self-serving agnostic and careerist who has earned a first-class degree. "Brown" is a typical name for a Graham Greene character; he used it for both the teenage gangster in *Brighton Rock* (1938) and the narrator of *The Comedians* (published in 1966, after *Ginger*). Spelled "Browne," the name echoes the spelling of Greene's own name. The Greene novel that *Ginger* most resembles is *The Quiet American* (1955). Both novels tell the story of a sexual triangle featuring two men of very different personality types. Lodge's novel also resembles Greene's by beginning near the end of the story, and alternating between flashbacks that gradually bring the story up to the opening point and sections which advance the story in the narrative present. There is something confessional about both of these first-person narratives, and the beginning of Jonathan Browne's story includes a sentence which could easily have been written by Graham Greene: "I could never again write so unflattering an account of myself as the following, because it would open up so many awful possibilities of amendment" (*Ginger*, 9). Similarly, there are echoes of *The Heart of the Matter* in Jonathan's description of soldiers at King's Cross station, "disconsolate shades on the banks of the Styx waiting to be ferried across to Hades" (133).[15] Another passage, describing Jonathan's feeling on being demobbed, is again from the world of Greene, both in the idea of feeling nostalgia for suffering and in the specific use of the hospital as an analogy: "Who has left a hospital, in which he has suffered misery, pain and embarrassment, without a sudden, treacherous pang of regret, an irrational surge of affection for the fellow patients who kept him awake with their selfish groans, for the nurses who only got the hypo in properly at the third attempt, for the surgeon who let his wound get infected?" (190–1). In both of these examples, there is something a bit overwrought about the analogy, especially since Lodge's novel is written in a much more realistic mode than are Greene's, and there is little of the latter's metaphysical melodrama. Perhaps one should attribute this rhetoric to Jonathan's literary education, but he still seems to have a more Catholic imagination than would be expected from an agnostic – for example, he applies John Henry Newman's theory of the development of doctrine to regimental discipline in the army (66). These examples suggest that the influence of Greene has still not been fully assimilated, although *Ginger* is a significant advance on *The Picturegoers* in terms of control of tone and voice.

Jonathan and Mike were not really friends at college, but they band together when they meet on the way to basic training in Yorkshire, united by their resentment of the army. Mike's resistance is of a more active, but also self-destructive nature, and he mocks Jonathan for his timidity and "unchristian" prudence (152). When Mike deserts and is ultimately arrested, Jonathan again demonstrates this self-serving quality by telling his commanding officer that although he once knew Mike, he is "not what you might call a friend, sir" (200). Jonathan is dimly aware that this constitutes a betrayal of friendship, especially since he has taken up with Mike's girlfriend Pauline in his absence. He justifies himself with the thought that he is better suited to her self-contained femininity than Mike is, with his "barmy" boyish recklessness.

Betrayal, especially the archetype of betrayal among schoolboys, is one of Greene's most abiding themes, or perhaps obsessions might be a better word. Lodge identifies it as such in his monograph on Greene, where he lists a number of Greene's preoccupations, from dreams to dentistry to his own name. Lodge emphasizes among these "the impact of childhood experience" and "the obsession with treachery and betrayal – the 'Judas complex' which Greene has detected in Henry James, but which is far more evident in his own work" (*Graham Greene*, 9). In the famous conclusion to *The Quiet American*, Thomas Fowler seems to be looking for God, or at least wishing that God existed: "I thought of the first day and Pyle sitting beside me at the Continental, with his eye on the soda-fountain across the way. Everything had gone right with me since he had died, but how I wished there existed someone to whom I could say that I was sorry" (189). At the end of *Ginger*, Jonathan is preparing to welcome Mike, who is going to stay with him after being released from prison. Jonathan has married Pauline after getting her pregnant, and things have not been going well. "Somehow I must learn to love her," he says (211). It is not really a religious conversion, and certainly not a conversion in the mode of Mark's in *The Picturegoers*, but it is a turning towards responsibility in a manner that suggests the provisional theological framework of *The Quiet American*, rather than the world of Greene's earlier and more overtly Catholic novels.

In *Ginger, You're Barmy*, Lodge handles the narrative point of view in a manner that allows him much greater control over the ironies generated by the text than is the case in *The Picturegoers*. Although Jonathan is telling the story, the reader does not feel compelled to accept his interpretation of events. *The End of the Affair* and *The Quiet American* would have been powerful examples of the effective use of an unreliable first-person narrator. Bendrix and Fowler are sometimes self-deceiving, and their motives are often suspect, but they never lose the reader's sympathy. Like them, Jonathan Browne seems to be on the threshold of redemption as his story comes to an end. Thus the early, one might say immature, influence of Greene reflected in the overtly religious plot of *The Picturegoers* is overcome in *Ginger* by the imitation of a different aspect of Greene's achievement. It is interesting how unconscious this seems to have been, for in the afterword to the Penguin reissue of *Ginger*, Lodge confesses that it was only after the novel was completed and published that he realized that he had borrowed both the narrative structure and the story of sexual rivalry from *The Quiet American* (*Ginger*, 215).

For most of his career Lodge has alternated critical books and novels; initially the critical books were academic literary criticism, whereas after he retired from teaching they have been collections of essays, often based on invited lectures or reviews in the *New York Review of Books*. The relationships between the fictional and critical books are sometimes striking. In the late 1950s, Lodge was finishing *The Picturegoers* while at the same time writing his MA thesis on the Catholic novel. In the mid-1960s, he produced both *Language of Fiction*, the book that established his reputation as a critic, and *The British Museum Is Falling Down*, a novel whose parodies of modern novelists are closely connected to the stylistic analysis in *Language of Fiction*. Lodge's study of the methodology of stylistic analysis may have helped to free him from Greene's influence by allowing him to see more clearly the stylistic means by which Greene expressed his characteristic themes and obsessions. Once Lodge was able to parody Greene effectively, as he does in *British Museum*, he had gained some valuable distance from him. This is not to say that Lodge turned against Greene. He continued to be an advocate for his work, as he was in the early pamphlet on Catholic writing and his master's thesis. In the 1990s, Lodge wrote several reviews of biographies and memoirs of Greene, notably one in which he defended him against the attacks in Michael Shelden's very hostile biography (1994). He also wrote a review in the TLS of Neil Jordan's 1999 film adaptation of *The End of the Affair*, and his continuing interest in Greene is evidenced by his involvement in the activities of the Graham Greene Birthplace Trust.[16]

David Lodge's third novel is a departure from the realistic techniques that dominate in the first two. *The British Museum is Falling Down* is more of a metafiction than either of its predecessors, and it is also more fundamentally comic in nature. *British Museum* is about Adam Appleby, a graduate student at London University who is trying to write a thesis which sounds like a parody of *Language of Fiction*, and whose consciousness is periodically taken over by the language of the authors that he has been studying. There are ten passages in the novel that parody famous novelists, mostly classics such as Conrad, Woolf, Greene, and Joyce, though C.P. Snow and Baron Corvo also make appearances. As Lodge explains it in an afterword of 1981, "no doubt the use of parody in this book was also, for me, a way of coping with what the American critic Harold Bloom has called 'Anxiety of Influence' – the sense every young writer must have of the daunting weight of the literary tradition he has inherited, the necessity and yet seeming impossibility of doing something in writing that has not been done before" (*British Museum*, 168). Lodge's linguistic studies and his acute critical sense inform his marvellous parodies. The parody of Greene is precipitated when Adam goes through "a green baize door," into an area of the Reading Room that is restricted to staff:

> He was in another country: dark, musty, infernal ... It was as if he had dropped suddenly from the even pavement of a quiet residential street into the city's sewers. He had crossed a frontier – there was no doubt of that; and already he felt himself entering into the invisible community of outcasts and malefactors – all those who were hunted through dark ways shunned by the innocent and the respectable ... Voices, sharp and authoritative, were raised on the other side of the door. He had a sudden vision of the capture, the indictment and the punishment, and stumbled blindly towards a flight of stairs. He grasped the bannister like salvation. (90)

Apart from being a pun on Greene's name, the "green baize door" is a recurrent phrase in his writing whose origin is explained in *A Sort of Life*, where he describes the frontier between his home, the headmaster's house of Berkhamsted School, where his father was headmaster, and the school itself, where he was a pupil: "The school began just beyond my father's study, through a green baize door" (60–1). The reference to treachery, the crossing of a border, the sewers (recalling the conclusion of Greene's film treatment, *The Third Man*), the reference to outcasts and malefactors, the use of the word "salvation" as a point of comparison in a simile involving a physical action, and the use of a sequence of three words or images (here "the capture, the indictment and the punishment") are all features of Greene's style and fictional world that are readily recognizable to anyone familiar with it. The passage continues with some parodic religious titles followed by another of Greene's most characteristic devices, a kind of cinematic montage by means of which he invokes a character's inner life or a mood through a series of briefly rendered, vivid details that are at once evocative of a particular place and symbolic of a spiritual state:

> His hand groped instinctively for a weapon, but lighted only upon books: *A Quiverful of Arrows against Popery, Plucked from the Holy Scriptures* and *The Sin Against the Holy Ghost Finally Revealed*. Holding the two dusty volumes limply in his hands, he remembered the oozing wall of the urinal in the school playground, the tough Middle English paper in Finals, the fly-specked oleograph of the Sacred Heart in the Catholic doctor's waiting-room, and Barbara crying on the unmade bed; and the will to resist any longer ebbed out of him like water out of a sink, leaving behind only a sour scum of defeat. (91)

Lodge is perhaps mimicking a passage from *Brighton Rock* that he quoted in his thesis on Catholic literature ("Catholic Fiction," 678), and in his subsequent critical study of Greene (*Graham Greene*, 21). It describes Pinkie, near the end of the novel, driving into the country as his world is collapsing around him:

> An enormous emotion beat on him; it was like something trying to get in, the pressure of gigantic wings against the glass. *Dona nobis pacem*. He withstood it, with all the bitter force of the school bench, the cement playground, the St Pancras waiting-room, Dallow's and Judy's secret lust, and the cold unhappy moment on the pier. If the glass broke, if the beast – whatever it was – got in, God knows what it would do. He had a sense of a huge havoc – the confession, the penance, and the sacrament – an awful distraction, and he drove blind into the rain. (*Brighton Rock*, 242)

In *The British Museum*, Lodge is able to overcome the influence of Greene in two different ways. By writing of domestic life, notably the experience of a married couple who attempt to follow the Catholic church's teaching on birth control, Lodge suggests the need for Greene's achievement to be supplemented, or completed. This is the second of Bloom's six "revisionary ratios," *tessera* (the name comes from a token of recognition in an ancient mystery cult, a fragment of broken pottery that completes the reconstitution of a vessel). This term describes the process by which the writer reads the precursor in a way that suggests the precursor "failed to go far enough" (*Anxiety of Influence*, 14). Through his masterful use of parody Lodge also effects what could be seen in Bloom's terms as an "emptying out" of Greene's achievement, a clearing of space to make way for something different. In *The Anxiety of Influence* Bloom calls this strategy *kenosis*, after the New Testament Greek word that refers to the "emptying out" or self-humbling of Christ (14–15).

Lodge says that his parody of Greene is more an act of sympathetic homage than of satire, and I do not doubt this. But the effect of *British Museum* is to extend Greene's Catholic themes into a very different social world, dealing in a comic mode with the challenges of everyday domestic life in the context of Catholic moral teaching. By incorporating the parody of Greene, Lodge shows his mastery of that novelist's characteristic style and fictional world, which is supplemented by the realistic aspect of the novel. Greene himself acknowledged the incompleteness of his knowledge of English Catholicism when he wrote to Lodge after the publication of *How Far Can You Go?*: "I have never encountered the kind of Catholic types you portray, perhaps because I belong to a much earlier period. I thought that the idea that contraception was wrong and a belief in hell vanished before the war" (qtd. in *Practice*, 76). Interestingly, Greene was sufficiently impressed with the topical relevance of the treatment of the contraception issue in *British Museum* that he suggested that Lodge should send a copy of the novel to the Cardinal Archbishop of Westminster, and he undertook to do so himself when Lodge raised objections (*Practice of Writing*, 73).

Lodge explains how he domesticated Greene's fiction in an insightful comment on his own work: "My own early novels transposed some characteristically Greeneian themes – belief and unbelief, transgression and guilt – into a less luridly lit, more suburban milieu, but not without some stylistic echoes" (*Practice*, 71). Greene's taste for extremity, both in his fiction and in his personal life, derives from a fundamental aspect of his temperament. This is revealed in an important and revealing letter that he wrote to his wife Vivien in 1948, at a time when their marriage was breaking down irretrievably: "the fact that has to be faced, dear, is that by my nature, my selfishness, even in some degree my profession, I should always, and with anyone, have been a bad husband … the disease, which has been going on ever since my childhood and was only temporarily alleviated by psycho-analysis, lies in a character profoundly antagonistic to ordinary domestic life. Unfortunately the disease is also one's material. Cure the disease and I doubt whether a writer would remain" (3 June 1948; *Life in Letters*, 159). For me, one of the best illustrations of Greene's antagonism to domestic life is his description of the teenage gangster Pinkie, in *Brighton Rock*, bleeding from a wound and hiding from his pursuers in the garage of a suburban house. The accumulations of a lifetime are piled in the garage, including "a pram which had been converted into a wheelbarrow" (109); one senses Greene's own hatred of domesticity behind Pinkie's hatred of the unremarkable life summed up in the junk piled around him. Greene writes, "And the Boy hated him. He was nameless, faceless, but the Boy hated him, the doll, the pram, the broken rocking-horse" (109).

One of the best-known lines in all of Lodge's fiction occurs in *The British Museum*, and it might also be considered a response, especially in the context of a novel about contraception, to the portrayal of sexuality and domestic life in the fiction of Graham Greene. Adam's friend Camel accuses him of not knowing the difference between life and literature, and he replies "Literature is mostly about having sex and not much about having children. Life is the other way round" (56). Adam's definition of literature certainly applies to the fiction of Graham Greene, where there are not many children, and where those who do exist often, like Scobie's daughter in *The Heart of the Matter*, seem to have been created only in order to die. Lodge's view of domestic life is very different from that of Greene. Like his near contemporary Margaret Drabble, he found much of the substance of his fiction in "ordinary domestic life"; he learned from Kingsley Amis and other neo-realists of the 1950s how to domesticate the vision of extremity that characterizes Greene and the modernists. This will be discussed in greater detail in chapter 4, with particular reference to the image of the pram. Lodge frequently mentions his wife Mary and their three children in his essays and in interviews, and he has clearly found domestic life no impediment to the creation of a sizeable oeuvre comprising both criticism and fiction, much of it written while he was also holding down a teaching position. In *The British Museum*, the protagonist Adam is burdened by his growing family, and his fears that it will increase in size, but this does not prevent him from thinking fondly of them, and his anxieties arise from his concern about providing for them.

Given Greene's distaste for domestic life, it is amusing that Adam's landlady, a comically interfering women, is called "Mrs Green," while in her interior monologue at the end of the novel Adam's wife Barbara remembers a schoolmate whose name was "Olive Green" (156). Lodge also includes the satirical portrait of a radical Dominican priest, Father Wildfire, in *The British Museum*. Adam does not want to trouble Father Wildfire with his own difficulties about the Catholic teaching on contraception, for the priest "lived at the frontiers of the spiritual life, where dwelt criminals, prostitutes, murderers and saints, a territory steaming with the fumes of human iniquity, from which souls emerged, if they emerged at all, toughened and purified by a heroic struggle with evil. In contrast, Adam's moral problem seemed trivial and suburban" (64). Father Wildfire is clearly a character who inhabits Greeneland, sharing Greene's interest in what Robert Browning called "the dangerous edge of things. / The honest thief, the tender murderer."[17] Here again we find Lodge using the favourite Greene image of the frontier.

His fascination with borders is often related to Greene's sense of crossing boundaries by being both the headmaster's son and an ordinary pupil at Berkhamsted School. This same double identity has also been linked to his frequent use of espionage motifs in novels such as *A Gun for Sale*, *The Confidential Agent*, and *Our Man in Havana*. At first Greene classified these books as "entertainments" rather than novels.[18] Lodge has always been regarded as a literary novelist who is also popular, whereas John le Carré, whom Harold Bloom has called "Greene's haunted disciple" (Introduction, 3), is seen as a popular writer who has literary merit. Le Carré has been popular since the 1960s. His novels of the sixties and seventies expressed the tensions and anxieties of the Cold War period; since then he has explored other issues, including the legacy of colonialism in Africa. In the aftermath of 11 September 2001, he has regained something of the standing he had in the 1970s, as witnessed by the high profile of *Our Kind of Traitor* (2010) and by the 2011 film *Tinker Tailor Soldier Spy*, which remade the popular 1979 miniseries. Like Greene and le Carré, Lodge is also fascinated with the idea of passing between different worlds and identities, though in a very different register that is largely restricted to everyday life, for example industry and the university in *Nice Work*, the humanities and science in *Thinks…*, or his recurrent use of the Jamesian international theme to explore the cultural differences between England and the United States.

Even the most realistic novelist will occasionally include melodramatic elements that are characteristic of genre fiction. For example, Margaret Drabble, who is associated in the public mind, fairly or unfairly, with the life of professional women in Hampstead and the experiences of maternity and adultery, incorporates elements of an espionage thriller in the latter part of her condition of England novel *The Ice Age* (1977). Lodge occasionally includes elements of popular fiction in his work as well, although they are always contained by a larger realistic or ironic structure. In *Out of the Shelter* he plays his own variation on John le Carré's *The Spy Who Came in from the Cold* or *A Small Town in Germany*, as two of the characters try to sell secrets to East Germany. Lodge is not wholly comfortable with this territory however, and the most significant parts of the espionage plot are reported at second hand. This is about as close as Lodge gets to imitating Greene's entertainments, though he does send up thrillers in *Small World* when Morris Zapp is briefly kidnapped by a gang of Marxist terrorists, before being released through the influence of a famous Marxist professor.

Also in *Small World*, Philip Swallow, the rather diffident and underachieving academic, suddenly finds himself acting out a romance plot straight out of film noir: "Three hours later, Philip paced anxiously up and down the broad platform of Ankara's main railway station beside the tall coaches of the Ankara-Istanbul express. The train had a period air, vaguely reminiscent of thirties' thrillers, as did the whole scene" (214).[19] Needless to say, Swallow's romantic interlude has an ignominious conclusion. Lodge's most recent novel, *A Man of Parts*, is for the most part concerned with H.G. Wells's life as a writer and with his romantic and sexual relationships. But towards the end, the possibility that his lover Moura Budberg is a Soviet spy is mentioned in a way that suggests how a wholly different novel, in the manner of John le Carré, could have emerged from this material, as Wells contemplates the possibility "that their long love affair had been from the start directed and determined by the expediencies of her personal survival" (549).

Lodge may have successfully dealt with influence of Graham Greene in *The British Museum* through the strategies that I have just discussed, but he was not finished with it. Greene plays a significant role in two of Lodge's best novels, *How Far Can You Go?* and *Therapy*. *How Far Can You Go?* is at once Lodge's most Catholic novel, and a work that charts the process by which Catholics lost their distinct identity within English society as a result of social changes in the second half of the twentieth century and changes in the church resulting from the second Vatican Council. The novel begins with nine Catholic undergraduates at the University of London, and the priest who oversees their college's Catholic society, and it follows them from 1952, through their various experiences of marriage (or in the case of one of the students, religious vocation), parenting, illness, marital difficulties, and bereavement, to 1975, with an authorial coda written in 1978. As in *The British Museum*, considerable space is devoted to domestic life and children. Lodge returns to the topic of the Catholic teaching on contraception, and looking back to *The British Museum*, he says that that work would depress him now "if I didn't know that my principal characters would have made a sensible decision long ago to avail themselves of contraceptives" (*How Far*, 74). It is remarkable how vividly each of the characters in the novel emerges, given its relative brevity (244 pages in the Penguin edition). Lodge incorporates various metafictional devices, including a number of examples of the kind of sudden shifts in time that are pervasive in Muriel Spark's *The Prime of Miss Jean Brodie*. These, in both works, serve to emphasize the power of the authorial voice over the chronological sequence of the characters' story.

Like the Catholic novels of Greene and Mauriac, Lodge's *How Far Can You Go?* is concerned with the relationship between human desire and the teaching of the church, but here the similarity ends. Greene characteristically explores these themes in extreme situations such as revolutionary Mexico, London during the Blitz, or an African leper colony. Violence and exotic settings are his trademarks (Martin Amis quotes his father as saying that the ideal title for a Greene novel would be *Visa to Darkness*[20]). In Lodge's novel, the settings are largely the provincial suburbs, and the characters belong to the professional middle class. Marian Crowe has observed of the people Lodge describes in *How Far Can You Go?*, "What is extraordinary about these characters is that they are so ordinary" (*Aiming at Heaven*, 148). In fact, this is the key to Lodge's success in the novel. Rather than presenting the extremes of rebel-saints, he is seeking to convey the nature of everyday religious experience in average people. The title refers to both sexual and religious experience, and the novel frequently makes analogies between them. The character Michael reflects on the mysteriousness of the sexual experience of other people, even his own spouse (70).

Lodge has written perceptively about George Eliot's first book, *Scenes of Clerical Life*, especially praising the first story in that work for the uncompromising way in which it makes "the commonplace and unglamorous figure the centre of attention," revealing "a confidence in the significance of the quotidian" (*Year*, 185). Lodge shares Eliot's interest in the quotidian, which would have been reinforced by the aesthetics of much of the new literature of his youth, and it is incorporated into *How Far Can You Go?* in dialogue with other voices in the text, such as those of literary theorists, or literary modernism, or Christian theology. Bergonzi's incisive discussion of *How Far* recognizes Lodge's achievement in this respect, but at the same time voices regret for the loss of the experience of transcendence in earlier Catholic literature: "Lodge has moved down from those dangerous peaks and that rarified air to the flat, populous plain where most of us live our daily lives"; his characters "are decent and likeable and one intimately understands and sympathizes with their struggles. But they are also *gens moyens sensuels* and, when all is said, a rather mediocre lot" ("Decline and Fall," 187; 186). In *How Far Can You Go?* the alienated individual exists primarily in the modern novels studied by Michael, a college lecturer whose career in some ways parallels Lodge's own, notably in his devotion to the works of Graham Greene. Although Michael's study of modern literature has given him a theoretical commitment to the quest for personal authenticity, he is not an adventurous person at heart, and it is his friend Dennis, a plant manager in the electronics industry, who leaves his wife for a younger woman. In a comic scene, Michael meets Dennis in the pub, feeling like "a nervous envoy from the world of bourgeois morality." Michael sees the situation, as he usually does, in terms of a literary reference: "'It's like *Heart of Darkness*,' he said. 'You're Kurtz and I'm Marlow'" (225). However Dennis is not at heart a rebel either, but a rather conservative and conformist person who is relieved when Father Austin Brierly, the young priest from the first scene of the novel, is able to bring him back together with his wife Angela.

At the beginning of the novel, Michael's guilt about his sexual feelings causes him to pose as an anguished Greene character, notably to his friend Polly, who is far more comfortable with her own sexuality. They discuss the relative merits of Greene and Waugh at a student party:

> Michael's favourite novel at the moment is *The Heart of the Matter*, and Polly's, *Brideshead Revisited.* "But Greene's awfully sordid, don't you think?" says Polly.
>
> "But Waugh's so snobbish."
>
> "Anyway, it said in the *Observer* that they're the two best English novelists going, so that's one in the eye for the Prods." (25)

Michael works on a postgraduate thesis on Greene, and realizes that his own religious identity is closely bound up with literary Catholics.[21] He is troubled by the way that in Greene's *Quiet American* (1955), "there was not the same stark contrast between the Church and the secular world that you got in the earlier novels. Michael's interest was more than academic: in some way the credibility of the Catholic faith was underwritten for him by the existence of distinguished literary converts like Graham Greene and Evelyn Waugh, so any sign of their having doubts was unsettling. Polly, however, didn't want to talk about Graham Greene, but about her love affairs" (41). Here as elsewhere, a reference to Greene is one of the ways in which Lodge signals the passage of time and the nature of the Zeitgeist; the increasing pressure towards liberalization within the church is paralleled by an increasingly skeptical or agnostic attitude towards the church in Greene's novels. This is exemplified by *A Burnt-Out Case* (1961), where Michael recognizes a move away from a version of Catholicism that he himself no longer accepts, as Greene reflects "the evolutionary Utopianism of Teilhard de Chardin" (82). Lodge also quotes from the first-person narrator of Greene's novel about Haiti, *The Comedians* (1966): "When I was a boy I had faith in the Christian God. Life under his shadow was a very serious affair ... Now that I approached the end of life it was only my sense of humour that enabled me sometimes to believe in Him" (*How*

Far, 102; ellipsis Lodge's). Both Greene and Lodge moved to more provisional views of their religious faith as they grew older. In an interview with Bernard Bergonzi first published in 1992, Lodge described himself as an "agnostic Catholic," a term he prefers to Greene's "Catholic agnostic" (Bergonzi, "Conversation," 203).

Michael's relationship with Miriam, the woman he marries, is partly presented by means of references to Greene. They have their first serious quarrel while attending a performance of his play *The Potting Shed*, which had its London run in the spring of 1958, featuring John Gielgud in a cardigan of a "peculiarly bilious green" (*How Far*, 59). The funniest scene involving Greene occurs on Michael and Miriam's wedding night, and the aspect of *The Heart of the Matter* that Kingsley Amis mocks in *Lucky Jim* is again the source of comedy. As a result of their inexperience, Michael and Miriam do not succeed in making love on their first attempt, and as they sit together sadly at dinner Michael turns to Greene in order to clarify his feelings: "Michael contemplated the prospect of a marriage without sex. After so long a wait, did he love Miriam enough to accept that heavy cross? He reached under the table and squeezed her hand, suffused with a Greeneian gloom, 'the loyalty we all feel to unhappiness, the sense that this is where we really belong,' as a favourite passage in *The Heart of the Matter* put it" (63). Here again, Lodge deals with Greene's legacy by an element of parody, for the gloom is soon dispelled, and Greene is not mentioned in the latter half of the novel. Michael moves on to write essays of cultural commentary, just as Lodge moves on to depict the social concerns, attitudes, and fashions of the early 1970s, employing language from structuralist criticism and modern theology to signal how far he has come as a novelist since his early days.

Greene is not an important presence in Lodge's academic trilogy, but his influence reappears in a productive way in *Therapy*, which is arguably Lodge's best novel. *Therapy* combines a number of Lodge's abiding interests: it contains significant Catholic elements, and the narrative of the protagonist's youth goes back to the south London world of *The Picturegoers*. The satirical comedy of the academic novels continues, but it is moved into the setting of the entertainment business, and farcical accounts of a holiday in Tenerife and a trip to Los Angeles show, more than is usual in Lodge, the influence of Evelyn Waugh. But *Therapy* is also something of a departure in that it commences a shift towards fiction based on extensive research as well as experience, and *Therapy* is more intellectually ambitious than Lodge's earlier books. Once again, Lodge reworks aspects of *The End of the Affair*, but he does so in the context of a serious engagement with the work of Søren Kierkegaard.

Comedy, Graham Greene, and Kierkegaard sound like a disastrous combination, rather like Woody Allen's attempt to make a "serious" film with *Interiors*, but Lodge is careful to insulate himself against the charge of excessive solemnity by parodying his own procedure within the novel. The narrator of *Therapy* is Tubby Passmore, a TV sitcom writer in the throes of midlife crisis. He proposes to his incredulous producers that he will make a TV documentary about the life of Kierkegaard. Lodge gave a lecture at a conference on Kierkegaard in which he discusses the writing of *Therapy*, and he says that he used the "risible" situation of a self-educated television writer becoming obsessed with Kierkegaard in order to generate comedy, for he "was determined from the outset to write a novel about depression that would not be depressing" (*Consciousness*, 274). To my mind, Lodge carried off his high-risk strategy in *Therapy* extremely well. One of the strengths of the novel is that it overcomes Greene's influence, and that of the Catholic novel itself, by infusing the ideas of Kierkegaard, an existentialist Protestant, into a story about confession, forgiveness, and pilgrimage. In the lecture on *Therapy*, Lodge says that he intended the Kierkegaardian elements to "yield a different perspective on [Tubby's] plight and a different language for talking about it" (*Consciousness*, 274). Kierkegaard provides a vocabulary for analyzing mid-life crisis; at the same time the plot is partially based on the story of Kierkegaard and Regine Olsen, and the various methods of narration that Tubby employs resemble the complex use of personae in Kierkegaard's own works.

Some scenes in *Therapy* return to the setting of *The Picturegoers* in order to explore themes of sexual fidelity and the search for faith. Lodge writes about the 1950s from the perspective of the 1990s, as Tubby looks back to his youth in order to understand his present anxieties (Tubby is fifty-eight in 1993, the year in which the novel is set, and thus was born in the same year as David Lodge). He has devoted much time and energy to various forms of therapy, psychological, pharmaceutical, and New Age, but in the end it is the journal he writes that allows him to understand himself sufficiently to resolve some of the issues that preoccupy him. Like *The End of the Affair*, *Therapy* is a first-person narrative about love, betrayal, and faith, and it too seeks to understand the present by a journey into the past. Greene's narrator, Maurice Bendrix, is a novelist, while Tubby Passmore is a television scriptwriter who has begun a journal as part of an assignment for his therapist. The significance of this is underlined by Lodge's use of an epigraph from Greene: "Writing is a form of therapy."[22]

There are numerous echoes of *The End of the Affair* in *Therapy*, many of which are small, but their cumulative effect seems to me significant. I have not found any comment by Lodge on this connection, and he may not be aware of its extent, since he emphasizes the role of Kierkegaard's life and thought as sources for his plot and some of the themes he explores in *Therapy*. He has written that he used Kierkegaard to provide "another discourse, another perspective, another (parallel) story," feeling that Tubby's own perspective was too limited to stand alone (*Consciousness*, 272). Greene and Kierkegaard have a number of concerns in common as essentially religious writers who focus on the dilemmas of human beings seeking to live authentic lives in the face of the alienating structures of social institutions and social conventions.

The End of the Affair and *Therapy* can be connected through some of the characters' names. Greene loved to play games with names in his fiction, and he once observed that "there is a magic quality in names – to change the name is to change the character" (*Ways of Escape*, 11). He often used his own first name, Henry, for characters in his novels, and sometimes the last name Brown, notably for "Pinkie Brown" in *Brighton Rock*. Numerous heroines continue the colour theme by having the names Rose or Coral, while *The Third Man* features the villain Harry Lime, whose name is a variation on Henry Graham Greene. In *Therapy*, Tubby befriends a homeless man called Grahame who sleeps in the entryway of his flat. Like Harry in *The Picturegoers*, Grahame is one of Lodge's rare characters from the wrong side of respectability, and he serves as a kind of double or conscience figure. The transference of the final "e" from "Greene" to "Grahame" is a joke that suggests Greene's ongoing influence in a manner that might have been employed by Greene himself. Grahame's presence on the threshold of Tubby's flat is a perfect visual representation of the place of Graham Greene at the threshold of David Lodge's novelistic imagination. It is noteworthy that Grahame and his friends eventually steal the contents of the flat while Tubby is away, but knowing that Tubby is a writer, Grahame leaves behind the computer containing his precious writing.

At the beginning of *The End of the Affair*, Maurice Bendrix comments that "For some reason I am a man known by his surname – I might never have been christened for all the use my friends make of the rather affected Maurice my literary parents gave me" (3). This observation first sounds the theme of baptism that will become important later in the novel, and Bendrix is distinguished from Henry Miles, Sarah's husband, who is always referred to in the novel as "Henry." In *Therapy*, Laurence Passmore is known to almost everybody as "Tubby" rather than by his actual name. When he first meets Maureen, the great love of his adolescence, she mentions the religious significance of the name Laurence, confusing him by responding "Turn me over" when he tells her his name. She then tells him the story of St Laurence, who "was martyred by being slowly roasted on a gridiron" (*Therapy*, 229). Thus in each novel the narrator's name is associated with the Christian significance of naming, before each begins a journey towards faith.

At a turning point in Tubby's relationship with his "platonic mistress" Amy (31), he takes her to Rules, a restaurant that bills itself as the oldest in London, and the place where Bendrix and Sarah Miles eat in *The End of the Affair*.[23] As the story of *Therapy* unfolds, Tubby is trying to understand his pervasive unhappiness, and he begins an obsessive reading of Kierkegaard. When his marriage breaks up he starts trying to find Maureen, whom he cruelly abandoned many years ago. His quest, like Maurice Bendrix's quest to find out why Sarah Miles ended their relationship three years earlier, eventually becomes a journey towards God. In this case, it is Lodge rather than Greene who makes use of the motif of foreign travel, for Tubby's search takes him on the pilgrimage to Santiago de Compostela. This was one of the major medieval pilgrim routes, going from various points in Europe to Santiago in northwestern Spain, and it has had something of a revival in recent decades. Lodge provides the reader with quite a bit of information about the pilgrimage in the last part of *Therapy*.[24]

Both novels represent physical and spiritual healing that may or may not be a sign of the operation of divine grace; this theme is at the centre of *The End of the Affair* and is present in a more oblique way in *Therapy*. In Greene's novel, Sarah Miles dies and several coincidences or surprising turns of events following her death can be regarded as miracles, though Greene presents them in such a way as to allow for naturalistic explanations. After Sarah's funeral, Bendrix is "saved" from seducing Sylvia, the girlfriend of another writer, by the appearance of Sarah's mother. There are also two cases of healing. The rationalist Richard Smythe is cured of a disfiguring skin disease, and the detective Parkis's son is suddenly cured of a stomach ailment by reading a book that once belonged to Sarah.[25]

In *Therapy*, there are two parallel situations. After his marriage has broken up, Tubby travels to Copenhagen with Samantha, a young assistant, ostensibly for the purpose of researching his film about Kierkegaard but really with the intention of seducing Samantha. However, as a result of seeing Kierkegaard's desk in the city museum, Tubby has the strange sensation that the philosopher is somehow present in the room, hovering beside him. As a result, he abandons the erotic purpose of his trip: "Something held me back, and it wasn't the fear of impotence, or of aggravating my knee injury. Call it conscience. Call it Kierkegaard. They have become one and the same thing" (*Therapy*, 209). All through the novel, Tubby has been plagued by a mysterious knee pain that his doctor is unable to treat, and that seems to be a sign of his spiritual malaise; it "miraculously" disappears on the pilgrimage to Compostela, even though Tubby doesn't walk very much of the route. Maureen attributes the healing to the intervention of St James, but it also seems to be connected to the fact that Tubby tracked her down in order to ask for forgiveness and "absolution" for the way he treated her forty years earlier (*Therapy*, 297). It is striking that Tubby uses a "pea-Greene" simile at the end of *Therapy* when he and Maureen drive to Finisterre: "We sat down on a warm, flat rock, amid coarse grass and wildflowers, and watched the sun, like a huge communion wafer behind a thin veil of cloud, slowly decline towards the wrinkled surface of the sea" (315). The extravagant religious image may be attributed to the religious devotions Tubby has witnessed while accompanying Maureen on the pilgrimage, reviving memories of the days when he joined the Catholic youth club in order to court her.

The end of *Therapy* repeats the triangular situation of *The End of the Affair*, as Tubby has become a friend of both Maureen and her husband Bede, while he is occasionally Maureen's lover.[26] Lodge's conclusion to *Therapy* provides a comic resolution; none of his major characters dies, and the Catholic themes are muted, and blended with the references to Kierkegaard. He does not emulate the passionate extremity of Greene: one cannot imagine Lodge writing at the beginning of a novel, as Greene does on the first page of *The End of the Affair*, "this is a record of hate far more than of love" (1). Greene's influence seems to me pervasive in *Therapy*, but it is totally transformed into Lodge's own idiom. In terms of Bloom's analysis of influence, *Therapy* is an example of *apophrades*, or "the return of the dead" (*Anxiety of Influence*, 15). In this final revisionary ratio, the influence of the precursor returns, but in a manner that is under the full control of the later writer, as Lodge in *Therapy* seems in possession of both his own novel and of Greene's. Lodge's novel acknowledges the power and importance of love and sexual passion, but he represents forgiveness and reconciliation by opening up the possibilities of comedy. Tubby Passmore is self-deprecating and ironic in a way that Maurice Bendrix is not, and so Lodge is able to transform Greene's spiritual tragic drama into his own brand of domestic comedy while retaining something of the power of the informing influence. This act of creative appropriation may be one of the reasons why *Therapy* succeeds so well, and why it is one of Lodge's strongest works of fiction.

Lodge's next full-length novel *Thinks...* explores an adulterous relationship through the first-person narratives of the two lovers. One of them, Helen Reed, is a novelist, and she writes in her journal: "When I was fifteen I read Graham Greene's *The End of the Affair*, surreptitiously because I was fairly sure Daddy wouldn't think it was suitable. In fact of course it was the perfect book for a devout Catholic adolescent girl just beginning to be aware of her own sexuality ... Goodness how I cried over that book! How I yearned to be like Sarah when I grew up, to experience everything, and atone for my sins in a grand heroic gesture of self-sacrifice. Now I find myself in much her situation, but without her faith" (300). The novelist Monica Ali quotes this passage from *Thinks...* in her introduction to the 2004 Vintage Classics edition of *The End of the Affair* (Introduction, xv), and she goes on to argue that Lodge and Greene are both exploring, fifty years apart and in very different ways, the same "question of what it is to be human" (xvi).

Ali also wrote an afterword to *Dangerous Edges of Graham Greene*, the book of essays to which David Lodge contributed a foreword. This conjunction of Lodge with one of the best-known of the younger generation of contemporary British writers gives a nice symmetry to *Dangerous Edges* and demonstrates Greene's continuing appeal. Ali's discussions of Greene, along with Zadie Smith's 2004 introduction to *The Quiet American* and Pico Iyer's 2012 book on his relationship with

Greene's writing, *The Man within My Head*, are all signs of Greene's vitality.[27] In his foreword to *Dangerous Edges*, Lodge discusses the fact that Greene's work has endured even though it has not been held in high regard by the dominant schools of literary criticism in England. He adds that this is not the case in France, where Greene is highly respected (Foreword, xiii). It is a fascinating coincidence that Lodge's own work seems more highly regarded by general readers and by other writers than by academic critics, and he likewise has a great following in France. Once again in 2011, as in his 1966 study of Greene, Lodge seems to be describing himself when he describes Greene's critical reception. Monica Ali's invocation of David Lodge and *Thinks...* in her introduction to *The End of the Affair* suggests that Lodge will experience the same sort of enduring literary influence and popularity with readers that Greene so evidently enjoys.

3

Lodge Rejoyces: David Lodge, James Joyce, and Ireland

> Leavis declared that one must be for Lawrence or for Joyce, one could not serve both masters. I was unreservedly a Joycean.
>
> ~David Lodge, "D.H. Lawrence: Genius, Heretic, Classic"

David Lodge has described James Joyce as "a formative influence in my youth, when my own ambitions to be a writer were germinating ... He is, of all modern writers, the one I revere the most" (*Practice*, 124–5). The influence of Joyce can be seen in many of Lodge's novels, from the way that *The Picturegoers* is structured to the energetic linguistic play of *Small World*, but he suggests that Joyce's achievement is so far beyond what any successor can hope to attain that there should be no question of anxiety of influence: "Most of us have not dreamed of measuring up to that awe-inspiring genius, but have contented ourselves with reading and raiding his work for hints, models, blueprints and lessons" (*Write On*, 69).

Lodge describes his early encounters with Joyce in "My Joyce," an essay that he included in *Write On* in 1986. This is one of Lodge's most autobiographical essays, originally commissioned for a book that was never published, and it vividly evokes the world of his childhood: "I grew up within the intangible, but very real, walls of the Catholic 'ghetto.' I inhabited a world ideologically shaped and interpreted by Counter-Reformation Catholicism – which was not very different in England in the late 1940s from the Catholicism in which James Joyce grew up ... English Catholics were mostly Irish or partly Irish in origin, in the lower-middle-class social stratum to which I belonged, and many of the priests and teachers I encountered spoke with a thick brogue" (*Write On*, 58). This meant that Lodge first encountered Joyce not as the great example of high modernism, but as a chronicler of his own sociocultural world. He commented in the open discussion at a conference sponsored by the journal *Novel* that "one of the great books of my adolescence was *A Portrait of the Artist as a Young Man*" ("Windup Session," 353).

Lodge first read *Ulysses* as he approached his final exams for his undergraduate degree (*Write On*, 63). As for so many critics and writers of the twentieth century, *Ulysses* became for him a central point of reference, the indubitable masterpiece of modern fiction, and, quite simply, one of his favourite books.[1] In "My Joyce" he recalls the subversive, somewhat illicit status that *Ulysses* still had in the 1950s, prior to the *Lady Chatterley* trial of 1960, and he describes buying a copy from a bookseller in Charing Cross Road who displayed books of nude photographs in the window, after he had unsuccessfully asked for the book at several more reputable shops (*Write On*, 62). Lodge's description of the copy he bought, and still had on his shelf thirty years later, conveys a strong sense of its personal significance to him: "Just to handle the old Bodley Head edition was to feel a shiver of premonitory pleasure, a sense that this was no ordinary novel, but a magic book. It was heavy, and an unusual shape, squarer than the normal novel, with long lines of type stretching from margin to margin that imposed an appropriately deliberate pace upon the reader" (*Write On*, 62). Lodge implies that *Ulysses* is a monument of print culture, a kind of ultimate book with a special status. He presents it this way in *Ginger, You're Barmy* as well. On leave from his basic training, the agnostic narrator Jonathan Browne finds himself in a state of erotic frustration, jealous that his friend Mike has a girlfriend and he doesn't: "At home that night, I sat up late reading the last chapter of *Ulysses* for the dirt, which, in my morality, is a kind of mortal sin" (*Ginger*, 142).

There is no question then that Joyce was extremely important to Lodge. However, for him to become a successful novelist he had to come to terms with Joyce's influence, and I think that as in the case of Graham Greene this involved Lodge in some complex transactions with his precursor. Some of these transactions are more adversarial than Lodge suggests in his self-deprecating tributes to Joyce. Furthermore, Joyce raises questions of nationality and identity that are important to consider. Although Lodge's grammar school teachers may have been largely Irish by birth, he was born and grew up in England, and in his early fiction he would partially identify himself with the self-consciously

English literary movements of the 1950s. As an Irish writer and a modernist, Joyce is at odds with the literary values of the Movement, and he was not included by F.R. Leavis in his "great tradition" of the English novel. Lodge's use of Joyce is thus unavoidably connected to the question of national identity, and the second part of this chapter looks at Lodge's representation of Ireland and the Irish in his fiction. This is a place where religion, nationality, and politics are involved in a sometimes uneasy dialogue, which complicates the influence of Joyce in fascinating ways.

Joycean influences are readily apparent in Lodge's early fiction. For example, Mark Underwood, the student protagonist of *The Picturegoers*, introduces *A Portrait of the Artist as a Young Man* to Patricia Mallory, the teenaged daughter of the family with whom he boards: "she had read it through, soaking up like a dry sponge its sadness and revolt and rebellion and need to be free, and how she wished she could have met Stephen when he was her age, and talked to him and said how she understood" (32). Mark is an alienated young man from the suburbs and an aspiring writer. His rants against conformity and his quest for authenticity and meaning are thoroughly in the tradition of the literature of the 1950s, while his return to the faith in which he was baptized neatly reverses the structure of Joyce's novel. Lodge's response to Joyce in *The Picturegoers* can be elucidated by reference to some classic Catholic conversion narratives. By relocating Joyce in the religious tradition he rebelled against, and with which Lodge self-consciously identifies, Lodge is able to diminish his authority even while drawing on him as a literary model. This strategy resembles the revisionary ratio that Harold Bloom calls *daemonization*, which he explains as follows: "The later poet opens himself to what he believes to be a power in the parent-poem that does not belong to the parent proper, but to a range of being just beyond that precursor" (*Anxiety of Influence*, 15).

In Joyce's *Portrait*, Stephen Dedalus famously renounces the vocation of the priesthood for the vocation of artist after his epiphanic vision of the girl on the beach: "Her image had passed into his soul for ever and no word had broken the holy silence of his ecstasy. Her eyes had called him and his soul had leaped at the call. To live, to err, to fall, to triumph, to recreate life out of life! A wild angel had appeared to him, the angel of mortal youth and beauty, an envoy from the fair courts of life, to throw open before him in an instant of ecstasy the gates of all the ways of error and glory. On and on and on and on!" (*Portrait of the*

Artist, 145). Joyce's religious language here signals his reversal of the pattern of the Catholic spiritual autobiography, of which St Augustine's *Confessions* is the originating example. In Augustine's narrative, God speaks to him through the voice of a child, chanting over and over again "Pick up and read, pick up and read" ("*Tolle, lege*"), and, he writes, "I began to think intently whether there might be some sort of children's game in which such a chant is used. But I could not remember having heard of one. I checked the flood of tears and stood up. I interpreted it solely as a divine command to me to open the book and read the first chapter I might find" (*Confessions*, 152–3). Augustine picks up the book he had been reading, St Paul's Epistle to the Romans, and opens it to chapter 13:13–14 ("Not in riots and drunken parties, not in eroticism and indecencies, not in strife and rivalry, but put on the Lord Jesus Christ, and make not provision for the flesh in its lusts") and his conversion is complete: "it was as if a light of relief from all anxiety flooded into my heart. All the shadows of doubt were dispelled" (153). In Joyce's rewriting of Augustine, the voice of beauty speaks through the apparition of the girl on the beach, telling Stephen to dedicate his life to art: "Her eyes had called him and his soul had leaped at the call." He later articulates his new creed to his friend Cranly: "I will not serve that in which I no longer believe whether it call itself my home, my fatherland or my church: and I will try to express myself in some mode of life or art as freely as I can and as wholly as I can, using for my defence the only arms I allow myself to use – silence, exile, and cunning" (*Portrait of the Artist*, 208). Joyce's novel thus constitutes a counter-narrative to the archetypal story of Christian conversion, substituting aesthetic experience for divine grace, though retaining the sacramental language of Catholicism to describe the role of an artist.

Another influential spiritual autobiography in the Catholic tradition is John Henry Newman's *Apologia Pro Vita Sua* (1864). Newman was much admired by Joyce for his prose style, and he was the founder of the Catholic university in Ireland that later became University College, Dublin, the university James Joyce attended.[2] In the *Apologia*, Newman describes a pivotal moment in his conversion to the Roman Catholic church, when his theory of Anglicanism as a *via media* between the errors of Protestantism and Rome was radically challenged. In 1839, Newman was reading an article by Nicholas Wiseman, who would become the archbishop of Westminster when the Roman Catholic diocesan structure was revived in England in 1850. Wiseman quoted words from St Augustine: "Securus judicat orbis terrarum" ["the entire world judges with security"], and these words, Newman says, struck him with the force of the child's words to St Augustine: "they were like the 'Tolle, lege, – Tolle, lege,' of the child, which converted St Augustine himself. 'Securus judicat orbis terrarum!' By those great words of the ancient Father, interpreting and summing up the long and varied course of ecclesiastical history, the theory of the *Via Media* was absolutely pulverized" (*Apologia*, 116).

Though Joyce reverses the pattern of both Augustine and Newman, telling the story of a repudiation of Catholicism, his work never really left the church behind; in Lodge's words, "In many ways, Joyce was (and is) the most Catholic of all the novelists in the English language" (*Write On*, 61), or as Cranly puts it to Stephen Dedalus in the final chapter of *Portrait of the Artist*, "your mind is supersaturated with the religion in which you say you disbelieve" (202). Thus is not surprising that Joyce has appealed to Roman Catholic writers, whether converts or cradle Catholics. The story of Thomas Merton is a noteworthy example. As a student of literature at Columbia in the late 1930s, he became fascinated with the work of Gerard Manley Hopkins and found himself increasingly drawn to the church. It was in the fiction of Joyce that Merton made his first serious encounter with Roman Catholic doctrine. Merton became a Cistercian monk at the end of 1941, and in his own spiritual autobiography, *The Seven Storey Mountain* (1948), he records an experience that happened after he had entered the Abbey of Gethsemani in Kentucky. Merton encounters a new postulant to the order, and realizes that he is a Carmelite priest with whom he had previously discussed his vocation: "We both looked at each other with looks that said: 'You – here!' I did not actually say the words, but he did. And then he turned to Father Master and said: 'Father, here is a man who was converted to the faith by reading James Joyce.' I don't think Father Master had heard of James Joyce. I had told the Carmelite that reading Joyce had contributed something to my conversion" (386). This anecdote is well-known even to those who have not read Merton. William York Tindall alluded to it in an influential critical book on Joyce in 1950, and Lodge repeats it, without mentioning Merton by name, in "My Joyce."[3]

When he invokes Joyce in a novel that features a conversion to Catholicism, Lodge is thus following in a long tradition of autobiographical writing involving the relationship of the spiritual and the aesthetic, and more specifically a tradition featuring dramatically rendered moments of conversion. Perhaps the reason that Mark Underwood's conversion is not wholly convincing in religious terms is that its sources are more literary than spiritual: it is described in language deriving from Graham Greene rather than from Augustine or Newman. Though Catholicism was to remain a major theme for Lodge, it is its literary manifestations that he is most comfortable with. Mark's conversion is triggered by his failure as a writer; he tells Clare Mallory that he is overwhelmed by "the appalling multiplicity of life" (*Picturegoers*, 79). He is unable in his own writing to hold together or bring into balance "this infinite pullulating activity" (80). Eventually Mark comes to the same conclusion as that expressed in the poetry of Gerard Manley Hopkins, that it is only God who can comprehend and encompass the flux and diversity of existence. Finding unity in multiplicity, reconciling opposites, and holding tensions in balance are all functions of literature in the aesthetic theory of the New Critics, but for Mark Underwood, literature is not an adequate substitute for religion. *The Picturegoers* ends not with Mark defiantly going away like Stephen Dedalus, but with him returning to his stifling suburban home, and endeavouring to bear his mother's tiresome conversation with charity. The motif of the return home is crucially important in a number of Lodge novels, and I will discuss it in more detail in chapter 4; in this context the significant point is that Mark's effort to treat his mother more tolerantly is in marked contrast to Stephen Dedalus's rejection of his family as presented at the end of *Portrait* and the beginning of *Ulysses*. Similarly, Mark's ambition to be a writer is exchanged for the career in the church that Stephen renounces, as at the end of *The Picturegoers* Mark is about to try his vocation with the Dominican order.

In addition to the references to *Portrait*, *The Picturegoers* contains features that reveal the influence of *Ulysses*. Most notably, the point of view is divided among a large number of characters, and the places where Lodge cuts quickly from one to another were perhaps influenced by the "Wandering Rocks" episode of *Ulysses*. There are also a variety of discourses that are quoted or echoed within the discourse of the narrator, for example, sacred language, popular music, film, advertising, literary language, and entries from Mark's notebooks, which overlap with his speeches, both full of the posturing of the rebels without causes of the films and books of the 1950s. In his Bakhtinian analysis of Lodge's fiction, Robert Morace describes these effects as "stylizations," which he says operate within a larger dialogic structure (*Dialogic Novels*, 113). This, as Morace also points out, is something that *The Picturegoers* has in common with *Ulysses*. Furthermore, there is an interest in Lodge's novel in the conjunction of the sexual or scatological with the sacred or ideal that is typically Joycean. For example, Mark thinks of *Ulysses* while hearing Clare urinating in the overused family bathroom that is next to his bedroom, and he contemplates writing an ode "*On Hearing His Beloved's Urination*" (94). One recalls that Joyce reportedly connected the title of his early collection of lyric poems, *Chamber Music*, to the sound of urination in a chamber pot.[4]

Thus Lodge's first novel, like many written in the middle of the twentieth century, is strongly marked by Joycean influence. What Lodge may not have realized is the extent and strength of his own divergences from his precursor, by means of which he asserts the points of difference between them. What they have in common is a focus on language, a formalist approach to literature that corresponds to their essentially liberal and dialogical approaches to life. Stephen Dedalus rejects both the Catholic church and Irish nationalism, telling his nationalist friend Davin, "When the soul of a man is born in this country there are nets flung at it to hold it back from flight. You talk to me of nationality, language, religion. I shall try to fly by those nets" (*Portrait of the Artist*, 171). Lodge shares Joyce's dedication to literature rather than to ideology; we recall that he described himself as the kind of Catholic who does not want to convert others to his way of thinking and believing. But Joyce rebelled against what he saw as the insularity of Dublin and the confines of the Irish cultural tradition by embracing the international mode of modernism, and by a cosmopolitan life, while Lodge embraced an understated, self-consciously modest and English tradition according to which suburban and family life are central to his art.

Furthermore, unlike Joyce, Lodge did not find it necessary to reject the church; in fact, remaining within the church, supported by the examples of Greene and Waugh, could be seen as a rejection of the values of contemporary English society. In "My Joyce" he explains that when he left his Catholic school he went not to a religious institution but to a completely secular one, University College London. In fact, Lodge notes with macabre humour, the "wizened, mummified corpse" of Jeremy Bentham, the founder of the institution, is displayed in a glass case in University College, "as if in mocking commentary on the Christian doctrine of the resurrection of the body" (*Write On*, 60). Lodge recalls further that he was grateful for the sense of freedom that a university provided after his rather restrictive upbringing and education; nevertheless, to identify oneself in this self-consciously secular environment as a practicing Roman Catholic "was to strike a rather interesting, almost exotic pose before one's peers" (*Write On*, 60).

As an undergraduate, Lodge approached literature through the combination of historical and formalist analysis that prevailed in the 1950s, and as a graduate student he wrote a thesis on the Catholic novel. Joyce developed an aesthetic theory derived in part from Thomas Aquinas. His image of the artist as priest, transforming the everyday bread of common experience into art, celebrates the power and authority of the artist, who is seen as superior to others, whereas Lodge's fictional aesthetic and practice is modest and pragmatic. Both writers were intellectually and aesthetically informed by Catholicism, but the goal of Joyce's theory of art was independence from the church, while Lodge preferred to use the church as subject matter and as an aspect of his identity. Although Lodge regards Greene as the focus of his anxiety of influence, Greene may also be said to have provided him with the means by which he dealt with what otherwise would have been the overwhelming influence of Joyce. Thus Lodge found a way to combine a commitment to the church with a veneration for the work of the apostate James Joyce. To have left the church while attending a university founded by Jeremy Bentham would have been wholly unremarkable. In the cultural climate of England in the 1950s, remaining *within* the church was an act of self-assertion and self-definition.

Through his identification with this tradition, and by connecting with the English novel before and subsequent to high modernism, Lodge deflects the authoritative power of modernism over his career. But this is not the only way that he deals with Joyce; Joyce becomes a productive influence on the more carnivalesque Lodge of the mid-career books, which are probably the ones he is best known for. In addition to absorbing and contesting Joyce's influence in his own fiction, Lodge studied and taught Joyce as a literary critic and academic. There is a substantial section devoted to Joyce in one of Lodge's most important critical books, *The Modes of Modern Writing: Metaphor, Metonymy, and the Typology of Modern Literature* (1977).[5] This book is largely informed by structuralism, and Lodge uses Roman Jakobson's distinction between metaphor and metonymy in order to provide a powerful account of the dialectical alternation of these modes in modern literature. Joyce is even more central in the Bakhtinian turn that Lodge's criticism took subsequent to the publication of *Modes*. A key text in this regard is Lodge's essay "Double Discourses: Joyce and Bakhtin," presented at symposia in Dublin and Seoul in 1982 and published the following year.[6] This analyzes the use of various types of doubly oriented discourse in *Ulysses* and *Finnegans Wake*, showing how from a Bakhtinian perspective these works "appear not as eccentric digressions from the great tradition of the novel ... but the most complete fulfilment of the expressive potential of the novel that has yet been achieved" (1).

As Lodge explains in the introduction to *After Bakhtin* (1990), Bakhtin provided him with the means to go beyond the impasse that he had created by insisting that "all critical questions about a novel are reducible to questions about language" (4). Lodge came to perceive "the possibility of a formalist criticism of the specifically narrative elements of a literary text," elements that had been "downgraded by the Anglo-American New Criticism in whose methods of 'close reading' I had been trained, or had trained myself" (5). He refers to his exploration of the continental tradition of narratology and his use of structuralist concepts in *The Modes of Modern Writing*, noting that in that work he had not completely transcended the tendency of stylistic criticism to treat the language of a text "as if it were a homogenous entity" (6). Bakhtin, on the other hand, explains "that there is no such thing as *the* style, *the* language of a novel, because a novel is a medley of many styles, many languages – or, if you like, voices" (6). Lodge quotes a passage from Bakhtin's *Problems of Dostoevsky's Poetics* that he says had the effect on him "of a light bulb being switched on in one's head"; it includes the key sentence "For the prose artist the world is full of other people's words, among which he must orient himself and whose speech characteristics he must be able to perceive with a very keen ear" (*After Bakhtin*, 7).[7] This statement applies readily to many of Lodge's novels, and especially to *The British Museum Is Falling Down* and the campus trilogy. In these novels, which are significantly influenced by Joyce, Lodge is more overtly and pervasively dialogical than in his more socially realistic works, and parody, stylization, and the incorporation of a variety of linguistic registers are central features. It is as though in his identity as a critic, Lodge's study of Bakhtin provided him with a greater awareness and conscious understanding of what he had already been doing in his novels for some time.[8]

In discussing Joyce's influence on Lodge's campus fiction I will concentrate on *The British Museum is Falling Down* and *Small World*. As in Virginia Woolf's *Mrs Dalloway* and Joyce's *Ulysses*, the action of *The British Museum* is confined to a single day, and involves a number of characters interacting as they move about a large city. The language of various modern novelists is the object of representation, both in the set parodies and elsewhere. Lodge also satirizes the language of advertising, as Adam Appleby composes entries in a competition to complete the couplet "*I always choose a Brownlong chair*," e.g., "*For laying girls with long brown hair*" (19), or "*The answer to a bottom's prayer*" (147; italics Lodge's). The Brownlong motif recurs numerous times, rather like the Plumtree's Potted Meat motif in *Ulysses*, which may have suggested it to Lodge. Throughout Joyce's novel there are echoes of an advertising slogan that Bloom first reads in the newspaper in the street:

> *What is home without*
> *Plumtree's Potted Meat?*
> *Incomplete.*
> *With it an abode of bliss.* (72; italics Joyce's)

Both the Brownlong and the Plumtree's references are connected with advertising, and as they recur they are also both expressive of the sexual anxieties of the characters who obsess about them. Additionally, Lodge parodies theories of childrearing (10–11) and military conversation (27), and he recurrently parodies aspects of Roman Catholicism. One passage imagines an entry on Catholicism from a Martian encyclopedia. It is largely devoted to the matter of birth-control, and concludes "Other doctrines of the Roman Catholics included a belief in a Divine Redeemer and in a life after death" (*British Museum*, 12). As a final example of a parallel with *Ulysses*, we may take the micturatory prowess shared by the protagonist of each work. In the "Ithaca" section of *Ulysses*, Bloom and Stephen both urinate: "The trajectories of their, first sequent, then simultaneous, urinations were dissimilar: Bloom's longer, less irruent, in the incomplete form of the bifurcated penultimate alphabetical letter who in his ultimate year at High School (1880) had been capable of attaining the point of greatest altitude against the whole concurrent strength of the institution, 210 scholars" (655). At the beginning of *British Museum*, Adam Appleby wakes up and his consciousness is flooded with regrets and fears, remembering among other things "that at primary school he had proved so proficient in the game of who-can-pee-highest-up-the-wall of the boys' outside lavatory that he had wetted the biretta of the parish priest who happened to be visiting the playground on the other side of the wall at the time" (7–8).

Another way that *British Museum* resembles *Ulysses* is that it follows Adam on his peregrinations around London, which are punctuated by ineffectual efforts to work on his thesis in the British Museum Reading Room. In the course of the day he is tempted by a girl eager to lose her virginity, twice encounters Father Finbar Flannegan, and has several traffic mishaps involving his motor scooter, before he returns home to his wife and family. This of course repeats the homecoming or "nostos" structure that characterizes both Joyce's novel and its Homeric model. Lodge thus reproduces a number of the principal features of *Ulysses* in a novel of less than two hundred pages that is both amusing and highly readable, and that is also a satire of the church's teachings about contraception. It is in effect a *Ulysses* in miniature, an epyllion to place alongside Joyce's epic. It ends with Lodge's most overt homage to Joyce in the form of a chapter of stream of consciousness from Adam's wife Barbara, imitating Molly Bloom's soliloquy at the end of *Ulysses*; in a characteristic joke, Lodge repeats and concludes with the tentative, equivocating, liberal word "perhaps," rather than with Joyce's and Molly's more emphatic "yes." Some might argue that the novel ends weakly, with a pastiche of Joyce that follows a series of brilliant parodies of other modern writers. On the other hand, it would be at least as convincing to argue that Lodge places Joyce as one of a sequence of modern writers whose voice he has appropriated for his own purposes, and that by reaffirming the value of the realist tradition he is implicitly challenging the hegemony of the school of criticism that celebrates *Ulysses* as both the ultimate novel and the novel to end all novels.

In the essay "The Novelist at the Crossroads," first published four years after *British Museum*, Lodge says that "There is a good deal of evidence that the English literary mind is peculiarly committed to realism" (*Crossroads*, 7). In spite of its metafictional games and its high degree of intertextuality, *British Museum* shares that commitment. In fact, the "Crossroads" essay was written to defend the post-war English tradition with which Lodge identifies himself, in opposition to those who argued that the more experimental fiction that prevailed in France and in the United States represented the direction that the novel should take. Lodge concludes the essay with an explicit linking of the realist and the liberal traditions. He is responding to the practitioners of the new kind of fiction that Robert Scholes called "fabulation," who argued that their departures from realism were made necessary by the extreme conditions of the age. Today the most common term for such fiction is "postmodernism," though the forms haven't changed much and they are often justified by the same argument. Lodge replies in the "Crossroads" essay with what is in effect his fictional as well as ideological credo: "The realist – and liberal – answer to this case must be that while many aspects of contemporary experience encourage an extreme, apocalyptic response, most of us continue to live most of our lives on the assumption that the reality which realism imitates actually exists ... We are conscious of ourselves as unique, historic individuals, living together in societies by virtue of certain common assumptions and methods of communication ... we seek to adjust our lives, individually and communally, to some order or system of values which, however, we know is always at the mercy of chance and contingency" (*Crossroads*, 33–4). Lodge makes language central to his representation in *British Museum*, following in Joyce's footsteps, and at the same time, as Joyce does with early twentieth-century Dublin in *Ulysses*, he provides a realistic representation of aspects of London life in the early 1960s. He diverges from Joyce by making *British Museum* a readerly text in the mode of Kingsley Amis, the pioneer of the campus novel in modern British literature.[9] Amis and Joyce are two very different influences, and it is a sign of Lodge's originality as a writer that he can draw effectively on each of them.

In *Out of the Shelter* (1970) and *Changing Places* (1978), Lodge explores aspects of the Jamesian "international theme," and both of these novels have their Joycean aspects as well. *Out of the Shelter* is a Bildungsroman that uses some of the techniques of *A Portrait of the Artist* to represent the development and coming of age of Timothy Young. Like *Portrait*, it also contains many references to the historical and political background to the story, for Timothy's coming of age involves realizing that political questions are much more complex than he has assumed. Until his visit to Germany he has lived comfortably in a world of inherited Tory patriotism, shaped by the moral simplicities of his wartime childhood. Lodge follows Joyce in restricting the point of view to the consciousness of his hero, beginning with the limited perspective and simple language of early childhood and introducing more sophisticated discourse as Timothy's perceptions mature. The novel opens, like *Portrait*, with a sensory memory: "Almost the first thing he could remember was his mother standing on a stool in the kitchen, piling tins of food into the top cupboard. On the table there were more tins: pineapple, peaches, little oranges – you could tell by the pictures" (*Shelter*, 3). His mother explains that the tins are there because there is a war, but Timothy never remembers his mother's answer to his question, "What's a war?" In a sense, the whole novel is an attempt to answer that question, as *Out of the Shelter* incorporates many perspectives on the Second World War, from combatants, conscientious objectors, civilians who survived it, young people who can barely remember it, and of course the different attitudes of the British, American, and German characters.

With *Changing Places*, Lodge commenced what would become a trilogy of campus novels about Philip Swallow, the underachieving English academic who teaches at Rummidge University, and Morris Zapp, the overachieving American. Joyce's influence is apparent in the way that it uses a different narrative technique in each chapter, with the final chapter written as a screenplay. Chapter 4 is entitled "Reading" and it advances the story through a series of newspaper articles, paralleling Joyce's "Aeolus" section, and perhaps also referring to the Newsreel sections in John Dos Passos's *U.S.A.* trilogy. Thus Lodge continues the experiments with narrative technique, parody, and stylization of language that characterize *The British Museum Is Falling Down*, and that he will use extensively in *Small World*. In his review of *Changing Places* in the *Times*, Philip Howard recognized this use of stylization and parody, writing that "Mr Lodge is a virtuoso of such disparate dialects as Senior Common Room, chat show, and bed-room" (Rev.). Lodge captures the political ferment of the period very effectively, especially its radical discourse, as evidenced by the following passage from a fictional newspaper article in the "Reading" chapter, under the headline "Earthquake Cure": "Earthquakes, said a speaker at yesterday's Euphoric State teach-in on Ecology and Politics, were nature's way of protesting all the concrete that had been laid on top of the good earth. By planting things, one was liberating the ground, and therefore preventing earthquakes" (*Changing Places*, 165).

Small World, the sequel to *Changing Places*, is a pervasively intertextual and carnivalesque novel, whose Joycean dimension is advertised by an epigraph from *Finnegans Wake*: "Hush! Caution! Echoland!" (*Finnegans Wake*, 13). *Small World* is indeed an "echoland," stuffed with allusions to Arthurian romance and modernist literature, especially T.S. Eliot, and beginning with a paraphrase of the opening lines of Chaucer's *Canterbury Tales*. The naïve hero of Lodge's comic romance in prose is Persse McGarrigle, a young Irish academic, and in the first scene of the novel he responds to the bleakness of the campus of Rummidge University by quoting, as so many other teachers of English literature have done on similar occasions, from the opening line of Eliot's *Waste Land*: "April is the cruellest month" (3). *Small World* thus begins with a barrage of quotations from the literary tradition, while Joyce's *Ulysses* begins with a series of allusions to the Catholic tradition, including Buck Mulligan's intoning of the opening words of the Tridentine Mass.

Joyce is echoed again within the first few pages of *Small World*, when Persse sees "the most beautiful girl he had ever seen in his life" and responds with the exclamation "'Heavenly God!' ... quoting again, this time from *A Portrait of the Artist as a Young Man*" (*Small World*, 8). The quotation is from Stephen's epiphany of the wading girl on the beach: "– Heavenly God! cried Stephen's soul, in an outburst of profane joy" (*Portrait*, 144). Persse introduces himself to the girl and has to spell out his unfamiliar Irish name, to which she replies:

> "Oh, like in *Finnegans Wake*! The Ballad of Persse O'Reilley." "Exactly so. Persse, Pearce, Pierce – I wouldn't be surprised if they were not all related to Percival. Percival, *per se*, as Joyce might have said," he added, and was rewarded with another dazzling smile. (9)

The connection between Persse and the Arthurian knight Percival is an early hint of the pervasive parallelism between the action of *Small World* and Arthurian romance.

Lodge explains in an essay about the writing of *Small World* that he conceived it as a story about "the vanity of human wishes" as seen in the jet-setting behaviour of scholars attending international conferences. He aimed to deal "in a carnival spirit" with the competing literary theories which dominated literary studies at the time, and with the relations between the academy and the worlds of literary publishing and the media (*Write On*, 72). In trying to find a way to combine these elements in his novel, Lodge resorted to the modernist technique of employing a systematic parallel between a myth or classic work and the situation being represented. This is the method of Joyce in *Ulysses* and of T.S. Eliot in *The Waste Land*. In Eliot's celebrated phrase, Joyce's "mythical method," the elaborate structure of correspondences between Homer's *Odyssey* and Joyce's *Ulysses*, "has the importance of a scientific discovery ... It is, I seriously believe, a step toward making the modern world possible for art" ("*Ulysses*, Order, and Myth," 177–8). Parallels with *The Waste Land* are important to the overall structure of *Small World*. Many of Lodge's characters are sexually unfulfilled and are pursuing an erotic quest, and many of those who are writers and academics are suffering from writer's block. Presiding over them all is Arthur Kingfisher, the Fisher King of modern criticism, who is no longer "able to achieve an erection or an original thought" (*Small World*, 94). Like the Fisher King in *The Waste Land*, he awaits the rejuvenation of his domain, but he still has the power to award the UNESCO Chair of Literary Criticism, the most prestigious prize on offer in literary studies.

Lodge was inspired to write a novel about the international conference circuit as a result of attending a James Joyce symposium in Zurich (*Write On*, 71); in *Small World*, Persse McGarrigle attends a T.S. Eliot symposium in the same city. While in Zurich, the young Irishman is surprised by scenes of street theatre that enact episodes from *The Waste Land*, a poem by an American who turned himself into an Englishman. This confluence and confusion of identities is wholly typical of Lodge when matters Irish come to the fore in his fiction, and Persse is both a composite of English stereotypes about the Irish and an ingénu figure who exposes the contradictions and posturing of the academics whom he meets. *Small World* is a celebration of both difference and desire, as representatives of various schools of criticism and literary movements interact in a globalized marketplace of discourses. Adherents of Marxism, reader-response theory, structuralism, liberal humanism, and deconstruction vie for the UNESCO Chair. Lodge juxtaposes life in the English suburbs, quiet and predictable, where "today will be much like yesterday or tomorrow" (94), with the globe-trotting existence of the principal characters, who inhabit the world of postmodern metafiction. At the culminating conference in the book, the MLA Convention in New York, Ronald Frobisher, once an Angry Young Man novelist and now a writer of television scripts, is talking to Persse McGarrigle: "He filled Persse's glass and introduced him to a lean, shrewd-eyed, red-haired woman in a green trouser suit. 'Desirée Byrd, Section 409, "New Directions in Women's Writing,"' he said. 'I'm Section 351, "Tradition and Innovation in Postwar British Fiction". Strictly speaking I'm just the Tradition bit'" (*Small World*, 330).

Another way that Lodge carnivalizes literary and critical discourse is by having it reproduced in absurdly garbled form in the essays of Sandra Dix, a very weak student who blackmails her professors for marks by having sex with them and then threatening to tell their wives. Her essay for the Australian professor Rodney Wainwright is entitled "Matthew Arnold's Theory of Culture," and Lodge provides this excerpt for the reader: "According to Matthew Arnold culture was getting to know, on the matters that most concerned you, the best people. Matthew Arnold was a famous headmaster who wrote 'Tom Brown's Schooldays' and invented the game of rugby as well as the Theory of Culture. If I don't get a good grade in this course I will tell your wife that we had sex in your office three times this semester, and you wouldn't let me out when there was a fire drill in case somebody saw us leaving the room together" (*Small World*, 299). Through such parodic devices, Lodge reinvents and reinvigorates the genre of the academic novel, as some of the many enthusiastic reviewers who first hailed the novel pointed out.[10]

Nothing that Lodge has written since *Small World* is as pervasively Joycean, but before moving on to other influences it may be useful to enlarge the scope of the present chapter by moving from Joyce to the wider but related question of Lodge's representation of Ireland and Irishness in his fiction. The complicated relationship of British and Irish literature in the twentieth century reproduces the difficult political relationship between the two nations. For example, Yeats and Joyce are major figures in modern Irish literature, yet are also essential figures in modern British literature. Ireland is closely involved with the complexities of Lodge's personal identity as well, and therefore issues of nationality come up frequently in his novels.

The poetry of Philip Larkin is relevant as a point of comparison with

Lodge. Larkin is a writer who is important to Lodge, and whose poetry is widely seen, both for better and for worse, as exemplifying the qualities of Englishness. His plain style and commonplace subject matter correspond to post-war ideals of realistic liberalism and disillusion with ideology, though the bigotries revealed in his letters indicate a more sinister aspect of English nationalism. At the same time, there is a powerful undercurrent of Romanticism in Larkin. As an undergraduate at Oxford, he heard the poet Vernon Watkins talk about the poetry of W.B. Yeats (Motion, *Philip Larkin*, 83). In the introduction to a 1966 reissue of his first book of poetry, *The North Ship* (first published 1945), Larkin wrote "I spent the next three years trying to write like Yeats, not because I liked his personality or understood his ideas but out of infatuation with his music (to use the word I think Vernon used)" (*North Ship*, 9). He refers to this infatuation, at the end of the introduction, as a "Celtic fever" (*North Ship*, 10).

Larkin's mature style was formed in reaction against poets like Yeats and Dylan Thomas, and in emulation of an English tradition that he identified in Hardy and the Georgian poets. In 1966, Larkin maintained that his feeling about Yeats was one of "*Revulsion*" (qtd. in Motion, *Larkin*, 344); writing to an Oxford University Press editor about his *Oxford Book of Twentieth-Century English Verse* Larkin said, "I am interested in the Georgians, and how far they represented an 'English tradition' that was submerged by the double impact of the Great War and the Irish-American-continental properties of Yeats and Eliot" (*Selected Letters*, 380). In 1969, shortly after his forty-seventh birthday, Larkin visited Ireland, where he felt anxious about his status as an English Protestant driving an expensive-looking car, given the riots that were taking place in the north. Nevertheless, he and his companion Monica Jones travelled to Sligo to visit "the grave of that old blatherer Yeats" (qtd. in Motion, *Larkin*, 392). It is characteristic that he both undertook the trip, and undercut its significance by abusing the object of his pilgrimage.[11]

One of Larkin's most archetypally English poems is "MCMXIV," an evocation of England before the so-called "Great War" of 1914–18. The life that Larkin conjures up seems both archaic and desirable, like a distant childhood memory, as he moves through a series of tableaux of the society that was lost irretrievably in the war, a world, he suggests, that was more innocent, slower, and rooted in the past:

> … the shut shops, the bleached
> Established names on the sunblinds,
> The farthings and sovereigns,
> And dark-clothed children at play
> Called after kings and queens,
> The tin advertisements
> For cocoa and twist, and the pubs
> Wide open all day. (*Collected Poems*, 99)

Along with its nostalgia and conservative sense of Englishness, I think there is in this poem a subliminal struggle with a precursor, namely Yeats's "Easter, 1916." Both poems have a date as their title, though Larkin's, by using Roman numerals, suggests that the date is engraved on a town cenotaph such as were constructed all over England to commemorate the dead of the First World War. As Christopher Ricks has pointed out, Larkin's title is really unpronounceable; its meaning depends on being seen rather than heard (*Force of Poetry*, 302). Yeats's poem is about a rebirth, and looks to the future; Larkin's is concerned with the passing of an era and looks to the past. In Yeats, the monochrome world of commercial Dublin, seen by Joyce in *Dubliners* as spiritually paralyzed, is transformed into something noble, just as the "drunken, vainglorious lout" John MacBride is transformed into someone heroic ("Easter, 1916," 203). The transformation comes at a cost, as Yeats is aware: the poem ends by affirming that the revolutionaries whom it celebrates "Are changed, changed utterly: / A terrible beauty is born" ("Easter, 1916," 205). Larkin's poem also ends with transformation, but not of a kind that is celebrated. "MCMXIV" is conservative in contrast to Yeats's revolutionary poem, autumnal rather than eastertide in its tone, as it concludes by emphasizing the innocence that was irretrievably lost as a result of the war.

Lodge is an admirer of both Yeats and Larkin. The poetry of the former is quoted by the protagonists of *Paradise News*, *Therapy*, and *Deaf Sentence*, and Bernard Walsh in *Paradise News* also quotes Yeats.[12] In 1993, Lodge identified Yeats's "Among School Children" as his favourite poem in an anthology where a number of famous people each contributed a brief note on the poem they chose (MacMonagle, *Lifelines*, 109). Since the anthology had its origins in the project of an Irish school to raise money for Ethiopian famine relief, there was perhaps an element of diplomacy in Lodge's choice of Yeats. It is interesting that in 1998, in a *Sunday Times* question and answer feature, Lodge selected as his favourite poem Larkin's "The Whitsun Weddings," whereas for "favourite quotation" he listed "The best lack all conviction, while the worst are full of passionate intensity," from Yeats's "The Second Coming" ("Bibliofile"). These literary preferences embody a kind of doubleness in Lodge which I want to explore in some detail, as they reveal not only the complexity of his religious, national, and ideological identities, but also the split in his literary affinities between the realistic tradition and modernism, or what he called in *Modes of Modern Writing* the metonymic and metaphoric poles of literary discourse. One can think of Yeats as the representative of the Romantic, visionary tradition of poetry, open to mythological influences from a diverse variety of sources; it is no accident that the book in which he sets out his system of myth is called *A Vision*. Larkin, on the other hand, is identified with the anti-Romantic poetics of the Movement, poets of the era of logical positivism, finding their subject matter not in art or mythology but the ordinary experiences of provincial life.[13] The title of Larkin's second book of poetry, *The Less Deceived*, sums up perfectly the ironic and skeptical stance of the Movement, while the title poem of his third book, "The Whitsun Weddings," exemplifies the celebration of ordinary middle-class experience and has numerous affinities with the realistic pole of Lodge's fiction.

Like Larkin, Lodge is often seen as an archetypally English author, in the tradition of the English comic novel: Fielding, Austen, Dickens, Waugh, and Kingsley Amis. Nevertheless, Lodge's identity is complicated by his Roman Catholicism. It was centuries after the Reformation before Roman Catholics gained full civil rights in England, and for a long time after that they were still regarded with suspicion by many in a country where the Church of England is the legally established religion. To this day the sovereign of England cannot be a Roman Catholic, and effigies of Guy Fawkes, the most notorious of the conspirators in the Catholic Gunpowder Plot of 1605, are burned throughout the country on 5 November. In the nineteenth century, both John Henry Newman and Gerard Manley Hopkins found it necessary to assert the Englishness of the Catholic church in England. In the *Apologia*, for example, Newman writes that "when I became a Catholic, nothing struck me more at once than the English out-spoken manner of the Priests … I have ever found it in the priests of this Diocese; did I wish to point out a straightforward Englishman, I should instance the Bishop, who has, to our great benefit, for so many years presided over it" (240–1). Furthermore, English Roman Catholics have always had a problematic relationship with Ireland. Both Irish immigrants to England and English Catholics who found work in Catholic institutions in Ireland often felt that they were not accepted by their co-religionists. Newman had a deeply frustrating time trying to found a Catholic university in Ireland in the 1850s, and indeed his celebrated *Idea of a University* is not so much a Platonic idea of a perfect institution as it is a visionary blueprint for what a Catholic university could and should be in mid-Victorian Ireland. Hopkins taught at University College, Dublin from 1884 to 1889, and described himself in one of his "terrible sonnets" as being "at a third / Remove" from his home and family ("To seem the stranger," *Hopkins Reader*, 27). He complained about Home Rulers to Newman, who replied "If I were an Irishman, I should be (in heart) a rebel" (3 March 1887; Hopkins, *Further Letters*, 266).[14]

To explore this question of religious and national identity further, it may be helpful to compare David Lodge to a near contemporary who shares an Irish immigrant background and Roman Catholic upbringing and secondary education. Terry Eagleton, Britain's most prominent literary critic and theorist in the late twentieth and early twenty-first centuries, was born in Salford in 1943, making him eight years younger than Lodge. Both writers attended Roman Catholic grammar schools, although Eagleton was more thoroughly immersed in the "Catholic ghetto" than was Lodge, and more involved in the activities of the church. For both, however, the experience of Roman Catholic education was dominated by Irish clergy and lay-brothers. Eagleton describes his school experience in his vivid memoir *The Gatekeeper* (2001): "My North-of-England grammar school was almost wholly populated by Irish teachers and clerics, along with second-generation Irish pupils. But I was unaware that names like Doyle or Farrell or O'Dwyer were in any sense out of the ordinary, since I have no memory of the words 'Irish' or 'Ireland' being used throughout the whole of my school career. Naturally not: the task of these raw-boned, huge-handed Brothers, themselves refugees from small farms in Clare or Kerry, was to wipe the last traces of bog from our souls and pack us off into middle-class England … We were Irish, but we did not know we were, even if most of us came from families embarrassingly larger than the English sociological norm" (37–8). Eagleton emphasizes the un-English nature of Catholicism, and argues that growing up as a Catholic meant "lacking all instinctive feel for the liberal sensibility" (*Gatekeeper*, 34). For him, as for Graham Greene in various of his works, notably *The Power and the Glory* and *Monsignor Quixote*, there is a natural affinity between Catholicism and Marxism, or to quote from Eagleton in Chestertonian mode, "The path from the Tridentine creed to Trotskyism is shorter than it seems" (*Gatekeeper*, 35). Of course, Eagleton was just young enough to have no personal memories of the Second World War, and to still be in his twenties during the radical years of the late 1960s.

Lodge reviewed *Exiles and Emigrés*, an early book by Eagleton, in 1970. While recognizing Eagleton's ability as a critic, Lodge distances himself from his method in a way that illustrates Lodge's own liberalism: "Mr Eagleton's aesthetic is based on the necessary; mine on the possible. I believe we should approach art predisposed to give it a conditional assent, in which case our own ideological preferences come into play only when the work has broken down in its terms, that is, rhetorically. Mr Eagleton, however, seems to approach the work with suspicion, intent on discovering whether it confirms his own social and metaphysical truths. More often than not, of course, it doesn't, and the limiting or dismissive judgment follows inexorably" ("Strangers," 1028). Eagleton discusses Lodge in the *New Left Review* in 1988. He objects to the "plain man" persona of Lodge's writing, and argues that he is not really a Catholic writer so much as an English liberal who happens to be a Catholic: "He is, in effect, a thoroughly secularized author, whose Catholicism makes little difference to his conventional liberal vision other than providing him with convenient materials for social commentary and comic satire" ("Silences," 96). Eagleton has identified himself in various ways with Ireland through his career, writing about Irish topics, and eventually living part of the time in Dublin.[15] He writes in the *New Left Review* article that "Lodge's own social background would not seem intensively Irish" ("Silences," 96). But as I have already shown, Lodge's background has a significant Irish element, and furthermore his wife, Mary, is the daughter of Irish immigrants. Irishness continually interacts with Catholicism in Lodge's fiction in ways that complicate any attempt to portray him as a pragmatic English liberal. Just as Eagleton has never claimed to be a liberal, but has a continuing and elusive relationship with Catholicism, so Lodge has never identified with Marxism, but has a continuing and complex relationship with Irishness, which I will now explore briefly with reference to several of his novels.

As has already been mentioned, Lodge suggests that he never felt any anxiety of influence in relation to Joyce. If we see Joyce as the pinnacle of international modernism, both a figure of Olympian remoteness and a repertoire of models for emulation, then this claim may have some plausibility. However, if one sees Joyce as in part shorthand for both Irishness in general and issues involving Irish Catholicism in particular, then the question of anxiety may seem rather different. Perhaps Lodge's affirmation of the English comic tradition, one similarly made in the face of modernist precursors by Kingsley Amis, is less of a self-evident self-description, and more of a defensive claim to an identity, than it appears at first sight. In the literary climate of the 1960s and 1970s, there was a striking lack of confidence in English literary discourse, evidenced in an anxiety over what was widely seen as the more innovative and ambitious literary works being produced in the United States and the more radical experimentation of the French *nouveau roman*. Bernard Bergonzi's *The Situation of the Novel* (1970) is a good example of a critical book dominated by this concern. The same sort of anxiety about national decline marks the politics of the period. These issues form the context for the representation of national identity in Lodge's early novels. He negotiates his Irish affiliations and allegiance to the self-consciously English pose of writers such as Kingsley Amis and Philip Larkin in a delicate balancing act.

Early in *How Far Can You Go?*, in a scene dated precisely by the narrator as taking place in 1955, two characters who have recently graduated from university are discussing their Catholic upbringing:

> "Italians tolerate adultery and brothels because they're not allowed to divorce," Polly said. "English Catholics have the worst of both worlds. No wonder they're so repressed."
> Michael nodded … "It's the Irish Jansenist tradition," he said.
> "What's that?"
> "In the penal days, Irish priests used to be trained in France, by the Jansenists, so that over-scrupulous, puritanical kind of Catholicism got into their bloodstream – and ours too, because, let's face it, English Catholicism is largely Irish Catholicism." (*How Far*, 40)

This is not how English Catholicism generally appears in the novels of the convert authors Greene and Waugh. In *Brideshead Revisited*, Lord Sebastian Flyte explains to his friend Charles Ryder that Catholics are not, as Charles thinks, just like other people: "that's exactly what they're not – particularly in this country, where they're so few. It's not just that they're a clique – as a matter of fact, they're at least four cliques all blackguarding each other half the time – but they've got an entirely different outlook on life; everything they think important is different from other people" (87). The largest of these "cliques" would presumably be the Irish immigrant community, but Waugh is more interested in the upper-class recusant community and the world of fashionable converts. For Lodge, and for the reason mentioned by his character Michael in *How Far Can You Go?*, Irish Catholicism is a significant cultural and ethical force, and one that he must come to terms with in his fiction.

Irish priests abound in the world of David Lodge, including the fanatical Father Finbar Flannegan of *The British Museum is Falling Down*, who is regarded by Adam and Barbara Appleby as the "Priest Most Likely to Prevent the Conversion of England," and who thinks that John Henry Newman is a Protestant (28; 30). In *Small World*, Persse McGarrigle goes to confession after attending a pornographic film, and is absolved by Father Finbar O'Malley, who originates from the west of Ireland and who administers the "Our Lady of Knock Fund for Reverse Emigration" (50). Father Jerome, in *Therapy*, is treated less comically. The protagonist of the novel, Laurence "Tubby" Passmore, has become infatuated with Maureen Kavanagh, a Catholic girl whom he meets at the bus-stop on his way to his Church of England grammar school, and he is allowed to see her on condition that he attends a Catholic youth group. Father Jerome appears to Tubby disconcertingly different from a Church of England clergyman: "He was a gaunt, grizzled Dubliner, with nicotine-stained fingers and a shaving cut on his chin which he seemed to have staunched with a fragment of toilet-paper. He wore a long black cassock that reached to his scuffed shoes, with deep pockets in which he kept the materials for rolling his own cigarettes" (233). At the end of *Therapy*, Tubby is reunited with Maureen and they complete the pilgrimage to Compostela and visit the shrine of St James before commencing an affair. Referring to this passage in a review of *Therapy*, the Irish novelist John Banville asks, "Why wasn't I brought up in that kind of Catholicism?" ("Nice Work").

Banville's ironic question suggests that English Catholicism is more relaxed about sexual matters than Irish Catholicism, something that Michael denies in the passage I have quoted from *How Far Can You Go?* when he asserts the identity of the two nations, at least in terms of Catholic experience. In the space between these two statements lies the ambiguity of David Lodge's treatment of both Roman Catholicism and the Irish. That ambiguity is most fully exemplified in his novels *Paradise News* and *Ginger, You're Barmy*, and a discussion of these works will thus serve as an appropriate way to conclude this discussion of David Lodge and Ireland.

Lodge's most sustained exploration of the Jansenist tradition in Irish Catholicism comes in *Paradise News*, the story of a former priest named Bernard Walsh who now is an unbelieving teacher of theology at a college in Rummidge. Bernard and his elderly father Jack travel to Hawaii, where Jack's sister Ursula is seriously ill. Initially there is some comedy in the juxtaposition of the tense and serious Bernard and his Irish father, whose holy medal of Our Lady of Lourdes triggers the metal-detector in the airport security screening, and who leaves his boarding pass and passport on the Irish whiskey shelf in the Duty Free shop. However, the presentation of the Walsh family becomes progressively darker as Lodge explores "the baggage of guilt and failure" (97) that Bernard carries around as a result of a repressed Irish Catholic upbringing, a joyless life as a priest, and an unsuccessful attempt at a relationship with a woman that precipitates his leaving the church.

Bernard's earlier life is narrated in brief flashbacks and in a journal he keeps while in Hawaii. Through these devices, Lodge economically suggests a life hemmed in by prohibitions, anxieties, and unmentionable secrets. Ursula has had a lifelong aversion to sex after her oldest brother Sean used to expose himself in front of her, something that Jack knew about, but that they have never mentioned to one another, and that has been further repressed because Sean died heroically in the Second World War and is revered in the family. From a conversation with his sister Tess, Bernard realizes belatedly that because he was destined for the priesthood, he had a sheltered and privileged life at home. In another scene, Bernard recalls visiting his father at the transport company where he worked as a despatch clerk, and being told never to come there again: "Bernard had realized then for the first time that his father was ashamed of his humble job, and of its sordid setting. He had wanted to say something healing and reassuring, but couldn't find the right words. He had slunk off feeling guilty and ashamed himself. It had been a kind of primal scene, very Irish, exposing a secret of status, not sex" (*Paradise News*, 64–5). Bernard experiences a personal transformation and reconciliation with his family as a result of the Hawaiian trip. As in *Out of the Shelter* and *Changing Places*, Lodge represents the United States largely positively, as a place of material plenitude and emotional openness. In place of the dour Catholicism of Britain and Ireland, the church in Hawaii is vibrant and effective. Bernard meets a priest serving as a hospital chaplain who is a member of the charismatic movement, and who has an enthusiasm for his vocation that Bernard has never experienced. The novel concludes with Bernard back in England, reading a letter describing his aunt's death and the ceremony of scattering her ashes at sea, after a folk mass that fuses the Roman liturgy with indigenous cultural traditions. Both the English caution represented by Bernard and the Irish repressiveness of his family background are transformed by this encounter with the United States, and the novel suggests that, in however demythologized a form, there is something truly catholic in Catholicism that transcends any specific cultural manifestation. Lodge reinforces his use of sacramental imagery with allusions to *The Tempest*, a play all about forgiveness and reconciliation, though characteristically he tempers these with a reference to Larkin's "This Be the Verse." Bernard recites the opening lines to his sister to characterize their childhood: "They fuck you up, your mum and dad / They may not mean to, but they do" (*Paradise News*, 307).

Lodge's fullest treatment of the complexities of the relationship between England and Ireland is found in his second novel, *Ginger, You're Barmy*. In the afterword to the novel, Lodge explains how national identity was incorporated into its structure of binary oppositions: "My response to the Army shifted from an indignant moral resistance to its values … to a pragmatic determination to make myself as comfortable as possible and to use my time as profitably as possible … For the purpose of *Ginger*, I split these reactions into two characters, and set them interacting. To heighten the contrast between them I gave the rebel an Irish Catholic republican background (and flaming red hair) and made the conformist pragmatist an agnostic" (*Ginger*, 214). At the beginning of the story, Jonathan, the narrator of the novel, is on his way to Catterick, the large army camp in Yorkshire, for basic training, and he deeply resents what he sees as a waste of two years of his life. He has just obtained a first-class degree in English, and is looking forward to graduate studies. On the train he meets the red-haired Mike Brady, the "Ginger" of the title, who was at the same college of the University of London and who failed his degree. Mike's father, a doctor, possesses something of the republican glamour of Mr Casey in Joyce's *Portrait of the Artist as a Young Man*: "The Bradys were a politically conscious clan, fervently nationalist and anti-clerical. Mike's great-uncle had been a friend of Parnell. His father, a medical student at the time, had been closely associated with the Easter Rising of 1916. He still treasured a piece of rusty thread with which he had stitched a flesh-wound of Pearse's" (31). While Mike's father is political, his mother is devoutly religious, a gender split also found in *Portrait*, where it is significant in the Christmas dinner scene. As Mike's Protestant girlfriend Pauline explains, "In some ways, [Mr Brady] seems to dislike his religion. He's always making cracks against the parish priest over Sunday dinner, and Mrs Brady gets quite angry because she thinks he shouldn't say such things in the presence of a non-Catholic" (159).

The awkward friendship that develops between Jonathan and Mike is based on various stereotypes of Englishness and Irishness: Jonathan is characterized by pragmatism, common sense, timidity, and diligent application when it suits his own interests. Mike is passionate, religious, courageous, and wildly impractical, "just a wild Irish boy that never grew up," in Pauline's words (155). Interestingly, Lodge introduces a third character whom he places between Jonathan and Mike. Percy Higgins is "a slender, willowy boy whose physical appearance suggested that he was a product of aristocratic inbreeding" (33), and he comes from a family of "Old Catholics," that is, Roman Catholics who kept the faith during the period of persecution, and who are described as "a tightly-knit, conservative, clannish group, who regarded Irish and convert Catholics with rather more suspicion than they did Protestants" (51). Percy is in several ways a parody of an Evelyn Waugh character, as the passages I have just quoted illustrate. Mike befriends him and tries to protect him as much as possible, out of a feeling of solidarity with a fellow Roman Catholic. Percy's general ineptitude suggests a critique of Waugh's romanticization of the recusant gentry and aristocracy.

Ginger explores the differences between Mike and Jonathan in terms of their attitudes to the army, to their education and potential careers, to religion and ultimate questions, and to love and sex. Mike is in many ways the more attractive character, but he is a failure in worldly terms, and is lazy by nature, "barmy" in terms of the popular song which gives the book its title. As Jonathan says, "My temperament was prudence and my destiny success, as surely as Mike's were foolhardiness and failure" (205). When a sadistic corporal is indirectly responsible for Percy's death, Mike and Jonathan discuss what they should do. Jonathan's main goal is to stay out of trouble, whereas Mike wants to teach the corporal a lesson. In a passage redolent of the 1950s, their discussion leads to the ultimate question of why they exist on earth, which Mike answers by quoting the Catechism: "To exercise my free will, and save my soul" (150).

On a leave in London, Jonathan is invited to meet Mike at O'Connell's, "an Irish drinking club occupying a dingy basement in a narrow passage off the Tottenham Court Road" (127). There he meets two friends of Mike, Brendan Mahoney and Peter Nolan, and is made uncomfortable by what he terms their "Celtic fanaticism" (129). There are echoes of the Cyclops episode in *Ulysses*, where Bloom's liberalism is confronted with the rabid nationalism of the Citizen. Peter Nolan is identified as one of the organizers of a historical occurrence, the theft from the Tate Gallery in 1956 of a painting from the contentious Lane Bequest. Sir Hugh Lane's will had bequeathed an outstanding collection of modern paintings to the British National Gallery, but in an unwitnessed codicil to his will he left them to the City of Dublin, which had been his earlier intention until he had a dispute with the Dublin Corporation about how the pictures would be housed. That dispute lies behind W.B. Yeats's poems "To a Wealthy Man" and "September 1913." When Lane died in the sinking of the *Lusitania* in 1915, the courts upheld his gift to the National Gallery, and the ensuing conflict over ownership of the paintings continued throughout the twentieth century, a thread in the network of conflicts between Britain and Ireland during that period.[16] Lodge incorporates the theft of the painting into his novel as a recent example of Anglo-Irish tension, just as he incorporates the Irish Republican Army, whose Border Campaign, consisting of raids against targets in Northern Ireland, lasted from 1956–62.

Peter Nolan turns up again later in *Ginger*, when Mike deserts from the army. Before he leaves, he gives Jonathan a letter to post to "Gordiano Bruno," which Jonathan later realizes is a Joycean pun, a pseudonym for Peter Nolan: "Bruno of Nola! It was a favourite pun of Joyce's" (201).[17] The price for Nolan's assistance is that Mike is recruited into the IRA, and required to take part in a raid on an army camp, during which Jonathan, on the one occasion that he shows initiative in his army career, is responsible for Mike's arrest. When Jonathan is briefly permitted to visit him, Mike comments "Funny really: out of one Army and into another. There's not much to choose between them" (203). From Jonathan's pragmatic perspective, "surely anyone of Mike's intelligence could see that nowadays the I.R.A. was nothing but a bad joke" (201), but Mike's father takes some pleasure in contemplating his son's actions. I do not think that Lodge is as easily dismissive of the IRA as is his narrator Jonathan, for *Ginger* represents the British army as being ill-equipped and poorly trained, and Jonathan embodies some of the least attractive features of Britain in the late 1950s in his narrow self-interest and cautious timidity. From the perspective of hindsight, we know that the Provisional IRA campaign that began in 1969, only seven years after the publication of *Ginger* and the end of the Border Campaign, was a sustained struggle that continued until the peace process of the late 1990s.

The novel ends in an impasse. Mike's attitudes and values have caused him not only to fail at university but to serve a prison sentence for his role in the IRA raid. He is, in the words of the novel's title, "barmy." Yet at the same time, he has an integrity of purpose and a generosity of spirit that the novel connects to his Catholic beliefs. Jonathan, on the other hand, though he has survived the army and won Pauline for himself, has betrayed his friend and lacks a coherent ethical framework within which to conduct his life. He sums up what he has learned from his military service in the following way: "All human activity was useless, but some kinds were more pleasant than others. The Army had taught me that much philosophy. There was no such thing as communication operating over the whole of society. In fact, *there was no such thing as society*: just a collection of little self-contained boxes, roped untidily together and set adrift to float aimlessly in the waters of time … Success consisted in determining which box would be most pleasant for you, and getting into it" (186; emphasis added). Here again, Lodge is attentive to political trends that would only come to the fore in future decades. In an interview in 1987, Margaret Thatcher commented that "There is no such thing as society" – although one should note the statement was taken out of a context that softens its impact considerably.[18] Thatcher's words were widely quoted in the late

1980s as summing up her radical individualism and lack of compassion, and came to symbolize in short form the attitudes of extreme neoliberalism. At the end of *Ginger*, we see Jonathan trying to make amends, as Mike is about to be released from prison, just as Thomas Fowler, at the end of Greene's *The Quiet American*, wishes there were some way he could atone for his betrayal of his American friend Alden Pyle. *Ginger, You're Barmy* implies that it is difficult to reconcile English pragmatism and liberalism with Irish Catholicism, but also that each set of values is deficient, and needs to be corrected by the other. In his effort to learn to love his wife Pauline and to atone for his betrayal of Mike, Jonathan is embracing a version of Christian charity. In political terms, he moves to a version of liberalism with a social conscience, rather than the radical individualism that would come to the fore in the 1980s, and that Lodge would depict again in *Nice Work*, his novel of the Thatcher era.

In Lodge's continuing effort to reconcile the claims of religious and national identity and liberal temperament, it is ironically fitting that it was an Irish writer, Colm Tóibín, who gave Lodge one of the most difficult experiences of his literary career by publishing an acclaimed novel about Henry James only months before Lodge's *Author, Author*, a novel on the same topic, was scheduled to be released. Lodge describes in the essay "The Year of Henry James" how he and Tóibín both spoke about their books at the Rye Festival, and afterwards met for lunch. Lodge was not keen to discuss their mutual experiences in publishing novels about Henry James, and he records that he was glad of his wife Mary's presence to keep the conversation on other topics: "She is of Irish parentage, and I am a quarter Irish, so discussion of recent changes in Irish culture and society occupied a lot of the time" (*Year*, 93). Suddenly, in the year of Henry James, circumstances had made Irish politics a safer topic than English literature.

4

"Dante and Beatrice in a Suburban Key": David Lodge and the 1950s

"But they don't exist!" Helen exclaims.
"For a novelist you're very literal-minded," Ralph says.
"I'm a realistic novelist."
~David Lodge, *Thinks...*

Lodge has described Kingsley Amis's *Lucky Jim* (1954) in the same way that he describes *Ulysses*, as a "magic book for me" (*Write On*, 64). In this chapter, I follow Lodge by using *Lucky Jim* as a synecdoche for a type of fiction that emerged in his formative years and that was vitally important for his development as a writer. In 1987 Lodge gave the keynote address to a conference at Brown University sponsored by the journal *Novel* and focussing on the topic "Why the Novel Matters: A Postmodern Perplex." He describes teaching a course at the University of Birmingham on contemporary British fiction: "Taking Kingsley Amis's *Lucky Jim* as a benchmark to represent the kind of social realism typical of British fiction in the fifties, I selected seven texts to illustrate subsequent developments" ("The Novel Now," 133). The other novelists on the syllabus included John Fowles, Muriel Spark, and Martin Amis.

Amis's *Lucky Jim* was influential on Lodge and on other writers in several ways. First, it was the best-known example of the realistic fiction about young men from the lower middle class or working class, often from the midlands or the north of England, that has been summed up by the label "Angry Young Men." This group includes novelists such as John Braine and Alan Sillitoe. *Lucky Jim* is important for at least two other reasons. It is the foundational British example of the campus novel, the genre for which Lodge is still best known. It also is a comic novel, both in terms of its generic structure, with Jim Dixon triumphing over those who would frustrate him in his career and in his romantic life, and in its frequent use of farcical action, parody, and carnivalization of official discourses. The connection between *Lucky Jim* and *Ginger, You're Barmy* is suggested by the titles of the works. Amis's title is from an "Old Song" quoted in the epigraph to the book: "*Oh, lucky Jim, / How I envy him,*" while Lodge's comes from a song adapted into a playground chant that features in the text as well as serving as an epigraph: "*Ginger, you're barmy, / You'll never join the Army, / You'll never be a scout, / With your shirt hanging out, / Ginger, you're barmy*" (*Ginger*, 130). The choice of a phrase from a distinctly non-literary source is typical of the stance of the "Angry" writer. There are various other connections, for example the strong resemblance between Captain Pirie's poor driving skills in Lodge's novel (70) and the celebrated opening chapter of *Lucky Jim*, featuring Professor Welch's appalling driving.

Lucky Jim was published by Victor Gollancz, a prominent and left-leaning firm who had published authors such as George Orwell, Elizabeth Bowen, and Ivy Compton-Burnett, and who would later publish E.P. Thompson's *The Making of the English Working Class* (1963). With the help of a clever promotional campaign, *Lucky Jim* was an instant success, and it soon was regarded, along with John Osborne's play *Look Back in Anger* (first performed in 1956), as one of the defining works of English literature in the 1950s. Even before Amis had obtained a publisher for *Lucky Jim*, an extract was broadcast on a book program entitled *First Readings*, produced by John Wain (Leader, *Life*, 270–1). The dust-jacket of the first edition (in the distinctive Gollancz bright yellow) featured a quotation from C.P. Snow: "For promise and achievement combined, it is the best first novel I've read in the last two years."

From its first publication, *Lucky Jim* has divided readers on the questions of its success as a novel and its historical significance. For example, in a review of a book of verse by Amis in 1956, the poet and critic A. Alvarez said of *Lucky Jim*, "Though I thought the novel very funny and well done, I couldn't quite see the hero as the great voice of our predicament. Except for less money and more resentment, he seemed to me essentially the same sort of figure as Bertie Wooster, an excellent comic type" ("A Joke's a Joke"). The lack of money and the resentment are of course among the defining qualities of Amis's novel, along with the remarkable stylistic control with which the author conveys them. The novelist and critic D.J. Taylor, in his survey of post-war fiction, confesses that he is not fond of Amis's novels, finding them "slackly written and intellectually disingenuous" (*After the War*, xxv). At the same time, he concedes "the fact remains that no discussion of the post-war novel can journey very far without acknowledging Amis's enormous importance" (xxv). For Taylor, Amis is a representative figure of all of the former Labour supporters who "regarded the Conservative victory of 1979 as a national deliverance. For these reasons, whether we like it or not, *Lucky Jim* is a key post-war English novel whose resonance – both as a social and a literary artefact – endures even forty years after its first publication" (xxv). As an author in an English comic tradition, preoccupied especially with issues of social decorum and class difference and the linguistic manifestations of these matters, Amis has often been mystifying to American readers. John Updike notoriously wrote in the *New Yorker* in 1983 "If the postwar English novel figures on the international stage as winsomely trivial, Kingsley Amis must bear part of the blame ... His universe is claustrophobically human, and his ambition and reputation alike remain in thrall to the weary concept of the 'comic novel.' There was something unabashedly sophomoric about *Lucky Jim*" ("Jake and Lolly," 293). Similarly, William H. Pritchard wrote in the *Hudson Review* in 1995 that "most American novel readers gave up on Kingsley Amis awhile back" ("Appreciating Kingsley Amis," 103).

David Lodge belongs firmly in the camp of Amis's admirers, and in his critical writing he frequently acknowledges the importance of Amis to his own career as a novelist. In 1963, Lodge published "The Modern, the Contemporary, and the Importance of Being Amis," one of the earliest critical essays on Amis, in *Critical Quarterly*. Lodge's article became the final chapter of *Language of Fiction*, and it is more personal in tone than the other essays in that book, and really as much about the situation of the novelist in the 1960s as it is about the language of Amis's novels.[1] It sounds a note that will recur in major essays such as "The Novelist at the Crossroads" and "The Novel Now: Theories and Practices." Lodge writes that the "importance of being Amis" exceeds the aesthetic qualities of his fiction, for in his writing and in his persona, Amis has played a vital role in the self-definition of many "middle-class intellectuals of the post-war period" (*Language*, 249). He continues, "If I may cite myself as an example, I suppose that, as a Roman Catholic, I could scarcely be more distant from Amis's view of the eternal verities.

And yet I constantly experience a strange community of feeling with him, and find that he speaks to me in a way that the great classic novelists do not, in an idiom, a tone of voice, to which I respond with immediate understanding and pleasure and without any conscious exertion of the kind required by critical reading" (249). Tracing the sources of this "strange community of feeling" is a way of clarifying what is distinctive in each of the two writers, and of clarifying aspects of the literary history of the second half of the twentieth century in Britain.[2]

Lodge frequently identifies himself as a member of the first generation to take advantage of the 1944 Education Act, which facilitated access to higher education for the working and lower middle classes, and which produced the phenomenon of the "scholarship boy," whose educational success meant that he was no longer comfortable in the social world of his childhood, but whose background made him ill at ease in the professional world he had entered.[3] For Lodge, the achievement of *Lucky Jim* was that it established, for people of his ambivalent position, "precisely the linguistic register we needed to articulate our sense of social identity, a precarious balance of independence and self-doubt, irony and hope" (*Write On*, 64). He expands on this comment in an introduction to the Penguin Twentieth- Century Classics edition of *Lucky Jim* in 1992, where he recollects his first reading of the novel in 1955 as a "long-postponed treat" after completing his undergraduate degree, adding that "I consumed it with exquisite pleasure" (Introduction, v). Looking back after many years and with the critical detachment those years have afforded, Lodge spends much of his introduction noting the aspects of *Lucky Jim* that link it to the venerable conventions of the English comic tradition. For example, the prominence given to the episode of the college summer ball is a structural parallel to the fiction of the eighteenth century. In addition, Lodge shows that in spite of its publication date of 1954, *Lucky Jim* is in ethos a novel of the immediate post-war period. It is full of military references, and the characters, especially Jim Dixon, live austere lives and have few possessions. Meanwhile, in the Welch family we see the survival of aspects of pre-war modes of life that are already unusual, such as the fact that they have maidservants, or the Bloomsbury poses of the two sons with French names. Lodge identifies a number of surprisingly literary allusions for such an apparently iconoclastic novel (and there are others that he does not comment on). But in spite of all these conventional aspects, *Lucky Jim* appeared as a boldly original book when it was first published. Lodge argues that this was because Amis found the perfect style to express the sense of social indeterminacy that was so common for educated people of his generation, and he characterizes the style of *Lucky Jim* as "educated but classless," eschewing "all the traditional devices of humorous literary prose" (vi).

Lodge relates Amis's style to Oxford ordinary language philosophy in the way that it strives for precision and plays skeptical variations on the stock phrases and idioms of everyday usage.[4] The following example is from a conversation between Jim Dixon and Professor Welch, in which Jim is trying to get some idea of when a decision will be taken on renewing his lectureship: "Any statement that could be battered out of Welch was invariably trustworthy, so that Dixon was back where he started. But how lovely to be back where he started, instead of out in front where he didn't want to be. How wrong people always were when they said: 'It's better to know the worst than go on not knowing either way.' No; they had it exactly the wrong way round" (*Lucky Jim*, 86–7). Another good example occurs in an exchange between Jim and his troublingly keen student Michie:

> "What are your main ideas so far, sir, if you don't mind my asking?" Michie asked as they turned downhill into College Road. Dixon did mind, but said only: "Well, I think the main emphasis of the thing will be social, you know." (28)

The writers of the Movement valued linguistic precision and understatement, and they opposed themselves to "affected, pretentious, obscure, and unintelligible usage" (Cameron, "'Virtues of Good Prose,'" 148), which they identified with modernism and especially with their bête noire, Dylan Thomas. Thomas's neo-romanticism, his extravagant use of language, and his self-dramatizing qualities were all objectionable to writers such as Amis, who satirizes Thomas in his second novel, *That Uncertain Feeling* (1955). It is often noted that George Orwell was an important influence on, or precursor of, the Movement.[5] Lodge's own critical prose, written largely in ordinary language, has much in common with the values of the Movement, even if he has incorporated numerous aspects of continental theory into his thinking. When Terry Eagleton describes Lodge's literary persona as that of an "educated plain man" and objects to his practice of "domesticating and defusing otherwise disruptive European insights for the purposes of home consumption" he sounds very much like a leftist intellectual writing about Orwell ("Silences of David Lodge," 96; 97).[6]

A major theme throughout Lodge's criticism, beginning with some of the essays in the second part of *Language of Fiction*, has been the opposition between modernism and realism in British literature from the late nineteenth century to the present, and his inaugural lecture as Professor of Modern English Literature at the University of Birmingham in 1976 continued this exploration under the title "Modernism, Antimodernism and Postmodernism." In this lecture, Lodge designates as "antimodernist" the kind of writing "that continues the tradition modernism reacted against. It believes that traditional realism, suitably modified to take account of changes in human knowledge and material circumstances, is still viable and valuable. Antimodernist art does not aspire to the condition of music; rather it aspires to the condition of history. Its prose does not approximate to poetry; rather its poetry approximates to prose" (*Working with Structuralism*, 6). This account serves as a very good summary of the fictional aesthetic of Amis and other writers of the 1950s, and also of some of Lodge's own writing. In his major contribution to literary theory and history, *The Modes of Modern Writing* (1977), Lodge presents the dialectical opposition between modernism and antimodernism as part of a larger structural opposition between metaphorical and metonymic modes of writing. In a rare instance of Lodge writing about poetry, the book includes an analysis of Philip Larkin as a metonymic poet (*Modes*, 212–20). The idea that post-war fiction was averse to experiment was challenged by Malcolm Bradbury in the same year that *The Modes of Modern Writing* appeared, and recent scholarship continues to complicate our picture of the literature of mid-century Britain.[7] Nevertheless, the overall narrative in Lodge's book retains its explanatory power, because the fact is that some of the most influential post-war writers repudiated the legacy of modernism for both artistic and ideological reasons. They sought to re-establish what they saw as a native English tradition, and to reject the cosmopolitanism and elitism of modernism for a more straightforward literary voice that would represent the experience of "ordinary people" who suspected ideological systems.

The phrase "Angry Young Men" gained currency after the controversial premiere of Osborne's *Look Back in Anger*, and was soon associated not only with with *Lucky Jim* but also with Colin Wilson's *The Outsider*. Amis dissociated himself from the label, though it has endured, no doubt because it not only served a need at the time, but still serves to articulate the combination of social discontent and assertive masculinity that characterizes a number of the writers of the period. Lodge argues that the "Angry" movement was not really political or ideological in nature, but rather an expression of frustration "at the slow rate of change in British society" (Afterword, *Ginger*, 216).[8] Lodge was just a few years too young to be part of the movement, not to mention the fact that his style and persona tend to be temperate, always aware of other perspectives and of counter-arguments. Anger does not play a large role in Lodge's literary personality, but if he was never an Angry Young Man, he was certainly sympathetic to aspects of the movement. In the afterword to *Ginger, You're Barmy*, he recalls going to a production of *Look Back in Anger* during a weekend leave from his National Service. He comments that he remembers "well the delight and exhilaration its anti-establishment rhetoric afforded me, and the exactness with which it matched my own mood at that juncture in my life" (215–16). It is appropriate that Lodge saw the play while on leave from the army, for his National Service seems to have been the experience that provoked the strongest feelings of resentment and class consciousness during his young adulthood. (By the time that he did his two years in the army [1955–57] the days of compulsory service were clearly numbered, and it was discontinued in 1960.) Jonathan Browne seems to speak for his creator when he reflects on the experience of basic training, where he felt that he had been forcibly removed from the meritocracy of the educational system and "thrust into a small archaic world of privilege, for success in which I was singularly ill-endowed" (*Ginger*, 49). As Lodge told an interviewer from the *Guardian*: "It wasn't until I was drafted that I found out about that sense of class inferiority, that other secret code of manners and connections and so on, and then it hit me like a brick wall ... From being a free spirit with my first-class degree, suddenly I was nothing. The Royal Armoured Corps was full of public-school types of a very offensive kind" (Turner, "Words Never Fail Him"; ellipsis in original).

Lodge's first two novels do contain a number of "angry" elements, including Mark Underwood's alienation and the critique of suburban conformity in *The Picturegoers* and the satire of bureaucratic incompetence and class privilege in *Ginger*. Furthermore, Lodge's first publishers, MacGibbon and Kee, were associated with the Angry Young Men, having published Tom Maschler's 1957 anthology of "Angry" writers, *Declaration*. In 1962, the Pan paperback reprint of *The Picturegoers* emphasized this aspect of the novel. The blurb on the front cover reads: "Love and brute desire ... cynicism and faith – a compassionate, realistic and even shocking novel of urban Britain today" (ellipsis in original). This is printed in yellow across a picture in muted nighttime tones of a young couple, presumably Mark and Clare, walking down a gritty urban street with a wooden fence on one side and the cinema dimly visible in the background. It is very much in the style of the covers of books by novelists such as John Braine and Stan Barstow. *The Picturegoers* was reviewed by the Movement poet Elizabeth Jennings, who was, like Lodge, a Roman Catholic, and she commented that: "*The Picturegoers* is an unusual combination in that it is a genuinely religious novel which is written and presented in the unillusioned, sometimes brutally direct manner of many of the younger novelists writing today" ("New Novels, 273).

As Lodge says in the Birmingham inaugural lecture, antimodernist art aspires towards the condition of history, and one of the strengths of Lodge's fiction, viewed as a whole, is the way that he has documented so precisely and effectively the way things were in England at various specific points in history. According to *Consciousness and the Novel*, the function of the novel is to create "fictional models of what it is like to be a human being, moving through time and space" (14). Lodge's fiction tells us, for example, what it was like to be an adolescent immediately after the war (*Out of the Shelter*), what it was like to be a professional-class person in the early 1970s (*How Far Can You Go?*), to be a young academic in the late 1980s, the period of university restructuring in England (*Nice Work*), or to experience mid-life crisis in the 1990s (*Therapy*). As a sign of his commitment to the documentary aspect of novel-writing, Lodge calls the first chapter of *How Far Can You Go?* "How It Was"; for a reader some thirty years after the first publication of this novel, that chapter title could equally refer to the whole book, with its remarkable ability to document social change through the telling selection of details of fashion, culture, politics, and social behaviour, connecting them to larger forces.

The antimodernist writers of the 1950s were not always subtle theorists, and in *The Novelist at the Crossroads* Lodge suggests that "the literary theorizing behind the 'Movement' was fatally thin" (18). Nevertheless, in their practice they showed him how to make literature out of his own experience, by writing about what was actually happening around him, unremarkable though that may have been by the standards of writers he admired such as Greene and Waugh. In critical discussion of the writing of the 1950s, two key words that recur are "suburban" and "provincial." Both Kingsley Amis and Elizabeth Jennings commented on the suburban setting in their reviews of *The Picturegoers*. Amis refers to the "lower-middle-class suburban habitat" of the characters ("Insolent Chariots"); Jennings notes that the novel "is set in a suburb on London's south bank" ("New Novels," 273). As Lodge writes in his essay about the Movement, "to get into this new literary scene one did not need the advantages of a privileged, cultured background, or to have exotic, unconventional, or heroic experience to write about. A lower-middle-class South London suburban upbringing, such as I had, was suddenly an almost fashionable background for a young novelist – though not quite as fashionable as a working-class upbringing in a Northern industrial town" (*Write On*, 105).

In his Marxist critique of Lodge in the late 1980s, Terry Eagleton uses the word "suburban" in the sneering way characteristic of both aristocrats and leftists (and Eagleton reveals a sneaking fondness for a lord in his memoir *The Gatekeeper*). He writes that "Sex provides Lodge with a suburban substitute for the high emotional currents which the careful comic distancing of his fictions otherwise expels," and he suggests that Lodge's novels "are largely innocent of political or spiritual passion" ("Silences of David Lodge," 98).[9] I have sometimes wondered whether Lodge was replying to Eagleton's comment when in *Therapy* he has Tubby Passmore, in his memoir about his adolescent love for Maureen Kavanagh, declare that his feeling "was the purest, most selfless romantic devotion. It was Dante and Beatrice in a suburban key" (225).[10] It is true, as Eagleton asserts, that Lodge's fiction practices "comic distancing"; that is a function of the genre he chooses, just as it is in Fielding or in Amis. But I think Eagleton is wrong to assert that Lodge leaves politics out of his novels (a reading of *Out of the Shelter*, *Nice Work*, or *Therapy* itself would suggest the contrary), just as he is wrong to argue a lack of "high emotional currents." The memoir of Maureen is a fine rendering of adolescent passion, and the reference to "Dante and Beatrice in a suburban key" nicely captures the intensity of the feelings involved, while bringing in both the religious context of Maureen's Catholicism and the background of the streets of the London suburb of Hatchford, from which Maureen journeys to the Sacred Heart Convent school and Tubby to the Lambeth Merchants' grammar school.

In chapter 2 of the *Vita Nuova*, Dante first sees Beatrice and falls in love: "She appeared dressed in the most noble of colours, a subdued and decorous crimson, girded and adorned in a style suitable to her years ... Let me say that from that time on Love governed my soul" (*Vita Nuova*, 4). This passage from Dante is paralleled in *Therapy*. Maureen appears at the tram stop every morning, while Tubby (then known by his real Christian name of Laurence) is waiting for a tram going in the opposite direction to hers. For a year or so, they do not speak, and like Dante's *Vita Nuova*, Tubby's memoir describes the dress of the beloved: "Even in her school uniform – a pudding-bowl hat, a gaberdine raincoat and pleated pinafore dress, all in a dead, depressing shade of navy blue – she was beautiful" (224). The next significant episode in Dante's narration is that, nine years later, Beatrice is walking down the street in the company of "two ladies of high bearing both older than herself," when she with "indescribable graciousness ... miraculously" greets him, "the first time her words had entered my ears" (6). Tubby doesn't have to wait quite as long as Dante, but nevertheless months pass before he and Maureen re-enact Beatrice's greeting of Dante. On her way to the tram stop, Maureen trips and falls; after Tubby has helped her to pick up her things, he finds an expensive pen she has dropped, which gives him an excuse to talk to her the next day. In recollecting the scene, Tubby makes a Graham Greene allusion, comparing Maureen walking down the hill with the scene at the end of *The Third Man* "when Harry Lime's girlfriend walks towards Holly Martins along the avenue in the frozen cemetery, except that she walks right past him without a glance, and this girl was not going to, because I had a flawless pretext to stop her and talk to her" (228).

Much of Lodge's fiction could be described as being in a suburban key. He uses the fictional south London suburb of Brickley to good effect in *The Picturegoers*, and versions of it reappear in a number of his novels, notably the south bank district of Battersea where Adam Appleby and his family live in *The British Museum*, the neighbourhood where Desmond Bates's father still lives in *Deaf Sentence*, and the scenes in Lodge's two novels of the 1990s where the childhood homes of the protagonists are revisited. In both *Paradise News* and *Deaf Sentence* he reuses the fictional name Brickley, which is mentioned once in *Therapy* as the neighbouring parish, against whose football team Tubby's club plays a match. In *The Picturegoers* we first see Brickley through the eyes of the middle-class student Mark Underwood, whose attitude towards it is a usefully explicit (perhaps overly explicit) compilation of the attitudes I have been discussing in the writers of the Movement:

> its ugliness held him with an obscure fascination that was to grow more and more insistent, until it entirely occupied the vacant space in his mind that should have held an affection for home. In future years, he felt sure, when he experienced a pang of homesickness, it would not be for the neat, clean villas and smug, dull shop-fronts of Blatcham, but for the grimy, arid streets of Brickley; for the tall, decaying Victorian houses, from each of whose windows sagged the washing of a different family; for the long, maddening rows of squat, identical nineteenth-century workers' homes with big new cars parked outside in incongruous opulence; for the worn, soft pavements; and for the honourable scars of the blitz, of the suffering he knew only by repute, the patches of new bricks, slates, paving-stones, the pre-fabs sprouted like mushrooms from the dung of destruction, new raw blocks of flats, and even the occasional neglected bomb-site, its stark outlines softened by the work of weather and vegetation, a playground for children, and for him a kind of shrine too. (42)

The influence of Richard Hoggart's *Uses of Literacy* is evident here, in the way that the ugliness of Brickley nevertheless embodies a more meaningful community than the middle-class suburb where Mark grew up.

Another interesting descriptive passage occurs in *Out of the Shelter*, as Timothy Young travels by bus to Victoria station before going abroad to stay with his sister in Germany:

> From the window of the bus the familiar streets took on a strange visual clarity and resonance of association. He felt that he was seeing them for the first time as they really were, that he was responding with all his senses to the special character of South-East

> London, its soiled, worn textures of brick and stone, its low, irregular skyline, its odours of breweries and gas and vegetables and tanneries. He noticed how old and neglected it all was: if you raised your eyes above the modern shop-fronts, you saw that they had been pasted on to buildings crumbling into decay, with cracked, grimy windows and broken-backed roofs and chipped chimney pots. The predominant colours were black, brown and a dirty cream. Guinness tints. (69)

Timothy is seeing his city with an artist's eye, as though for the first time, and rather like Des Esseintes setting off on a trip to London in Huysmans's *A Rebours* he wonders why he needs to go all the way to Germany if his perceptions have already been renewed. But in *Out of the Shelter*, Timothy must learn more than a new way of seeing; his experience in Heidelberg will transform his understanding of politics and human relationships, and these changes can only come about through immersion in another culture and conversation with people whose perspectives and opinions are very different from those he has absorbed in England. His careful observation of the architecture of the shops illustrates the preoccupation with the urban landscape that was an important part of post-war social planning. In the novel's brief epilogue, set in the mid-1960s, we learn that Timothy has become an academic in the new discipline of environmental studies, specializing in urban renewal (264).

In addition to writing about London, Lodge has created the fictional midlands city of Rummidge, a comically distorted version of Birmingham, where he has lived ever since he took up a temporary lectureship there in 1960. In *Changing Places* and *Small World*, Rummidge is the archetypal provincial city, still in some ways mired in the 1950s. Philip Swallow's reflections on departing from Rummidge to California on an academic exchange provide a good summary:

> No need ... to go for a walk on Sunday afternoon. No need to rouse himself, heavy with Sunday lunch, from his armchair, to help Hilary collect and dress their querulous children, to try and find some new, pointless destination for a drive or to trudge out to one of the local parks, where other little knots of people wander listlessly, like lost souls in hell, blown by the gritty wind amid

> whirlpools of litter and dead leaves, past creaking swings and deserted football pitches, stagnant ponds and artificial lakes where rowing boats are chained up, by Sabbatarian decree, as if to emphasize the impossibility of escape. *La nausée*, Rummidge-style. (*Changing Places*, 28)

Rummidge is treated more seriously and realistically in *Nice Work*, as a complex industrial city at a time of economic recession and political change. *Nice Work* is Lodge's condition of England novel, modelled on Victorian industrial novels such as Elizabeth Gaskell's *North and South* and alluding as well to *Howards End*, a novel that Lodge has introduced for Penguin Classics.[11] Rummidge appears once more in *Paradise News* as the city where Bernard Walsh teaches at a theological college after leaving the priesthood, and it has by this time accumulated, for Lodge's habitual readers, a richly resonant set of associations. It exists in his fiction as vividly as Barchester does in the novels of Trollope, or Middlemarch in George Eliot's greatest novel. Lodge's long residence in Birmingham, a large and unpretentious city with a long history as the hub of British manufacturing, has enabled him to remain in touch with ordinary English life in a way that gives his novels their rich specificity. Although he now owns a flat in London, he has not followed the example of Kingsley Amis by making London his permanent home, but has persisted in the spirit of the literature of the 1950s in finding a wealth of subject-matter in provincial existence. This commitment to Birmingham has been praised by David Edgar, a fellow Birmingham writer (Wroe, "Seriously Funny").

Reviewing *Therapy* in the *Observer*, Valentine Cunningham wrote that Tubby Passmore's memoir of Maureen is "the best account of working-class school-child amours back in the Fifties Dark Age that you're likely to meet in a very long day's journey through current fiction" ("How Tubby Got the Grail"). One of the reasons it is so effective is that Lodge is revisiting the world of his early fiction, so that the memoir is a kind of Movement novel in miniature whose effect is heightened by the fact that we have already become well-acquainted with its author, the likeable, mid-life-crisis-afflicted TV writer Tubby Passmore. At the age of fifty-eight, Tubby seeks to resolve his present difficulties by returning to the past, first keeping a diary, then eventually writing the memoir, transforming himself from a scriptwriter to what he calls a "book writer" (18). Lodge himself also makes a cameo appearance in *Therapy*, as part of a BBC crew filming a documentary about the Compostela pilgrimage (304).

Therapy provides an interesting perspective on shifts in political opinion from the 1950s to the 1990s. A number of the Angry Young Men who were on the left in the 1950s identified themselves with Margaret Thatcher's version of conservatism in the 1980s, which is not so surprising when one compares the trajectory of her career to theirs: from grocer's daughter to Oxford undergraduate to national figure. Kingsley Amis explained why he abandoned the Labour party in "Why Lucky Jim Turned Right" (first published in the *Sunday Telegraph*, 2 July 1967), noting that he had already "started getting reactionary" about education in the 1950s, as evidenced by chapter 17 of *Lucky Jim*: "It is never very difficult, as a colleague remarked, to be modern-minded and forward-looking in approaching questions of which one knows nothing. Here, as elsewhere, experience is a Tory" ("Why Lucky Jim," 202).

Lodge sets *Therapy* in 1993, the year after John Major led the Conservatives to their fourth consecutive election victory. Tubby Passmore confesses to his therapist that although he voted Labour, he is secretly glad that the Tories won the last election (86–7). Here Lodge identifies what seems to have been a common psychology among supporters of the Labour party in the 1980s whose social compassion was at odds with their rational analysis of the political situation. D.J. Taylor admits in *After the War* that "There must have been several million electors who voted Labour in June 1983 – I was one – in the not quite conscious hope that Labour would lose" (271). Tubby is the classic example of a working-class boy who has achieved, and who enjoys having an expensive car and being able to access private health services, but at the same time feels guilty about his advantages. The political genius of Tony Blair and New Labour was that they were able to appeal to people like Tubby, and those who had gone one step beyond him to become Tories. Blair writes in his memoirs that the credibility of New Labour rested on accepting that many of the changes that Margaret Thatcher had made were necessary and inevitable: "Saying this immediately opened the ears of many who had supported the Tories in that period – not because they were instinctively or emotionally Conservative, but because Labour had seemed so old-fashioned and out of touch with individual aspiration" (*A Journey*, 101). Lodge's novel is an excellent context for understanding the rise of New Labour. Tubby is an empathetic person who often imagines the sufferings of others, and who makes generous donations to various charities. At the same time, when he needs surgery he goes to a private doctor because he is aware of the problems in the National Health Service. These problems are reflected in other aspects of society, leading to his running motif of "Internal Derangement," a phrase he gets from one of his therapists and applies to anything that is not functioning as it should, from his own knee joint to the government to the national psyche. *Therapy* is profoundly insightful about the psychology and sociology of political opinion, and especially about the contradictions that can exist within an individual on political questions.

I discussed in chapter 2 Graham Greene's antipathy to "ordinary domestic life" (*Life in Letters*, 159), and his affinity, like that of other modernist writers, with visions of extremity. It was an article of faith for the modernists that bourgeois domestic life was characterized by deprivation and inauthenticity, so that the artist had to become a rebel, an exile, a bohemian. This attitude is exemplified in a notorious phrase in Cyril Connolly's *Enemies of Promise* which became proverbial for a generation and more. Since the context is much less well-known than the phrase, I will quote at some length from Connolly:

> In general it may be assumed that a writer who is not prepared to be lonely in his youth must if he is to succeed face loneliness in his middle age. The hotel bedroom awaits him. If, as Dr Johnson said, a man who is not married is only half a man, so a man who is very much married is only half a writer. Marriage can succeed for an artist only where there is enough money to save him from taking on uncongenial work and a wife who is intelligent and unselfish enough to understand and respect the working of the unfriendly cycle of the creative imagination. She will know at what point domestic happiness begins to cloy, where love, tidiness, rent, rates, clothes, entertaining, and rings at the doorbell should stop, and will recognize that *there is no more sombre enemy of good art than the pram in the hall.* (127; italics added)[12]

In offering a choice between literary endeavour and domestic life epitomized by the iconic image of a pram, Oscar Wilde anticipated Connolly in *The Importance of Being Earnest*, where the governess Miss

Letitia Prism leaves the home of Lord Bracknell "in charge of a perambulator that contained a baby, of the male sex." She disappears, as does the baby, and the pram is later found in "a remote corner of Bayswater" containing "the manuscript of a three-volume novel of more than usually revolting sentimentality" (303).[13]

However, for Lodge, as for Kingsley Amis in his early novels, domesticity is part of the subject matter for fiction; Amis's second novel, *That Uncertain Feeling* contains numerous descriptions of the living arrangements of John Lewis, his wife Jean, and their two children. The following is an especially detailed example:

> Around them was a multitude of objects, such as might, in a memory test, be shown to spectators for one minute and then withdrawn. Apart from clothes, adult and juvenile, male and female, ironed, newly washed, and fit to be washed, there were a half-eaten, browning apple, several broken biscuits, a plastic doll, the torso of a rubber doll, some children's books with pictures of clothed animals on the covers, a cup, a card of blue safety pins, an orange with one of my pencils stuck into it, a bottle of cod-liver oil, a pair of plastic pants, a lot of string unwound from a ball, a can of powder, a spoon, a wooden locomotive, some diapers in varying states, the defaced cover of my *Astounding Science Fiction*, and a lot of other things. (61)

Amis was not one to let the pram in the hall interfere with his personal pleasure or with his writing, as is revealed by an anecdote concerning a visit of Philip Larkin and his fiancée Ruth Bowman to Kingsley and Hilly Amis after the birth of their son Philip. As Zachary Leader tells the story, the two women set out on a walk, leaving the baby for Amis to look after: "The sleeping infant was put in his pram in the garden and Amis was instructed to bring him in immediately if the weather turned. In the middle of the walk there was a sudden, heavy thunderstorm and Hilly, worried, insisted that they return home straight away. On opening the front door the two women were hit by the sound of jazz at full volume, 'but of pram and baby there were no sign. Poor Hilly dashed outside to find a very wet baby lying in sodden blankets. Kingsley was mildly surprised at his wife's rage. He assured her that he had no knowledge of rain'" (Leader, *Life*, 224).

Domestic life figures prominently in David Lodge's fiction from the beginning, and in *The British Museum Is Falling Down* he initiates a recurring motif characterized by Peter Widdowson, in a rather hostile critical discussion of Lodge and Malcolm Bradbury, as "a crucial return (or *nostos*) for the main characters from the wide-open spaces, the fleshpots, the global campus, to a marriage which has to be remade" ("Anti-History Men," 23).[14] Brian Wicker recognized this structure when he wrote that *British Museum* tells the story of a day in the life of its characters, "Adam's Odyssey, with Barbara his Penelope waiting at home for his return" ("Sex, an Academic Question"). Within all the stylization and parody of *British Museum*, I think that one can identify a distinctive David Lodge voice, that of a comically heightened domestic realism, representing the anxieties of a Roman Catholic couple who are attempting to follow the church's teaching on birth control. In the opening chapter Adam has to negotiate making breakfast for his precocious children while trying to find a pair of clean, dry underwear. He then has a day filled with mock-heroic adventure, and at one moment tries to phone his wife Barbara. When she is not there he imagines that she has taken the children to the park: "Adam thought of his wife pushing their creaking, lop-sided pram through the grey damp afternoon in Battersea Park, past the ghost-town of the Fun Fair, closed for the winter, brooding on her possible pregnancy, and a pang of pity and love transfixed him" (82). Another reference to a pram in the novel comes in the middle of the parody of Henry James, as Adam is negotiating with Mrs Rottingdean, the possessor of unpublished material by a minor Catholic writer that Adam hopes to be able to edit: "They had touched bottom at last; and like most bottoms it was muddy and a shade disillusioning, littered with the pathetic shapes of old broken things – prams, kettles and bicycle wheels" (106–7). The items mentioned suggest the world of domestic realism which is Adam's reality, from which he periodically is transported into one or another novelist's fictional worlds.

Thus Lodge can be said to domesticate the world of the Catholic novels that were his early models, practicing a form of realism that sought to incorporate "having children" into literary representation, thereby undoing Adam Appleby's distinction between life and literature.[15] Though in this respect he was preceded by the Amis of *That Uncertain Feeling* and *I Like It Here*, Lodge goes beyond Amis through his use of a multiple perspective that allows him in the final chapter to represent Barbara Appleby's perspective on sexuality and family life. In her monologue she reflects "the trouble is this myth of the large family what's so marvellous about a large family I'd like to know there was only one child in the Holy Family" (159).

While Lodge was publishing *The British Museum* in 1965, Margaret Drabble was beginning her career as a novelist. She may be taken as representative of the generation of women writers who, in Lodge's formulation, took up the challenge of telling the story of Margaret Peel in *Lucky Jim*, that is, the challenge of telling the story of women from a female point of view (see Introduction to *Lucky Jim*, xvi–xvii). In the 1970s Drabble enjoyed not only literary eminence but celebrity status, as her novels about the lives of women spoke to the urgent concerns of a whole generation and permeated the culture of the period. She was one of the contemporary writers discussed in the last chapter of Elaine Showalter's pioneering work of feminist literary history, *A Literature of Their Own* (1977), where Showalter says that "Drabble is the novelist of maternity, as Charlotte Brontë was the novelist of the schoolroom" (305). The phrase "novelist of maternity," which would be recycled endlessly, expresses an essential truth about Drabble's early fiction. In novels like *The Millstone* (1964) and *The Waterfall* (1965), she describes the experiences of pregnancy, childbirth, and motherhood with an unprecedented detail and inwardness.[16] In various of Drabble's novels the image of the pram features with sufficient emphasis that one may legitimately wonder whether she is making the point, in response to Connolly, that art can indeed coexist with the pram in the hall (and indeed for the female writer who is a mother it has no other choice but to do so).

The first of these novels is *The Garrick Year*, which is the story of Emma Evans, a woman who is married to an actor. They are spending a season in the Shropshire town of Hereford, where a drama festival celebrates the opening of a new theatre. They have a baby named Joseph, and his pram comes to represent the duties and burdens of motherhood for Emma, who is a rather self-absorbed woman. Joseph lies in his pram "in the downstairs garage, which faced directly on the street and occupied what ground floor our house possessed" (69), because Emma has made a poor choice of houses, passing up a new house with a garden for one with the "dignity" of antiquity (32). As Emma, who is the novel's narrator, reflects, "Only those with small children can appreciate how little and how much they occupy the mind and the day" (120). Later, in one of several episodes of domestic crisis that conclude *The Garrick Year*, the pram serves as a vehicle to transport laundry to the laundrette, but is an inconvenient one because it must be left outside (147). When Emma has to jump into the river to rescue her daughter Flora, who has fallen in, she and her friend Wyndham push the baby's pram to the nearby theatre so that she can dry herself; the pram and the baby must be left with the doorkeeper. In *The Realms of Gold* (1975), a minor character, Janet Bird, feels confined by an unhappy marriage; Part Two of *The Realms of Gold* begins, "Janet Bird née Ollerenshaw was pushing her pram along Tockley High Street. The fact that she was doing this, as she was some 24 pages ago, does not indicate that no time has passed since that last brief encounter. Nor does it indicate a desire on the part of the narrator to impose an arbitrary order or significance upon events. It is simply a fact that Janet Bird spent a great deal of time pushing her pram up and down Tockley High Street" (127).

Lodge has not written any extended criticism about Drabble, though he did review two of her novels, and he mentions her very briefly in the first essay in *The Practice of Writing* as a writer who, like Lodge himself in *How Far Can You Go?* or Malcolm Bradbury in *The History Man*, writes novels about "developments in contemporary society" that contain "a strain of metafiction" (9).[17] In *The Writing Game*, a play first performed in 1990, Lodge creates a female writer called Maude Lockett, who resembles Margaret Drabble, or at least popularly received ideas about her. Maude is described by another writer as "A woman who has brought up four children, writes a weekly book review in *The Times*, seems to be on TV or radio every other day, and has published ten bestselling novels" (10). The organizer of the creative writing course that constitutes the action of the play says that he doesn't care much for Maude's novels: "I can take just so much about periods and miscarriages and breast-feeding and so on" (7). In *Thinks...* Lodge creates another female novelist character, Helen Reed, who again has some resemblances to Margaret Drabble, though she is not as successful as Maude Lockett. A male character who reads one of Helen's novels tells her that "It's what used to be called 'a woman's book,'" and his private opinion is that "It's a rather tedious story of a woman going into and coming out of a depressive illness" (*Thinks*, 255; 253). One scene involving Helen is itself somewhat metafictional: at a party, she meets the

Vice-Chancellor of the University of Gloucester, where she has taken a term appointment as a creative writing instructor. The Vice-Chancellor's wife confuses Helen's book *The Eye of the Storm* with Margaret Drabble's *The Needle's Eye*:

> "Well, it was the Eye of something," says Lady Hibberd.
> "I wrote a book called *The Eye of the Storm*," says Helen.
> "That's it," says Lady Hibberd. "It begins with a man in an off-licence."
> "Well, no, actually that's *The Needle's Eye*, I'm afraid," says Helen apologetically. (*Thinks*, 132)

The novel ends with Helen overcoming her writer's block and publishing a new novel "which one reviewer described as 'so old-fashioned in form as to be almost experimental.' It was written in the third person, past tense, with an omniscient and sometimes intrusive narrator" (340). This description is humorous without being dismissive, and might be applied to a number of novels by women in the latter part of the twentieth century, including *The Radiant Way* (1987), the novel that marked Drabble's return to the novel after a seven-year hiatus.

Having considered Kingsley Amis and Lodge in relation to social realism, I will conclude this chapter with a discussion of Lodge's campus novels. *Lucky Jim* was, as Lodge says in his Penguin introduction, the first British novel "to take as its central character a lecturer at a provincial university, and to find a rich seam of comic and narrative material in that small world" (vii). Lodge, like Amis, was a university lecturer and novelist, but he had a much fuller academic career, publishing critical books as well as novels and rising to the rank of Professor, so it is not surprising that the university has played a pivotal role in Lodge's fiction. His campus novels include *The British Museum Is Falling Down*, the trilogy of novels featuring Philip Swallow and Morris Zapp, *Thinks...*, and *Deaf Sentence*. However, *Thinks...* is also concerned with the problem of consciousness and the profession of authorship, so that it is rather more than, and less than, a campus novel in the full sense; similarly, the most memorable and interesting parts of *Deaf Sentence* are about Desmond's deafness and his relationships with his wife and his father; the campus plot is definitely secondary, both in terms of the amount of space it takes up and in terms of its fictional energy.

University life is represented in his first two novels, but it is with *The British Museum* that Lodge properly joins the ranks of the campus novelists. He includes a parody of the style of C.P. Snow, whose *The Masters* (1951) is an academic novel, but one with more in common with Anthony Trollope's *Barchester Towers* than with *Lucky Jim*.[18] Snow, like Trollope, is preoccupied with the struggle for power among men belonging to a prestigious, self-contained institution, though he lacks both the humour and the strong element of romance that run through Trollope's work. Snow's preoccupation with technology and administration set him apart from the romantic and humanistic literary tradition. He was an important figure in the emerging literature of the 1950s, and his iconoclasm and rejection of the techniques of modernism give him some affinities with Amis. His novels are written in a straightforward, unmetaphorical style that some might call pedestrian.

Snow is very much a writer of the Oxbridge world, presenting an idealized Cambridge in *The Masters*, whereas Lodge, the product of a grammar school, graduate of the University of London, and long-time member of the faculty of the University of Birmingham, has never shared the nostalgia for Oxbridge that is to be found in many English writers. Lodge's parody of Snow is devastating, highlighting his literary inadequacies, and the way that everything in his world reduces to questions of power. The other parodies in *The British Museum* may be seen as celebrations of the stylistic strangeness and uniqueness of their authors, while the Snow parody seems to me an act of critical demolition, taking on a writer who in the mid-1960s was highly regarded, and by implication suggesting that Lodge's own university novel has far greater interest for its use of language and for the range of human experience that it encompasses. Chapter 2 of *The Masters* begins with the following brief paragraph:

> When I woke the next morning, the bedroom seemed puzzlingly bright. Round the edges of the blind a white sheen gleamed. Then, half-awake, I felt the chill against my face, remembered the snow, drew the bedclothes higher. Like a pain returning after sleep, the heavy thought came back that that morning I was obliged to call at the Lodge. (17)

The snow will reappear in Lodge's parody, where it does dual duty as a signal of the identity of the author who is being parodied, so let us see what happens when C.P. Snow is obliged to stand before the parodic gaze of Lodge:

> It was cold and damp on the pavement outside Student Christian Hall. The leafless trees in Gordon Square stood black and gaunt against the façade of Georgian houses. The sky was cold and grey. It looked like snow. (65)

Adam Appleby here narrates in the first person, in the manner of Snow's Lewis Eliot. He is going to meet his supervisor, Briggs, whom he finds in the midst of a dispute with a colleague over the allocation of office space. Appleby reflects,

> I felt a certain thrill at being witness to one of those classic struggles for power and prestige which characterize the lives of ambitious men and which, in truth, exhaust most of their time and energy. To the casual observer, it might seem that nothing important was at stake here, but it might well be that the future course of English studies in the University hung upon this conversation. (67)

The parody of Snow ends with Adam leaving the English department to walk back to the British Museum: "When I finally made my departure, the trees were still there in Gordon Square, bleak and gaunt against the Georgian façade" (69). Lodge has authoritatively placed Snow as a repetitive writer with a profound grasp of the obvious.

Another scene in *The British Museum* is clearly inspired by Amis, namely the English department sherry party, which brings to the surface Adam's anxiety about his academic career and his young family. His professional worries have much in common with those of Jim Dixon, and as the scene develops other intertextual connections with Amis are established. Adam is accosted by "a bald-headed man in a pale striped suit" (*British Museum*, 118) whose comic mispronunciations of the names of various contemporary authors recall a scene in Amis's *I Like It Here* where Graham Greene and Evelyn Waugh are rendered as "Grim-Grin" and "Ifflen-Voff" (46). Also reminiscent of Amis is the fact that there is no food at the party, and Adam is very hungry: "His stomach, which was empty, made a noise like old plumbing. He looked around for food, but could only find a plate thinly covered with the crumbs of potato chips. These he ate greedily, picking them up on the moistened tips of his fingers" (*British Museum*, 118). One recalls Jim's adventures while staying at Professor Welch's house, or the scene when he takes Margaret out for drinks at a pretentious roadside hotel: "Dixon felt he could recoup himself a little for the expensiveness of the drinks by eating steadily through the potato crisps, gherkins, and red, green, and amber cocktail onions provided by an ambitious management" (*Lucky Jim*, 21).

Lodge dedicated *The British Museum* to Malcolm Bradbury, with whom he collaborated on a theatrical revue in 1963. He credits Bradbury with helping him to discover "a zest for satirical, farcical and parodic writing that I had not known I possessed." Comedy, Lodge adds, "offered a way of reconciling a contradiction, of which I had long been aware, between my critical admiration for the great modernist writers, and my creative practice, formed by the neo-realist, anti-modernist writing of the 1950s" (Afterword to *British Museum*, 169; 170). Bradbury and Lodge have been consistently linked, both by general readers and by Marxist critics hostile to their liberalism, but they are really quite different writers. Bradbury's novels are much more novels of ideas, and his best-known academic novel, *The History Man* (1975), is a satire with a far sharper edge than Lodge's comedies, while *Rates of Exchange* (1983), which I think is Bradbury's finest novel, operates in a mode of bleak absurdist satire, magic realism, and play with ideas and language that suggests a combination of Saul Bellow, Milan Kundera, and Thomas Pynchon. Bradbury and Lodge were often confused in the popular imagination, and according to a newspaper article from 1984, "Someone phoned David Lodge once to ask him to settle a bet, whether he was or was not the same person as Malcolm Bradbury" (Hebert, "Signs of Love and Laughter").[19] Each writer has included in an academic novel a scene that alludes to this comic confusion. In Lodge's *Small World*, Persse McGarrigle attends a party at the MLA Convention in New York, at which "his glass ... was refilled in an absent-minded fashion by a shortish dark-haired man standing nearby with a bottle of champagne in his hand, talking to a tallish dark-haired man smoking a pipe. 'If I can have Eastern Europe,' the tallish man was saying in an English accent, 'you can have the rest of the world.' 'All right,' said the shortish man, 'but I daresay people will still get us mixed up" (331–2). Persse is told that they are novelists, presumably Lodge and Bradbury. In *Rates of Exchange*, Bradbury's protagonist Petworth is asked by a woman in the eastern European country he is visiting, "Do you know also a campus writer Brodge? ... Who writes *Changing Westward*? I think he is very funny but sometimes his ideological position is not clear" (268–9). The title fuses Lodge's *Changing Places* with Bradbury's *Stepping Westward*, just as "Brodge" neatly collapses their names into one.

David Lodge's *Small World* was published in 1984 and is the definitive British campus novel of that decade, just as *Lucky Jim* is for the 1950s and *The History Man* for the 1970s. *Small World* captures the excitement of the global conference circuit and of the arrival of literary theory at the moment just before the financial constraints of the 1980s really began to bite, taking the romance and high spirits out of academic life. Lodge's hero Persse McGarrigle is a neophyte in the ways of the academy, and in that sense resembles Jim Dixon, but whereas Jim's insecurities are the natural product of the changing nature of English society after the Second World War, Persse's innocence is of an extent that defies the norms of realistic fiction. *Lucky Jim* is structured according to the archetypal conventions of comedy, as Bruce Stovel has argued ("Traditional Comedy"). As such, its resolution comes about when Jim finds a way to incorporate himself within the existing social order. But at the end of *Small World*, when Persse abandons his quest for the beautiful and elusive Angelica that has been a central part of the novel's structure, he immediately sets out in search of another woman. *Small World* is structured according to the pattern of romance rather than comedy, and as Angelica explains near the end of the novel, in one of a number of excerpts from academic papers by the various characters, romance "has not one climax but many ... no sooner has one adventure been concluded than another begins" (322–3).

The narrative exuberance of *Small World* can be seen as corresponding to the material exuberance that characterized the early 1980s, and that would be most memorably expressed in the quotation "Greed is good," taken from a speech by the corporate raider Gordon Gekko in Oliver Stone's 1987 film *Wall Street*.[20] By the time that Lodge published the third instalment of the *Small World* trilogy, *Nice Work*, in 1988, the British university scene was, like the nation as a whole, undergoing a painful transformation. It was during this period of cutbacks and restructuring in the academic world that Lodge retired from the University of Birmingham. He told an interviewer in 2004 that "It was the right time to leave. All my former colleagues say: 'You are well out of it.' There's a weary disillusion to university life now and that's a shame because, when I was there, there was excitement, a joie de vivre. Now it has become like a machine, servicing large numbers of students, and much less attractive and interesting" (Llewellyn, "Bad Reviews"). Thus for those who were graduate students or junior faculty in the 1980s, *Small World* retains a special status, as a romance or fantasy about the way that universities could be. To echo Lodge, it was a "magic book" for many, serving in part as a guide to the varieties of literary theory, in part as a conduct book for aspiring global academics, and in part as a repository of anecdotes and jokes with which to enliven academic conversation. Elaine Showalter recalls in *Faculty Towers*: "In an era before there were handbooks, self-help guides, or advice columns for graduate students and junior faculty in the *Chronicle of Higher Education*, novels taught me how a proper professor should speak, behave, dress, think, write, love, succeed, or fail" (2). For those seeking to understand post-structuralism, Morris Zapp's "*every decoding is another encoding*" (*Small World*, 25; italics Lodge's) was as helpful a brief guide as Jonathan Culler's aphorism "Meaning is context-bound, but context is boundless" (*On Deconstruction*, 123). The ongoing saga of Rodney Wainwright's unfinished conference paper is a cautionary tale for any academic with a tendency to procrastinate. The fate of Persse McGarrigle's book proposal on the influence of T.S. Eliot on Shakespeare, like that of Jim Dixon's article on developments in fifteenth-century shipbuilding techniques, resonates with every academic's paranoid fear of having his or her ideas plagiarized.

It is worth repeating, as a final point concerning Lodge's campus novels, that they reveal an openness to American culture that was unusual among British writers and intellectuals until quite recently. Contemporary writers such as Salman Rushdie and Martin Amis may look to New York and find inspiration in the novels of Vladimir Nabokov and Saul Bellow, but through much of the twentieth century the United States was viewed with great suspicion. The writers of the Movement notoriously cultivated an insular attitude, although that sometimes concealed an attraction to things American.[21] Writers such as Greene and Waugh expressed hostile attitudes to the United States (and wrote successful books embodying them, namely *The Quiet American* and

The Loved One). But in *Changing Places*, and especially through the character of Morris Zapp, Lodge celebrates the vitality and amplitude of American culture and literature, encapsulating this memorably in the passage in *Changing Places* where Philip Swallow "understood American Literature for the first time in his life ... understood its prodigality and indecorum, its yea-saying heterogeneity" (195). This "international theme" is central in David Lodge, and it will be explored in more detail in the next chapter, as it is one of the things connecting him to Henry James.

Kingsley Amis was undoubtedly an influence on the comic dimension of Lodge's fiction, though it is difficult to distinguish between instances of influence and instances of a common vision of life and language. *Lucky Jim* is full of descriptions of comical and farcical action, often involving Jim's unsuccessful attempts to conform to the social codes of the academic world. Among the most memorable examples are his repertoire of faces, his visit to the Welches, especially the incident with the bedclothes, and his Merrie England lecture. *The British Museum* is the first of Lodge's novels with extended comic episodes, and Adam's incompetence with his scooter is very much in the mode of Kingsley Amis. From *Changing Places* one could instance various mishaps, such as Morris Zapp and the cascading tobacco tins, or Philip Swallow's wife Hilary talking to him on the phone about their marriage while he is being interviewed live on a radio talk show, or Morris Zapp thinking that the mentally ill former chair of the Rummidge English department is trying to kill him. *Therapy* is in some ways a very serious novel, but it also contains some of Lodge's most effective comedy. I am especially fond of the brief incident when Tubby blindfolds himself with an airline sleeping mask in order to try to find out what it would be like to be blind (13), while the holiday from hell that he and Amy spend in Tenerife is one of Lodge's best pieces of comic writing (151–62).

In his obituary notice for Kingsley Amis, Lodge identifies as one of his favourite Amis passages the scene in *That Uncertain Feeling* when John Lewis meets two foreign sailors in the street, one of whom seems to ask him:

> "Where is pain and bitter laugh?"
> This was just the question for me, but before I could strike my breast and cry, "In here, friend" the other little man had said:

> "My cousin say, we are new in these town and we wish to know where is piano and bit of life, please? (146)

There is a comparably amusing and revealing misunderstanding in *Therapy*. The depressive Tubby is doing some errands: "I was standing impatiently in line at the Post Office when I heard a woman's voice say at my shoulder, 'Are you desperate?' I swivelled round, thinking she was addressing me, but it was a mother talking to her little boy. 'Can't you wait till we get home?' she said. The little boy shook his head miserably and pressed his knees closer together" (100). The mishearings of the partially deaf Desmond Bates in *Deaf Sentence* are in the spirit of Amis's comically mispronounced English, for example, when he hears "non-stick saucepan" as "long-stick saucepan" (84).

Kingsley Amis has a reputation for not having admired modernism, and he is often quoted as having characterized experiment in fictional technique as "obtruded oddity" ("Fresh Winds," 565). While it is true that Amis does not write like Joyce or Woolf, his fiction is surprisingly literary, in ways that it often takes pains to conceal, and it is not averse to using the techniques that are characteristic of the modernists.[22] There are a number of occasions in *Lucky Jim* when Jim Dixon recalls books he had once read, or looked into; these are never named, for Jim is anxious to avoid appearing pretentious, "artistic," or intellectual. Lodge has pointed out how Jim thinks of Greene's *Heart of the Matter* at a key moment of crisis in his relationships with Margaret and Christine: "He remembered a character in a modern novel Beesley had lent him who was always feeling pity moving in him like sickness, or some such jargon" (*Lucky Jim*, 185). This is an effective parody of the imagery of Greene's novel, but Lodge argues that there is also a significant parallel between Scobie's situation in *Heart of the Matter*, caught between pity for his wife Louise and love of his mistress Helen, and Jim Dixon's feelings of guilt and pity towards Margaret that inhibit him from following up on his attraction to Christine (Introduction to *Lucky Jim*, xv).

Lodge did not pick up another literary allusion in *Lucky Jim*, one even more confounding to one's preconceptions about the novel than the reference to Greene. Greg Londe analyzes a scene involving Jim Dixon and Bertrand Welch. During an uncomfortable moment, Jim "thought of a sentence in a book he'd once read: 'And with that he picked up the bloody old towser by the scruff of the neck, and, by Jesus, he near throttled him'" (50). As Londe says, "believe it or not," the sentence is from the Cyclops section of James Joyce's *Ulysses* ("Reconsidering *Lucky Jim*, 130).[23] It is echoed later, in the scene of Jim's fight with Bertrand, when Jim finally expresses in words to Bertrand what he has been thinking of him all along: "The bloody old towser-faced boot-faced totem-pole on a crap reservation, Dixon thought. 'You bloody old towser-faced boot-faced totem-pole on a crap reservation,' he said" (*Lucky Jim*, 209). Amis appropriates the violent language of the bigoted narrator of the Cyclops episode, and puts it to the service of class justice in his own novel. This is every bit as allusive as anything we would find in one of Lodge's own novels, and suggests that the version of Amis that critics as subtle as Lodge himself have constructed, following hints given out by Amis himself, underestimates the complexity of Amis's fiction.

Lodge does make a different comparison of Amis to a modernist that is on the face of it surprising, but that illuminates the reason that Amis's novels have become "progressively darker, to the disappointment of many readers of *Lucky Jim*, but also deeper" (Introduction to *Lucky Jim*, xvii). In his obituary for Amis, Lodge says that Amis's style "is a kind of English equivalent to the prose of Samuel Beckett (though Amis would have spluttered derisively at the comparison). In each case, language, denied the luxury of metaphysical affirmation and romantic afflatus, coils back upon itself, mocking its own pretentions as well as the follies and foibles of human behaviour" ("Obituary"). Lodge has suggested that Beckett dealt with the anxiety of influence in relation to Joyce by moving in the antithetical direction of negation and silence (*Write On*, 69); Amis's stylistic precision could be read as a similar exercise in disconfirmation. The *Ulysses* allusion, which has remained buried in *Lucky Jim* until recently, may hint that Amis was responding to Joyce in a manner that parallels on a much smaller scale Beckett's strategy in the face of the same anxiety of influence.

Amis and Beckett share an unflinching ability to face the realities of "disease, madness, addiction, depression and death" (Lodge, Introduction to *Lucky Jim*, xvii). Lodge reviewed Amis's novel about old age, *The Old Devils* – which won the 1986 Booker Prize – for the *New York Review of Books*, and here again he compares Amis to Beckett: "It would seem one is not, in Yeats's phrase, a soul fastened to a dying animal, but just a dying animal" ("Closing Time," 16). Lodge has preferred to write novels with comic resolutions, but he too has explored the darker territory that Amis came to occupy. For example, *How Far Can You Go?* begins with a group of university students who are at the beginning of their adult lives, but as they attend the St Valentine's Day mass with which the book opens, they are in the company of two old women who are near the end of life's journey. The young people pay no attention to the old women, because "none of them actually believes he or she is going to die" (16). By the end of the novel, more than twenty years later, they have experienced physical and mental illness, the death of parents and in one case the death of a child, and they have moved much closer to the position of the old women. The closest thing Lodge has written to *The Old Devils* is *Deaf Sentence*, where Desmond Bates, who is partially deaf, has retired from his university teaching position, but is still caring for his aging father, whose final illness and death are portrayed in an unsparing manner near the end of the novel. *Deaf Sentence* has its share of comedy and even farce, but it is comedy with a despairing edge, given the situation in life of the principal character. The underlying sombre tone deepens as *Deaf Sentence* progresses. At about the midway point, Desmond records his memory of being in London on 7 July 2005, the day of the bombings on London's public transit system. Near the end of the novel, Desmond visits Poland to give a British Council lecture, and there is a laconic and moving description of his visit to Auschwitz, which underlines the seriousness of the novel's concern with ultimate questions.

As someone who has read a great deal of narrative theory, Lodge is very self-conscious about beginnings and endings. He likes to begin a novel with a character in bed, waking up to face the day: this is how he opens both *British Museum* and *Nice Work*, and he uses a similar scene to commence the main action of *Out of the Shelter*. *Author, Author* begins with the dying Henry James in his bed in the "master bedroom" of Lamb House (3) during the First World War, while Lodge's most recent novel, *A Man of Parts*, similarly begins at the end of the story, as H.G. Wells's family talk about how he is dying, and the Second World War still rages in the background. By beginning these novels at the end of the two writers' lives, Lodge foregrounds the metaphorical implications of the "death of the author," an influential concept in post-structuralist literary theory that he has never fully endorsed; he also forces the reader to think about the issues of both personal and literary afterlife. Lodge said in his essay on Kingsley Amis that he has a very different view of "the eternal verities" from that writer, but in his most recent works he has deepened his novelistic vision and turned it towards some of the same dark questions that increasingly occupied Amis through his long career.

In both *Small World*, in the character of Ronald Frobisher, and in the play and novella *Home Truths* in the character of Adrian Ludlow, Lodge portrays writers who enjoyed success and fame as young men but are now unable to produce anything new. By absorbing new influences and dealing with new subjects, he has avoided this fate, but his essays and fiction of the last twenty years or so have been preoccupied with the disappointments and difficulties of the life of a writer. Lodge has mentioned in several interviews how he was a much less anxious person as a young man than he became later in life, and he presents himself, like Amis's Jim Dixon, as someone who was "lucky."[24] The same word occurs in his 1993 introduction to the reissued *Picturegoers*. Recalling the circumstances of that novel's publication, Lodge describes buying a copy of the weekly magazine *The Listener* in Paddington station and reading Elizabeth Jennings's review of *The Picturegoers* while standing on a crowded train to Birmingham, where he had just been appointed to a temporary lectureship: "I was married, I had a child, a foot on the academic ladder, and now a novel, 'an ambitious and arresting achievement,' Elizabeth Jennings said. That seemed quite enough to be going on with. I felt lucky. I *was* lucky" (*Picturegoers*, xvi). It is a pleasing coincidence that *Lucky Jim* ends with Jim meeting Christine at the railway station where he will be taking the train to London to start his new job. The parallel is not quite exact: Jim is leaving his temporary job at the unnamed university for a job in business, and he is leaving a provincial city presumably in the midlands for London, while Lodge is beginning an academic career and moving *to* the kind of provincial city beloved in the novels of the 1950s, but in both cases the protagonist, through the workings of luck, has achieved a kind of comic resolution. The railway station is the perfect setting, for "the railway train … is an inherently metonymic product of technology" (Lodge, *Modes of Modern Writing*, 205), and therefore appropriate for neo-realist fiction, dominated by the metonymic mode – or indeed for a metonymic poet like Philip Larkin, who describes a railway journey in one of his best-known poems, "The Whitsun Weddings." Thus Lodge's memory of his first success as an author is presented in one of the central images of the literature of the 1950s, and one that especially recalls the ending of *Lucky Jim*. We could call this moment a description of "Lucky Dave."

5

"The Art of Fiction": David Lodge and Henry James

He smiled politely, thinking that a knowledge of Jamesiana, plus the possession of Jamesian texts, certainly befitted an indisputably major talent.
~Kingsley Amis, *I Like It Here*

Henry James was one of the two set authors on the syllabus for the modern option of the English honours course at the University of London when David Lodge was a student there (*Write On*, 61).[1] But Lodge has admitted in an interview that "I didn't really enjoy and appreciate James until I became an academic and started to teach him and write criticism about him" ("Conversation"). From those early teaching days onwards, James has been a significant presence in both Lodge's critical writing and in his fiction. James is exemplary for his commitment to the craft of fiction and for his conception of the novelist as an artist. His whole life was lived in service to this ideal, and some of his most interesting shorter works explore the paradoxes, anxieties, and ethical dilemmas of artistic life. He thus served as a model of the novelist as dedicated professional, and of the writer who was both great novelist and major critic.

Lodge's formalist tendencies make for a strong affinity between him and James on the question of the art of the novel. At the same time, there are significant differences between them that may explain why Lodge came to appreciate James later than others whose influence has already been discussed. James was an upper-class American who wrote about a social world far removed from that in which Lodge grew up. So there is a national difference, compounded by the difference of class. In addition, Lodge shares with Evelyn Waugh and Kingsley Amis a comic vision of the world which makes them observers of society and human behaviour, whereas James's concerns are profoundly interior, and he specialized in representing human consciousness. Among Lodge's early literary enthusiasms, both Waugh and Greene belonged to a different class, but both were Roman Catholics, like Lodge. Greene did not restrict himself to the socially privileged in his novels, and while Waugh largely depicted the upper classes, he did so in a comic and anarchic way that is more immediately accessible than James's tales of international intrigue among the gentry. Joyce also writes about an intensely Catholic world, and furthermore Lodge was familiar with aspects of Irishness from his family background and his Catholic schooling. Amis does not share the Catholic world view of these writers, but Lodge responded powerfully to the representation of a social experience that in many ways was his own. H.G. Wells, whom I will discuss in the next chapter, shares with Lodge a London suburban background and an interest in the comic possibilities of language and of class distinctions.

Nevertheless, for anyone interested in writing fiction in the late 1950s, Henry James loomed as an unavoidable figure, as we can see in his influence on Philip Roth, another writer whose characteristic concerns are quite different from those of James. Adeline Tintner, in *Henry James's Legacy*, says that Roth "has engaged in a long struggle with James" (202), one that she discusses in some detail in her book.[2] Roth's first full-length novel, *Letting Go* (1962), begins with the protagonist Gabe Wallach visiting the church in Chelsea that contains a plaque commemorating Henry James. When he receives the last letter written by his mother on her deathbed, he tucks it into his copy of *The Portrait of a Lady*, and the action of the novel is precipitated when Gabe lends this book to a fellow graduate student, forgetting that he has left the letter in it (*Letting Go*, 234). Graham Greene was a dedicated Jamesian; he wrote several critical essays on James and he had a large collection of first editions of James's fiction.[3] Greene writes in "Henry James: The Private Universe" that James "is as solitary in the history of the novel as Shakespeare in the history of poetry" (*Collected Essays*, 40).

Lodge's interest in travel, and his exhilarated response to his first visit to the United States, may have helped him to appreciate James. This chapter will trace Lodge's increasing admiration for and engagement with Henry James, culminating in the transformation of James into a fictional character in *Author, Author*. It is relevant to recall at the outset that Graham Greene's critical essays turned James into an honorary Catholic novelist. In *The Catholic Side of Henry James*, Edwin

Fussell shows that Catholicism held a strong fascination for James, in spite of his superficial knowledge of it. The Roman Catholic church is represented in James's writing as part of the picturesque backdrop of old Europe. But more than that, in at least some of James's novels it symbolizes an ethical system that is set in opposition to the world described by Lord Mark in *The Wings of the Dove* as "the groping and pawing, that of the vague billows of some great greasy sea in mid-Channel, of masses of bewildered people trying to 'get' they didn't know what or where" (107). It is no accident that Milly Theale, the dove of the title, is a Roman Catholic, nor that Merton Densher, at the end of the novel, chooses to visit Brompton Oratory on Christmas Day (477). These are unobtrusive details, but they do conform to a pattern, as Fussell's book demonstrates, and a pattern that Lodge would have been quick to recognize. In *Author, Author* James confesses to his friend George Du Maurier that he feels "a kind of emotional attraction to the Roman Church – emotional and aesthetic ... I believe there is such a thing as evil – original sin if you like – and that perhaps humanity needs religion as a bulwark against it. And I rather envy the Romans their rituals and symbolism – the sung masses, the votive candles, the anointing of the sick" (90–1). However, he is quick to reassure Du Maurier that he has no interest in converting: "Consciousness is my religion," he tells him, "human consciousness" (91).

James had a great influence on both the practice and the theory of fiction in the twentieth century. He has a major role in the Anglo-American tradition of theorizing about the novel due to his own essays and prefaces, and also due to the influence he exerted on Percy Lubbock's *The Craft of Fiction* (1921) and on subsequent criticism of the novel, down to Wayne Booth's *The Rhetoric of Fiction* (1961) and beyond. Given the weight of James's presence, it is not surprising that there was a backlash against his influence. Both Kingsley Amis and Philip Larkin disliked certain established reputations, as can be documented, often amusingly, from their letters, especially when writers such as Yeats or Dylan Thomas are mentioned. Larkin refers to James as "the old bore" in a letter to Monica Jones in 1951 (*Letters to Monica*, 72). In his *Memoirs*, Amis recalls being surprised by the obligation to teach a class during his year at Princeton in 1958–59, for which the textbook was a collection of short stories that included "The Aspern Papers," which he says "is the only work of [James] I have ever read to its conclusion" (197). Whether or not Amis is exaggerating in this claim (in 1950 he did profess to have read *The Bostonians*[4]), James plays a significant role in *I Like It Here* (1958), a novel that vaguely repeats the pattern of *The Ambassadors*, as the journalist and lecturer Garnet Bowen is sent to Portugal by a publisher friend to try to ascertain the genuineness of a new novel that has been submitted from the long-silent writer Wulfstan Strether. Lambert Strether is of course the principal character in *The Ambassadors*. Amis's Strether is an effete and pretentious figure, whose "dialogue recalled Charles Morgan rather than anything Downing College would approve – though the distinction was admittedly a fine one" (82). Amis includes a very effective parody of the style of James, or one of his disciples, describing an encounter under the bougainvillaea of two characters called Frescobaldi and Yelisaveta: "He reached towards her with 'How can you be so sure?' and the moment he had awaited, his words barely out, came" (111). Although Bowen smiles politely when Wulfstan Strether refers to James (see the epigraph to this chapter), his private opinion of *Portrait of a Lady* is more contemptuous: "Uncontrollable laughter was the only dignified response to that. He vented some" (84).

The case against James was most powerfully made by Maxwell Geismar in *Henry James and the Jacobites* (1963), a hostile account of James that emphasizes his social elitism, his refusal to engage with empirical and historical reality, and his fastidiousness about sexuality and the physical in general. Geismar's book is full of vitriolic epigrams, such as the statement that *The Ambassadors* is "perhaps the *silliest* novel ever to be taken seriously in world literature" (297; italics Geismar's). Many of the observations that he makes are accurate as reductively literal-minded descriptions of James's novels, but somehow beside the point for any reader who has once become absorbed by their world. *James and the Jacobites* has a kind of gruesome fascination as the brief of a prosecuting attorney who spends well over four hundred pages assailing in minute detail the work of a writer he claims to find detestable, all in the name of a socially engaged, leftist, and realist conception of literature.

Lodge reviewed the British edition of Geismar's book, *Henry James and His Cult*, in 1965, during the first phase of his engagement with James, along with the more or less contemporaneous *Language of Fiction* and *British Museum Is Falling Down*. In the review, Lodge concedes that James "has been excessively praised in some quarters" (Rev., 102), but he spends most of his time showing that Geismar's attack is based on a crude theory of fiction. While Geismar chides James for not sharing his own views about American society and about sexuality, Lodge asserts that "literary art deals with what is possible, not what is probable, or verifiable, or healthy or normal. The only essential obligation binding on the novelist is that he should convince us that his action is possible and of human interest" (102). Lodge is somewhat confusingly reversing Aristotelian categories here, for in one of the best-known passages in the *Poetics* Aristotle pronounces that "the poet should prefer probable impossibilities to improbable possibilities" (chapter xxiv, 64). Lodge's point, however, is clear: the novelist should not be restricted to the socially typical, to the average, as some nineteenth-century theories of realism argued, and as the twentieth-century Marxist theory of Georg Lukács maintained. I think that by "possible and of human interest" Lodge means "convincing within the world of the novel." For example, Lambert Strether in *The Ambassadors* sounds absurdly naïve in a brief summary of the story, but within the world of that novel we accept his behaviour and his perceptions as possible and even likely, given the way that world is presented to us.

Apart from overt detractors like Geismar, the indirectness of James's technique, the extreme complexity of his prose style, and the fastidiousness of his characters, along with well-known anecdotes about Henry James's public persona in later life, have caused him to be the object of frequent parody even among his admirers. Max Beerbohm wrote two that are as much homage as parody: "The Mote in the Middle Distance," published in *A Christmas Garland* in 1912, and "The Guerdon," written on the occasion of James receiving the Order of Merit. Both of these pieces have the advantage of brevity, whereas James Thurber's "The Beast in the Dingle" goes on far too long, and seems more like a weak imitation of late James than an effective parody. Beerbohm's "The Guerdon" is included by Seymour Chatman in his study of *The Later Style of Henry James*, a book that Lodge reviewed in 1974.[5] In his review of Chatman's book, Lodge praises him for extending the critical vocabulary for the discussion of James, but regrets that Chatman did not move from stylistics to literary criticism, arguing that there is less of a discontinuity between these activities than Chatman seems to believe. Lodge provides his own parody of James in *The British Museum Is Falling Down*, and his own discussion of James's style in *Language of Fiction*. Though it was published a year later, I will look at the latter first, before analyzing the Jamesian presence in *British Museum.*

"Strether by the River" is the fifth of the seven essays on specific authors and texts that comprise Part Two of *Language of Fiction*, and that illustrate the practical application of the discussion of language and style in Part One. Lodge gives a general sense of the "linguistic norms" of *The Ambassadors* (*Language*, 204), then in a masterful analysis of the two key paragraphs of the recognition scene in Book XI, chapter iv, he shows how at the crucial moment James violates the linguistic norms he has established, while making ironical use of various metaphors that are central to the novel. One of the important points that Lodge makes is that James's later style is dominated by "heightened cliché" (*Language*, 196). Characters speak in a way that manages "to discuss, or at least to suggest, infinite complexities and discriminations in a vocabulary that is on the face of it remarkably impoverished, giving expressive force to platitudes and dead metaphors by devices of intonation, stress, placing, and repetition" (197). That sounds remarkably similar to what Kingsley Amis and other writers associated with the Movement did with ordinary language and conversational idiom.

F.R. Leavis had a high regard for James, seeing him, along with Jane Austen, George Eliot, Joseph Conrad, and D.H. Lawrence as part of the "great tradition" of the English novel. Leavis describes *The Portrait of a Lady* as "an original masterpiece" (*Great Tradition*, 141), but he maintains that something went wrong during the final phase of James's career. He continues, "We are asked to admire *The Ambassadors* (1903); and *The Ambassadors* seems to me to be not only *not* one of his great books, but to be a bad one" (142; italics Leavis's). In another example of the prestige of Leavis in the mid-twentieth century, Lodge begins his essay on *The Ambassadors* by disputing Leavis's negative judgment of the late style of James, though he concedes that ultimately such disputes over value are beyond proof: "Whether James displays a sense of what is valuable and significant in living, and whether he demands a disproportionate effort from the reader, are questions that can only be answered in a spirit of religious witness" (191). Lodge demonstrates his strength as a critic when he argues against Leavis's dismissal of *The Ambassadors* by a careful analysis of the novel in response to each of the points that Leavis raises. Lodge's straightforward commentary is so convincing as to seem self-evident, and yet it is a subtle, perceptive reading of the whole novel, embodied in some well-chosen examples accompanied by characteristically incisive analysis. A key point he makes is that we are meant to perceive some vagueness, some inadequacy, in Strether's impressions of Paris: "But if we feel a certain impatience with him, if we long for him to encounter some brute fact that cannot be beaten into a shimmering tissue of impressions, is this not precisely how we should feel? Is this not precisely the point of the joke about the vulgar domestic utensil manufactured by the Newsomes, which Strether refuses to name? Is this not the necessary effect of the whole narrative tone, a tone of humorous, affectionate irony?" (*Language*, 194).

The Ambassadors is often read as a solemn, earnest work, but Lodge recognizes that it is full of quiet humour.[6] The "joke about the vulgar domestic utensil" is one beloved by students of literature, especially, in my experience, those who love James, and it has given rise to much creative speculation. Lodge offers an amusing solution to the question of its identity in *The British Museum*, where Adam Appleby's fellow student Camel announces at the English department postgraduate sherry party that the "small, trivial, rather ridiculous object of the commonest use" that is the source of the Newsome family fortune is in fact a chamber pot (121). (Adam, preoccupied with the Vatican's teaching on contraception, suggests that the Newsomes made their money by manufacturing contraceptives.) I have heard Camel's comment repeated in all seriousness, attributed to a nameless scholar, as a plausible view of the nature of the object, so it has obviously floated free of the novel and into the oral tradition of the academy.[7] The humour in *British Museum*, prompted by James's humour in *The Ambassadors*, prefigures the affectionate manner in which Lodge portrays the Master in *Author, Author*, deflating his own reverence for James periodically by describing him in the lavatory or the bathtub. It is worth emphasizing that Lodge lists *The Ambassadors* among his favourite novels (M. Thwaite, "Interview"), and it is something of a touchstone in both his criticism and in his own fiction. In an interview with Jonathan Derbyshire, he notes that having avoided questions on James on his undergraduate exams, "When I started teaching at Birmingham one of the first things I had to do was write a lecture about *The Ambassadors*, and I got very enthusiastic" ("Conversation").

Lodge's formal parody of Henry James occurs during one of the most memorable episodes of *British Museum*. Immediately before

Camel advances his theory about *The Ambassadors*, Adam visits a genteel middle-aged Catholic lady called Mrs Rottingdean in order to examine an unpublished literary manuscript that she owns. It was written by Egbert Merrymarsh, an invention of Lodge's who is an effective lampoon of the belletrists of the Catholic revival. Adam hopes that he can advance his academic career by publishing this manuscript, and during his visit Mrs Rottingdean's teenaged daughter Virginia makes sexual advances to him. The situation is roughly parallel to that in *The Aspern Papers*. Then, in a brilliant stroke, Lodge juxtaposes the James parody with one of Ernest Hemingway.[8] Mrs Rottingdean rents out the basement rooms of her house to some Argentinian butchers who intimidate Adam with talk of bullfighting and macho posturing. Of course, Hemingway's paratactic style, not to mention his characteristic subject matter, is at the opposite literary pole from James, and indeed Hemingway mocks James in a passage in *The Sun Also Rises*. On the other hand, Hemingway's fiction continues the international theme so authoritatively established by James, and his novels and memoirs explore similar themes of personal integrity and sexual renunciation.[9] By placing the macho butchers in the basement and the genteel lady upstairs, Lodge neatly comments on the way that American fiction includes very different traditions, which are, to some extent, divided according to gender. James is more associated with a feminized world, even though he is a presence in writers such as Hemingway and Roth.

When Adam Appleby finally escapes from the basement and meets Mrs Rottingdean, the style switches back to that of James:

> It was with a, for him, unwonted alacrity that our friend, hearing the tinkle of china in the hall, sprang gallantly to the door.
>
> "I've been admiring your 'things'," he said, as he assisted her with the tea-trolley.
>
> "They're mostly my uncle's," she said. "But one does one's best." She gestured vaguely to a cabinet where reliquaries, statuettes and vials of Lourdes water were ranged on shelves, dim dusty devotional.
>
> She made tea in the old, leisured way, pouring the water into the pot from a hissing brass urn. (*British Museum*, 105)

The Jamesian features here include a number of characteristics analyzed by Lodge in "Strether by the River." We can begin with the parenthetical "for him" in the first line, creating an unusual word order, the periphrastic description of Adam as "our friend," and the quotation marks around the word "things." Here the word has the sense of valuable old possessions, antiques, such as are owned by Maria Gostrey in *The Ambassadors* and Madame Merle in *A Portrait of a Lady*. In fact, *The Old Things* was the original title for *The Spoils of Poynton* (*Spoils*, 19). The quotation marks create a hint of irony in the use of the word, perhaps indicating the low commercial value of the Catholic bric-a-brac that Mrs Rottingdean has on display. The word "thing" was a favourite of James's in a variety of contexts, and is an example of his use of the clichés and dead metaphors of everyday discourse as objects held up to scrutiny in his late prose.[10] Something similar is true of the phrase "one does one's best." The adverb "vaguely" is characteristic of James (see *Language*, 201), while the omission of the commas between the three adjectives "dim dusty devotional," along with the use of alliteration to link them, is a favourite Jamesian device (see *Language*, 193–4). The latter phrase partners with "in the old, leisured way" as locutions that in Lodge's words serve "to dissipate the sense of particular time and place and to synthesize the discrete items of local detail into a confused but evocative impression of a historical way of life" (*Language*, 193).

The Language of Fiction provides an excellent description of James's elaborately metaphorical style, noting that when he "invests a metaphor with that startling concreteness of elaboration which we associate particularly with *The Golden Bowl*" then "The effect is rather like that of the heroic simile in epic poetry, where the 'tenor' recedes from sight, and the 'vehicle' takes on an independent poetic life" (207). A good example can be found in the late short story "Crapy Cornelia": "He had ever felt that an indispensable presence – with a need of it moreover that interfered at no point with his gentle habit, not to say his subtle art, of drawing out what was left him of his youth, of thinly and thriftily spreading the rest of that choicest jam-pot of the cupboard of consciousness over the remainder of a slice of life still possibly thick enough to bear it; or in other words of moving the melancholy limits, the significant signs, constantly a little further on, very much as property-marks or staked boundaries are sometimes stealthily shifted at night" (821). There are several striking metaphors in Lodge's parody of James in *British Museum*. He demonstrates his mastery of the Jamesian idiom by bringing a dead metaphor to life, and moreover one that was a favourite of James, the monetary or financial metaphor: "The memory of Merrymarsh was evidently a tender one, and it seemed as though the question of manuscripts would have to be delicately broached. He fairly rattled the small change of conversation in his pocket without lighting on a single coin that wouldn't, in the circumstances, seem too soiled and worn, too vulgarly confident of being 'hard' currency" (105–6). Another example, quoted in part in the previous chapter, develops the image of a stream or river, a favourite metaphorical vehicle in James, into an enumeration of the items on the bottom of the water. These objects seem to be from Adam Appleby's consciousness, or from a typical novel of the 1950s:

> That was it, then. They had touched bottom at last: and like most bottoms it was muddy and a shade disillusioning, littered with the pathetic shapes of old broken things – prams, kettles and bicycle wheels. But he had to admire, as he shot back to the surface with bubbles trailing from his mouth in the form of a gay, "Then I envy the bachelors of your acquaintance," the brave effort with which, gasping only a little, she quickly rejoined him in the thinner element of polite conversation. (106–7)

The image of the trailing bubbles, with its suggestion of comic-book art, exaggerates the Jamesian manner for parodic purpose, but like Beerbohm's parodies, Lodge's is part homage. It is also clearly the product of the great care with which he had analyzed the text of *The Ambassadors* while working on *Language of Fiction*. The same elements that for the anti-Jacobites are the occasion for harsh critique are for Lodge the object of affectionate comedy.

H.G. Wells seems to have begun with admiration and affection for Henry James, who both flattered him and sought to make him into a more self-conscious artist, but the affection was increasingly tempered with resistance as Wells chafed under James's self-appointed mentorship, until he resorted to comic resistance and eventually outright mockery. The documents assembled in Leon Edel and Gordon Ray's wonderful *Henry James and H.G. Wells* allow one to trace this relationship through all of its vicissitudes until it finally ended as a result of Wells's withering satire of James in *Boon* (1915).[11] Wells's satirical description of a James novel in *Boon* is very often quoted, but a less well-known passage is equally interesting. In his *Experiment in Autobiography*, Wells notes that James "thought that for every social occasion a correct costume could be prescribed and a correct behaviour defined. On the table (an excellent piece) in his hall at Rye lay a number of caps and hats, each with its appropriate gloves and sticks, a tweed cap and a stout stick for the Marsh, a soft comfortable deer-stalker if he were to turn aside to the Golf Club, a light-brown felt hat and a cane for a morning walk down the Harbour, a grey felt with a black band and a gold-headed cane of greater importance, if afternoon calling in the town was afoot" (*Experiment*, 453). Here we see James, from the perspective of Wells the scientist and student of human culture, as someone mystified by a set of social conventions which Wells, as the child of a domestic servant and as himself a former draper's apprentice, had always seen for what they were, superficial rules that, as Thomas Carlyle had argued in *Sartor Resartus*, allow a tailor to make a gentleman. In a characteristic passage, attributed to Professor Teufelsdröckh, the propounder of the clothes-philosophy, Carlyle writes, "Nay, is it not to Clothes that most men do reverence; to the fine frogged broad-cloth, nowise to the 'straddling animal with bandy legs' which it holds, and makes a Dignitary of? Who ever saw any Lord my-lorded in tattered blanket, fastened with wooden skewer?" (*Sartor Resartus*, 182). Of course, James recognizes the superficiality of social forms in his fiction, but at the same time he has a profound reverence for them. For example, in *The Ambassadors* it matters a great deal that Chad Newsome has learned the correct way to enter an opera box, even if in the final analysis that is not the most important thing about him.

In 2007, Lodge published an edition of *Daisy Miller* (1878), the work whose popularity established James's literary reputation. The introduction to that edition was adapted into an essay that forms part of *The Year of Henry James*, and it provides a valuable indirect commentary on the influence of James upon Lodge. Lodge uses *Daisy Miller* to illustrate two aspects of James's importance in literary history. On the thematic level, he was "one of the first novelists to perceive the social significance of tourism" (*Year*, 111), while in terms of literary technique, "Henry James was arguably the first among English and American writers to understand, analytically as well as intuitively, the importance of 'point of view' in telling a story" (*Year*, 116).

James's international theme typically involved a relatively naïve American character negotiating the complex social codes and old world corruptions of English or continental European society, with his novels

The American (1877), *The Portrait of a Lady* (1881), and the three great novels of the last phase – *The Wings of the Dove* (1902), *The Ambassadors* (1903), and *The Golden Bowl* (1904) – all forming variations on the theme of *Daisy Miller*. In Lodge's version of the international theme, the typical pattern is that a somewhat repressed English protagonist, sometimes also a Roman Catholic, burdened by the cultural memory of wartime austerity, discovers the material abundance, generosity, openness of spirit, and freedom from class prejudice of America and Americans. This pattern begins with Timothy Young in *Out of the Shelter*, and proceeds through Philip Swallow in *Changing Places* to Bernard Walsh in *Paradise News*, with some minor examples in other novels. A number of Lodge's novels describe travel to different countries: *Small World* takes place in a variety of nations, *Therapy* includes trips to the Canary Islands, Denmark, and Spain, while *Thinks...* and *Deaf Sentence* feature visits to eastern Europe. However, for Lodge America was the great revelation.

He notes in the essay "The Bowling Alley and the Sun" (1968) that in the two decades after the Second World War Englishmen "have increasingly gone to America to discover themselves" (*Write On*, 3). The essay has the subtitle "Or, How I Learned to Stop Worrying and Love America," echoing that of the film *Dr Strangelove*, "Or, How I Learned to Stop Worrying and Love the Bomb." In it Lodge describes his first visit to the United States on a Harkness Commonwealth Fellowship in 1964–65. He spent the academic year at Brown University and then travelled extensively for the following three months. He sums up his feelings after the year in the United States in the following way: "I liked America very much, and I believe that most British visitors of my type have liked America very much. And although there are obviously and inevitably many things we haven't liked about America, we don't feel in the least superior on that account. This is something that an older generation of British intellectuals, educated in the Europe-orientated tradition, and a large number of American intellectuals, caught up in the occupational hazard of alienation, find difficult to understand" (*Write On*, 4). These words still ring true more than four decades after they were written, for the traditions of loathing America remain strong, although now they are more characteristic of the left, schooled in French thought, whereas in the first half of the twentieth century it was the right who frequently manifested disdain for what was seen as a brash and vulgar civilization without a cultural tradition. Graham Greene typified the older anti-Americanism, which is conveyed throughout *The Quiet American* in the attitudes of the narrator, Thomas Fowler, though qualified in the world of that novel by the fact of Fowler's sexual jealousy of Pyle, the "quiet American."[12] More recently, the litmus test has been responses to American foreign policy, and the literary detractors of America have included the late Harold Pinter and Margaret Drabble. Drabble revealed her devotion to British cultural traditions through her book on landscape and literature, *A Writer's Britain*, and through her editing of the *Oxford Companion to English Literature*; during the Iraq war she expressed her hostility to the USA in a controversial piece in *The Telegraph* in which she wrote that "My anti-Americanism has become almost uncontrollable. It has possessed me, like a disease. It rises up in my throat like acid reflux" ("I Loathe America").

In contrast with Drabble, Lodge, as a Londoner, has never exhibited the "almost mystic devotion to the land itself" (Drabble, *Writer's Britain*, 6) that characterizes many British writers (Ted Hughes and Geoffrey Hill would be good recent examples), and his portrayal of the exuberant American professor Morris Zapp in the *Small World* trilogy of novels embodies his fascination with the energy and vitality of the new world. Timothy Young, the first of Lodge's pilgrims to America, shares his last name with Felix Young, one of the European cousins who visit Boston in James's short novel *The Europeans*. That novel is a fascinating reversal of the usual pattern of the international theme, and James balances things so carefully that neither nation or culture can really be said to have the upper hand. Paradoxically, in *Out of the Shelter* Timothy experiences American culture by travelling to Heidelberg to visit his sister, who works for the American army. Lodge has named James's *What Maisie Knew* as an influence on the way that he handles "the naïve central consciousness" in *Out of the Shelter* (Afterword, 276). In the same way that the young girl Maisie does not understand the sexual intrigues by which she is surrounded in James's novel, Timothy does not always understand what is going on around him, whether as a young boy at the beginning of the novel, or as a teenager visiting his adult sister. Influenced by his mother's speculation about why his sister Katherine never comes home to visit, he jumps to the conclusion that a little girl she has befriended at an orphanage she visits is her illegitimate daughter (*Shelter*, 157).

Timothy is, like Lambert Strether, a kind of ambassador, as his mother encouraged him to visit Katherine in order to find out what is going on in her life, and just as Strether has to find his way in Paris, Timothy has to work out the social conventions of both the American and German worlds in Heidelberg. This is complicated by differences of class and political ideology among the various characters, from the porter Rudolf, whose father was a Nazi, to the American cold warriors who are Katherine's friends, to Don Kowalski, an American liberal intellectual whom Timothy meets on the train, and who questions his patriotic British and Tory assumptions. But beyond all these complexities, America represents abundance: for Timothy, with a PX card and access to everything that Heidelberg has to offer, "Every day seemed to be like Christmas" (104). Meanwhile England still has rationing in 1951, and as Timothy tells his sister, their mother still doesn't have a refrigerator. Lodge sums up the mood of what David Kynaston has called "austerity Britain" in his presentation of the reasons why Katherine Young has continued working for the American army after the war ended.[13] She tells Timothy that she hasn't been home because she didn't want to tell their parents

> that she hated their poky little house, with rooms so small that you kept bumping into furniture every time you moved, where everyone was trapped in the back living-room for half the year because the rest of the house was cold as a tomb, and as damp … Just to draw back the curtains of her bedroom in the morning was enough to give her a feeling of panic, as if she were drowning. Just to look at all those mean, shabby little back gardens with their sheds, coalsheds and toolsheds and bicyclesheds, sagging and rotting away in the damp. And to see the women in old jumpers and skirts, with scarves over their curlers, clutching themselves against the cold, gossiping over the fences about the cost of potatoes, or hanging out sodden washing, with smoke falling from a thousand chimneys, so that if you ran your finger along a window ledge an hour after it had been dusted it came off black. The cold and the damp and the dirt. (*Shelter*, 162–3)

During a visit to Baden-Baden, Timothy realizes the kind of deprived life he had been living in England: "It seemed to him that for years he had been doing things that he hadn't really wanted to do, out of timidity and ignorance of anything better. Now he had discovered that there was another world to join, one that was abundantly pleasurable"

(151). One could say that Timothy has learned to agree with Jim Dixon's "theory that nice things are nicer than nasty ones" (Amis, *Lucky Jim*, 140), but because Timothy's revelation comes through an international experience, I think that James rather than Amis is the important influence here. Katherine's revulsion from England could have come from the pages of a typical Angry Young Man novel, full of references to dirt, damp, and rotting, while Timothy's appreciation of his new experiences is rendered in a richer style, with a wider range of sensory perceptions. In good time, unlike Strether for whom it is already too late, Timothy has learned the lesson that Strether imparts to his young friend Bilham in Gloriani's garden in one of the key moments in *The Ambassadors*: "All the same don't forget that you're young – blessedly young; be glad of it on the contrary and live up to it. Live all you can; it's a mistake not to. It doesn't so much matter what you do in particular, so long as you have your life. If you haven't had that what *have* you had?" (153; italics James's). The carefree and privileged existence of the Americans is not wholly endorsed; another American character, the intellectual Don Kowalski, criticizes his countrymen as camp-followers profiting from the misfortune of others (151–2). In the same way, James in *The Ambassadors* does not regard Paris as beyond critique. But for both Timothy Young and Lambert Strether, it is the awakening of an aesthetic sense, a capacity for deeper and more complex experience, that is the most important thing.

Travel of all kinds, from academic conferences to package holidays, is a recurrent subject in David Lodge's fiction.[14] Among the many travellers, two others stand out as sharing with Timothy Young the Jamesian discovery of a richer and deeper experience of life. First, in *Changing Places* Philip Swallow escapes the gloom of the industrial city of Rummidge for the pleasures of the American west coast. He leaves behind an English department that seems stuck in the era of *Lucky Jim* for the intellectual and political excitement of an American campus in the late 1960s. Lodge also shows an American, the critic Morris Zapp, having to make his way in the unfamiliar academic and social world of England, but this is more an occasion for comedy than it is for a cultural education. In fact, Zapp considerably enlarges the horizons of the department in which he is a visiting scholar and of Swallow's wife, with whom he has an affair. Lodge's positive view of America is expressed with especial fervour in *Changing Places* in Philip Swallow's epiphanic moment when he

> felt himself finally converted to expatriation; and he saw himself, too, as part of a great historical process – a reversal of that cultural Gulf Stream which had in the past swept so many Americans to Europe in search of Experience. Now it was not Europe but the West Coast of America that was the furthest rim of experiment in life and art, to which one made one's pilgrimage in search of liberation and enlightenment; and so it was to American literature that the European now looked for a mirror-image of his quest. He thought of James's *The Ambassadors* and Strether's injunction to Little Bilham, in the Paris garden, to "Live ... live all you can; it's a mistake not to," feeling himself to partake of both characters, the speaker who had discovered this insight too late, and the young man who might still profit by it. (194–5; ellipsis Lodge's)

The second traveller who finds a richer and deeper life is Bernard Walsh, the former priest in *Paradise News* who experiences a life-changing trip to Hawaii, where he is able to overcome the accumulated repression and guilt of an Irish Catholic upbringing, a failed vocation, and a failed relationship. Hawaii is rendered as a mixture of sublime beauty and commercialism, and as somewhere radically different from Rummidge, where Bernard, like Philip Swallow, works as an academic. Lodge's description of Bernard's first perception of Hawaii is particularly vivid and effective at establishing this difference: "The night air at Honolulu airport was like nothing Bernard had experienced before, warm and velvety, almost palpable. To feel it on your face was like being licked by a large friendly dog, whose breath smelled of frangipani with a hint of petrol" (83). Even though his father and aunt are both in hospital and he is trying to make arrangements for the latter, who is dying, Bernard responds to the simple pleasures of Hawaii with an intensity which was lacking in his exercise of his vocation as a priest. He is, like Timothy Young, an ambassador of sorts, representing his family to his expatriate aunt. Just as Mrs Newsome sends a second group of ambassadors when it seems that Strether is taking too much time, so Bernard Walsh is joined by his sister partway through his stay in Hawaii. James may be considered a subliminal presence in *Paradise News*, but Lodge also renders Bernard's self-discovery through allusions to poetry and especially to Shakespeare's *Tempest*, a story of transformations of the self on a remote island.

Like Henry James, David Lodge regards point of view as central to the art of fiction. Lodge's discussions of his own work often focus on how, having established the organizing idea for a novel, he then worked out the way that the story would be told. In this concern with the manner of telling he resembles the James of the Prefaces. In *The Picturegoers*, *How Far Can You Go?* and *Small World*, Lodge uses a large cast of characters, dividing the point of view up among them. He traces his interest in polyphonic effects in literature back to both his reading of *Ulysses* and to hearing a radio performance of Dylan Thomas's *Under Milk Wood*, which he says "had a terrific influence on me" (Jarniewicz, "Interview," 54). But the majority of Lodge's novels either employ a first-person narrator or focalize their narrative through the consciousness of one or two primary characters, and these are the more overtly Jamesian of his works.

Lodge's *Author, Author* had its origins in the mid-1990s, so it is not surprising that there are frequent references to James in the criticism that Lodge was producing at the same time, collected in *Consciousness and the Novel* (2002). In 1999 he gave the Henry James lecture at the Rye Festival on the topic of "Henry James and the Movies" (*Consciousness*, 200–33). James's preoccupation with point of view derives from his preoccupation with consciousness, which is why, as Lodge notes in the title essay of *Consciousness*, "James is a crucial figure in the transition from classic to modern fiction" (50); for him the problem of representing character in fiction is essentially a problem of representing a consciousness other than one's own.[15] The novel *Thinks...* was written after Lodge had already begun to research *Author, Author*, and it alludes to James a number of times. The problem of representing consciousness dominates *Thinks...*, where the cognitive scientist Ralph Messenger and the novelist Helen Reed both attempt in their own way to understand the thoughts of others. Since each of them narrates part of the novel, the reader has access to the thoughts of both. At one point Helen quotes and then analyzes the opening paragraph of *The Wings of the Dove*, explaining that she had once started a doctoral dissertation on "point of view in Henry James" (43). Between them, James and Helen represent the humanist contribution to the understanding of consciousness, with Helen mentoring the next generation of writers through her creative writing class. There are several other allusions to James in the action of the *Thinks....* While shopping in the town of

Gloucester, Helen visits the cathedral, and she recollects that Gloucester is where Charlotte and Prince Amerigo begin their affair in *The Golden Bowl*, using a visit to the cathedral as a pretext to avoid returning to London with the other guests at a house party (88–9). Another scene is elaborately patterned after the discovery scene in *The Ambassadors*. Helen makes "a kind of Jamesian pilgrimage" (231) to see a church that James describes in a letter to Charles Eliot Norton as "a noble old church (with detached *campanile*)" (230). While having lunch in a pub in Ledbury, she is surprised to see Ralph Messenger's wife Carrie with Nicolas Beck, an art historian from the university, and to realize that, contrary to rumour, Beck is not gay, but is in fact Carrie's lover. To make sure that the reader perceives the parallel, Lodge has Helen reflect, "Oh, it was so like the scene in *The Ambassadors* where Lambert Strether, at the riverside inn in the country outside Paris, identifies what he at first took to be a pair of anonymous young lovers in a rowing boat as Chad Newsome and Mme de Vionnet, and realizes that their relationship, which he has believed and staunchly declared to be platonic, is after all an illicit sexual liaison" (234). Thus the novels of James serve as a frame for Helen's perception of the erotic triangles in which she finds herself entangled, and her affair with Ralph seems to be predetermined by the James novels that are alluded to in the telling of the story.

Henry James shaped the public's view of his life and literary career through his autobiographical writings, his critical essays and prefaces, his revision of his work, and the organization of it into the volumes of the New York Edition. David Lodge, like James, is a highly self-conscious writer, and he has written at some length about his own work, largely in introductions and afterwords, but also in some of his essays. He has furthermore discussed his life and work in numerous interviews, a genre which was just coming into its own during James's lifetime. James may well have provided Lodge with a model for the shaping of a writer's literary career. Just as James's terms such as "the middle years" or the "international" theme have become part of the vocabulary for discussing his books, so Lodge's accounts of his early work in the neo-realist mode, or of the influence of Greene and Joyce, are both illuminating and unavoidable for the critic of his work. Perhaps one of the reasons for Lodge's anguished reaction to the reception of *Author, Author* is that it was determined in part by circumstances beyond his control. Before turning to that work, I will further consider Lodge's work as a critic of the novel, a role in which he can be seen very much as an heir to Henry James.

As I have argued in chapter 1, I think that a just assessment of Lodge's significance as a writer must consider him at once as a novelist and as a critic. I think he tends to be undervalued: it is noteworthy that unlike, for example, Margaret Drabble and Anita Brookner, he doesn't get a chapter of his own in the recent Blackwell *Companion to the British and Irish Novel 1945–2000*, edited by Brian Shaffer, though he does figure as "the genre's most significant practitioner" in a chapter on the campus novel in the same work (Womack, "Academic Satire," 333). On the other hand, Lodge's criticism is referred to throughout the Blackwell *Companion*. He has contributed significantly to our view of the history of post-war fiction, with his early work on Amis, his influential commentary on Greene and Waugh, his championing of Muriel Spark, and the powerful critical model provided by the categories of his *Modes of Modern Writing*. Furthermore, in engaging with the thought of continental literary theorists, Lodge was always as interested in the implications of theory for the practicing writer as for the critic. When the full range of his work is taken into account, Lodge emerges as a central figure in British literature of the post-war period.

As a commentator on the novel, Lodge is a major thinker in an Anglo-American tradition that stems from James and Forster, and that includes some eminent academic critics whose work has had a wide cultural impact. In the same decade as Lodge's *Language of Fiction*, one could instance Wayne Booth's *The Rhetoric of Fiction* and Frank Kermode's *The Sense of an Ending*.[16] Lodge combines the roles of critic, theorist, novelist, and journalist in another major critical achievement that is a more recent contribution to the tradition I have identified. *The Art of Fiction* (1992) is a guide to the poetics of prose fiction that is aimed at the general reader, and that originated in a series of articles published in the British newspaper the *Independent on Sunday*, also under the title "The Art of Fiction." It is a book that the student, scholar, general reader, or creative writer can read with profit. *The Art of Fiction* is divided into fifty short chapters, each beginning with one or two illustrative quotations from works of fiction, and treating topics such as "Beginning," "Point of View," "Names," and "Intertextuality." In the preface to the book, Lodge acknowledges that "The Art of Fiction" is the title of "a venerated essay by Henry James." He admits to "some uneasiness at trespassing" on James's title, but given Lodge's long engagement with James's work and his self-conscious shaping of his career as a novelist, one can also see the title as a claim to be a similar kind of writer, a claim that would in my view be thoroughly justified (*Art of Fiction*, x).

In the preface to his own companion to the art of fiction, a book with the no-nonsense title *How Fiction Works* (2008), James Wood mentions John Ruskin's *The Elements of Drawing*, and says that "there are surprisingly few books like this about fiction" (xv). He mentions E.M. Forster's *Aspects of the Novel* and the criticism of Milan Kundera, but overlooks Lodge's *Art of Fiction*.[17] Wood's reviews appear regularly in *The New Yorker* and he teaches "the practice of literary criticism" at Harvard. A brief comparison of *How Fiction Works* with *The Art of Fiction* will help to highlight what is distinctive about Lodge as a critic of the novel. Point of view is a central concern for both critics, and they both analyze free indirect discourse effectively. Both are deeply involved in the realist tradition, though Wood emphasizes character more than Lodge, and is less interested in the elements of plot and story. Wood is an heir to F.R. Leavis in the intense seriousness with which he approaches the critical task, the forthright nature of his judgments, and sometimes also in the narrowness of his views of literature. In *How Fiction Works*, Wood is dismissive of what he calls "commercial realism" (230), in which category he includes John le Carré and Graham Greene. Wood rather strangely analyzes not an actual passage from Greene, but a parody of Greene that he has composed for the occasion (228–9). Wood finds little pleasure or value in genre fiction, like Leavis preferring to concentrate on a narrow canon of masterpieces. By contrast, the number of different topics covered in *The Art of Fiction* between "Beginning" and "Ending," including "Imagining the Future," "Lists," and "The Telephone," means that Lodge's book includes a wide range of literary examples, some from classics such as Austen and Dickens, some from frequently read authors such as Greene and Salinger, and some from more experimental figures. He discusses these writers in a style that is accessible and yet has something to say to professional literary critics. All Lodge's favourite writers are present, but there are surprises too: Samuel Butler, Leonora Carrington, William Cooper, Fay Weldon, and Lorrie Moore.

The key difference between Lodge and Wood is that Lodge always writes with a pedagogical purpose, seeking to make literature available to as many readers as possible. While intellectually rigorous, he remains accessible and inviting. As he says of himself in the Preface, "Once a teacher, always a teacher" (*Art of Fiction*, x). Although Wood is also addressing "the common reader" (xix), his tone is less inclusive, and his narrow focus on a personal canon that includes Tolstoy, Flaubert, and Bellow is off-putting to anyone with a different set of personal touchstones. In "The Novel Now," where he was consciously speaking as both an academic and as a novelist, Lodge says that much traditional criticism, and certainly that of the school of Leavis, assumes "that it is a finer thing to be a critic working on a major novelist than to be oneself a good minor novelist" (126), and Wood often implies a similar assumption. But as Virginia Woolf writes, "masterpieces are not single and solitary births," but rather rise out of a context of other work, "those forgotten poets who paved the ways" (*A Room*, 85; 84). Christopher Isherwood and Leonora Carrington may not be the greatest twentieth-century novelists, but Lodge's analyses of passages from their work bring out what is distinctive and interesting in each, showing how they are both, like the other writers he discusses, part of the same creative endeavour as are Jane Austen, George Eliot, and Charles Dickens. *The Art of Fiction* is the distilled wisdom of forty years of Lodge's study of British and American fiction, and it draws on Anglo-American and continental narrative theory without overloading the text with technical terminology. It is full of choice examples from a wide range of fiction, illustrating a wide range of fictional techniques. To my mind it is one of Lodge's most important and most characteristic books, exemplifying the qualities that make him a major critic and suggesting that he must have been an outstanding teacher. It is a worthy, and wholly distinctive, addition to the tradition of Anglo-American commentary on the novel.

Lodge's recent novels, and his plays *Home Truths* and *The Writing Game*, are preoccupied with writing as a profession.[18] They represent the lives of novelists (both fictional characters and historical figures), and they deal with issues such as celebrity, rivalry, and the disappointments and triumphs of a career in letters. Lodge identifies as among his favourite works of fiction James's stories about literary life, for example "The Aspern Papers" and "The Figure in the Carpet," and these undoubtedly provided models for Lodge's treatment of the same subject (*Year*, 39). One likely reason for this new subject is that Lodge became a full-time author in the late 1980s. Furthermore, he has commented on the increased media interest in the personal lives of writers, noting that literary novelists only began to become celebrities in the 1980s. *Home Truths* focusses on the role of journalism in the construction and debunking of celebrity. In 1995, Mark Lawson, writing in the *Guardian*, observed what he perceived to be a new preoccupation with the private lives of novelists, taking as a prime example the fact that after publishing *Therapy*, Lodge "was to be found assuring several newspaper interviewers that he had never been unfaithful to his wife during their 36-year marriage." Lodge is quoted by Lawson as saying, "I had to make a decision about *Therapy*, because certain aspects of it were very close to my own life. Either I refused to give interviews – leading people to assume that the book was heavily confessional – or I gave interviews, in which I tried to make points about the categories of fact and fiction. I chose to do the latter, but I do have concerns about it and I'm taking stock now of whether I would take the same approach again. There is a risk that the aesthetic status of the novel is diminished by all the gossip surrounding it" ("Always Connect").

The issues that Lodge raises about celebrity, the invasion of privacy, and the press, came to the fore in 2011 with the phone-hacking scandal in England that led to the closure of Rupert Murdoch's venerable tabloid the *News of the World*. Writing about that scandal, Anthony Lane cited George Flack, the fictional journalist in James's novel *The Reverberator* ("Hack Work," 29). In James's novel, the heroine confides some gossip about her fiancé's family to Flack, who then to her surprise publishes it in his paper, *The Reverberator*. Similarly Lodge has been aware of the tension that exists between the need for an ambitious writer, in today's literary marketplace, to promote himself or herself in the media, and the desire of the media to sell their own product by denigrating anyone who is successful. In *Home Truths* Adrian Ludlow, a formerly up-and-coming novelist who now spends his days editing anthologies such as the *Paragon Book of Cricket Writing*, tries to outwit Fanny Tarrant, a celebrity-profiling journalist. But of course Fanny gets her story, tricking Adrian's wife into revealing the secret of why he no longer publishes fiction. However, in a twist of plot that brings in the biggest news story of the 1990s in England, the profile of Adrian in the Sunday papers is eclipsed by the reports of the death of Princess Diana. By connecting the plot of *Home Truths* to the most spectacular example of a human life turned into a media phenomenon, the life and death of Diana, Princess of Wales, Lodge provides a parable for our time that is very much in the tradition of James's *Reverberator*. Similar explorations of the ethics of journalism and publishing are found in James's "The Aspern Papers" and "The Abasement of the Northmores," both of which are concerned with the fate of personal letters after the death of their famous author. James also included journalists as significant characters in *The Portrait of a Lady* and *The Wings of the Dove*.

I have argued that Henry James provided Lodge with a model of how an author can control not only the form of the individual work of fiction, but the public perception of the author's life and thus of the shape of an entire literary career. It is therefore a great irony that when Lodge turned to James as the subject for a "biographical novel" he experienced what seems to have been the most traumatic episode in his professional life, an episode that Lodge has dubbed "the year of Henry James." He is referring to 2004, the year that his long-planned novel about James was finally published, bringing to a conclusion "one of the most satisfying creative projects I have ever undertaken" (*Year*, 15). The release of *Author, Author* had to be delayed from the spring to the fall for a variety of reasons, and as a result Colm Tóibín's novel on the same subject, *The Master*, appeared first, to considerable acclaim. Reviews of Lodge's novel therefore frequently judged it in relation to Tóibín's. To compound the irony, Lodge portrays James in *Author, Author* as disconcerted by the remarkable success of his friend Du Maurier's *Trilby*, which became one of the best-selling novels of the nineteenth century, at a time when James's fiction was selling less and less. Lodge writes about all of these issues in the long essay "The Year of Henry James," giving a detailed account of the composition and reception of *Author, Author*. There have been numerous articles comparing *Author, Author* and Tóibín's *The Master*, some mentioning other James-related novels that appeared at the same time; since this ground is so well-trodden (including by an article of my own) I do not intend to revisit it here, except insofar as I discuss the anxieties of authorship resulting from Lodge's awareness of Tóibín's book.[19]

Lodge explains that *Author, Author* originated with his first reading of *Trilby* in 1995, which led to an interest in the relationship between James and Du Maurier (*Year*, 19). That friendship is indeed at the core of the *Author, Author*. But its most dramatic episode is the account of the first night of James's play *Guy Domville* in 1895 and the public humiliation James endured when he was booed off the stage instead of giving the speech he had expected to make. In Lodge's introduction to an edition of *The Spoils of Poynton,* we get a glimpse of what James would have called the "germ" of that episode: "The story of the first night of *Guy Domville*, superbly narrated by Leon Edel in his life of Henry James, is itself as full of suspense, pathos, comedy and irony as any novel" (Introduction to *Spoils*, 1). Lodge summarizes Edel's account, which he would develop at length in his *Author, Author*, and notes that when James was booed by the gallery patrons "It was one of the darkest episodes of his literary life" (2). This passage from the introduction to *Spoils*, when read subsequent to the publication of *Author, Author*, resembles an entry in James's notebooks, giving a glimpse into the originating idea behind a work of fiction. In his essay "The Art of Fiction," James counselled the aspiring novelist, "Try to be one of the people on whom nothing is lost" (53). Lodge has certainly followed this injunction in his career, for experiences as diverse as his National Service, a teenage trip to Germany, and a visit to a sick relative in Hawaii have all formed the inspiration for novels.

As a historical novel, *Author, Author* was a new departure for Lodge, and his account of its writing in *The Year of Henry James* reveals how much he thought of the book and what high hopes he had invested in it. He records that "I have never enjoyed writing a book more, and publishing one less" (15). But Henry James himself had sounded a warning against dealing with the legacy of a deceased author in his many ironic stories about literary life and literary afterlife. James also disapproved of historical fiction, viewing it as inherently problematic. In *Consciousness and the Novel*, Lodge quotes from James's letter to Sarah Orne Jewett (5 Oct. 1901): "You may multiply little facts that can be got from pictures and documents, relics and prints, as much as you like – *the* real thing is almost impossible to do, and in its absence the whole effect is as nought; I mean the invention, the representation of the old *consciousness* – the soul, the sense, the horizon, the vision of individuals in whose minds half the things that make ours, that make the modern world, were non-existent" (qtd. in *Consciousness*, 50–1; italics James's). Lodge observes that James's dislike of historical fiction "may have been an unreasonable prejudice" (50), but it is hard not to feel some sense of irony, even nemesis, at work when reading Lodge's account of the way that *Author, Author* seemed to be "an unlucky book," and he seemed to have become himself a character in one of the Master's ironic stories (*Year*, 39).

Author, Author received some very favourable reviews, notably one by the Booker Prize-winning novelist Anita Brookner in the *Spectator*. She calls it a "remarkable novel" and refers to Lodge's "brilliant chapter" about the *Guy Domville* episode ("Rising Far"). Brookner concludes her review "This is a compelling book, which reads seamlessly, organically, as a novel. Never has a character – Henry James himself – been so well-served by an author" ("Rising Far"). Anthony Thwaite's perceptive and positive short notice in the *Daily Telegraph* described *Author, Author* as "an odd and brilliant book" (Thwaite, "Curtains").[20] However, some reviewers compared *Author, Author* unfavourably with Tóibín's *The Master*. For example, Adam Mars-Jones in *The Observer* concluded "the chief obstacle to the success of *Author, Author* lies in its timing. It is Lodge's misfortune that his long-pondered novel about Henry James should be preceded by Colm Tóibín's remarkable *The Master*, so that a capable book is published in the wake of a dazzling one" ("James the Second"). A number of critics, including James Wood, commented on the hybrid form of the work. Writing in the *Sewanee Review*, Cushing Strout distances himself from the negativity of Wood's extremely harsh review in the *New Republic*, saying that Wood "seems to bend over forward to be as hostile as possible" (Strout, xxxvi). Nevertheless, Strout agrees with Wood that *Author, Author* is marred by hesitations in point of view between the perspective of a novelist and that of a biographer, and his own review is entitled, whether by an editor or by Strout himself, "Border Country: Novelist or Biographer?"

Wood asserts uncontroversially that for a novel such as *Author, Author* to succeed, the character "Henry James" must live as a fictional creation. But he spends much of his review objecting to Lodge's characterization on biographical grounds, arguing that the fictional "Henry" is too much a comically diminished figure when compared with the James that we know from his own writing. As an example, he asserts that "Lodge's James is more obsessed with fame and success than the evidence will bear" ("Spoils"). Whether or not this is the case on the biographical evidence, I would argue that Lodge's portrayal of the hopes and fears of an author is one of the most insightful and indeed moving aspects of *Author, Author* and its great strength as a novel. The fictional Henry is wholly convincing in his respect. One reviewer who shares my assessment is Anthony Thwaite, who says that "Reading the book, I increasingly felt that what interests [Lodge] is not the 'secret life' in any prurient sense, but the secret professional life: the life of a writer who often feels himself to have been neglected, misread, read for the wrong reasons" ("Curtains"). Thwaite then refers to Lodge's "more modest profile" compared with such contemporaries as Martin Amis and Julian Barnes. Lodge told John Haffenden in 1984 that in his early life he always felt that people underestimated him and "they were surprised when I came up with the goods" ("Interview," 150). The history of the reception of his fiction suggests that this practice of underestimating Lodge has followed him throughout his life.

In both *Author, Author*, and even more in the memoir of its composition, "The Year of Henry James," Lodge reveals the anxieties that authors experience about their standing in the "pecking order" of their contemporaries, as they all the while secretly hope that posterity will adjust things in their favour, as so triumphantly proved to be the case with James. In his lifetime, James's friends Constance Fenimore Woolson and George Du Maurier both sold far more books than he did, especially Du Maurier, and as James grew older he saw his following in the reading public diminish, even as writers of popular adventure fiction like Henry Rider Haggard were succeeding phenomenally. Du Maurier's success gave his name to a brand of cigarettes, while the name of the title character of his *Trilby* came to signify a style of hat. It is true that James remained a revered figure among his fellow writers, but as Lodge presents him in *Author, Author* he hopes to combine financial success with literary esteem. One of the epigraphs to *Author, Author* is a fragment of verse from an obscure memoir by Felix Moscheles, *In Bohemia with George Du Maurier*: "Who was to be lucky and who to be rich / Who'd get to the top of the tree." The epigraph suggests the role of luck in literary success, and Lodge perhaps remembered it ruefully when he later described *Author, Author* as "an unlucky book." The young man who in 1960 had shared the good luck of Jim Dixon came to portray himself in the new millennium as an anxious author whose temerity in turning his great precursor into a literary character was punished when he became a character in an ironic story about authorship that might have been written by James himself.

Lodge evidently projected quite a lot of his own anxieties and aspirations into the fictional Henry of *Author, Author*. In interviews with

Jonathan Derbyshire and Boyd Tonkin he explains how his frustrations and disappointments in writing for the stage and adapting works for screen and television enabled him to enter into James's frustrations with his theatrical career, while in another interview in the *Observer* in 2008 he speaks of the burden of being a writer: "You're constantly assessed, measured, judged. You're always aware of the league table, the virtual pecking order. You can't ignore it. If you do, you're not competing, and if you're not competing, you're not going to be very good. Nor are you ever wholly satisfied with what you've achieved. You have ephemeral moments of satisfaction, even euphoria, when you finish a good chapter, but they don't last long ... The danger is that you become obsessed and are constantly watching the graph of other people's perception. And that way madness lies" (Cooke, "Nice Work"). Lodge clearly thought, and still thinks, that *Author, Author* is one of his best novels (see M. Thwaite, "Interview"), so of course the fact that the judges for the Booker Prize and many reviewers favoured *The Master* was deeply distressing, given the coincidence of subject between the two novels. *The Master*, unlike *Author, Author*, was short-listed for the Booker Prize, and it won the prestigious and lucrative International IMPAC Dublin Literary Award. As Lodge writes in "The Year of Henry James," "There is a sense in which all literary novels published in the same year or season compete with each other – for readers, for sales (not quite the same thing, though the two are of course connected), for critical approval, and (a fairly new development, this) for prizes" (11). He sympathetically discusses the harsh reception of Martin Amis's *Yellow Dog* (2003), empathizing with another victim of the literary marketplace (*Year*, 64–8). Anxieties, humiliations, and compulsions of these kinds form the stuff of the narrative of *Author, Author*, a novel that is often melancholy, but that is also infused with a sense of the rewards of literary composition and the way its joyful moments can transfigure the everyday experiences of life.

Lodge's narration of the first night of *Guy Domville* and his handling of James's relationship with Constance Fenimore Woolson in *Author, Author* have been justly and widely praised. To further investigate his presentation of Henry James as a fictional character, I have chosen two less prominent passages that strike me as particularly successful, and that are revealing about the motives that may have attracted Lodge to write the novel, and to write it in the way he did. In the first he describes Henry at work, composing the memoir he had promised to write at Du Maurier's funeral, and has put off for too long.

Lodge's representation of the friendship between James and Du Maurier is convincing and often moving. He does a good job of both imagining the reasons why the two men were such good friends, and of conveying the undercurrents of rivalry that inevitably exist in a friendship between two writers, and that become pronounced with the unprecedented success of *Trilby*. Once his memoir of his friend is underway, Henry realizes that what really interests him is the way that this success "had seemed to cause [Du Maurier] more distress than joy, and what the whole phenomenon implied about contemporary culture and society" (*Author, Author*, 336). While on a holiday with the sister of his beloved cousin Minny Temple and her daughters, he dictates the memoir to his laconic Scottish secretary MacAlpine in the intervals of bicycling in the Suffolk countryside. Lodge effectively weaves James's words in with his own in the account of the writing of the memoir – this is one of the places in the novel where he does this most successfully. Lodge was of course aware of the present-day application of James's words about publicity, which appear increasingly prescient as each year passes, with the proliferation of social media, as James envisions "the senseless hum of a million newspapers and the irresponsible chatter of ten millions of gossips" (*Author, Author*, 337).

Immediately following the completion of the memoir, Lodge describes James's purchase of Lamb House in Rye, a new beginning that allows him to put the failure of *Guy Domville* behind him. The main part of the narrative of *Author, Author* comes to an end with Henry James in his new home, beginning a day of writing: "He had reached that point in *The Awkward Age* where Nanda was speaking to Vanderbilt in the garden of Mr Longdon's country house, and he intended to base his description of this setting on his own garden. He looked forward immensely to the morning's work" (352). In the end, it seems, writing is the only therapy for the disappointments of the literary life, and this passage, like Lodge's novel *Therapy*, endorses the therapeutic view of literary creation expressed by Greene in *Ways of Escape*.

The second passage I have chosen again involves the fad for bicycling, this time describing Henry tentatively attempting a solo ride after having had some lessons (bicycling was an interest that James shared with Wells). As he rides, he thinks that "a combination of Momentum and Balance was the secret – and one might draw an analogy here with the art of fiction" (303). At this moment he has to brake as a little girl, five year-old Agatha Miller, pursues her runaway doll's perambulator into his path, and Henry falls to the ground. He interprets the incident "as a warning against hubris ... with respect to the literary life" (304). I doubt whether Lodge was thinking of Cyril Connolly's notorious pram, but the coincidence is pleasing, and the whole incident is also a literary joke, because the little girl will grow up to become Agatha Christie, perhaps the best-selling novelist of all time. Henry's accident is thus not only a wonderful piece of comedy but an exemplary literary parable. It even obscurely alludes, via the bicycle, to the conversation about Henry James in *The Sun Also Rises*.

In critical discussion of *Author, Author*, the hybrid genre of the book has occasioned much comment. This question is central to Wood's very negative review. He begins by complaining about the style of the opening paragraph, pronouncing that Lodge's use of clichés and banalities "has lost the discriminating reader before his novel has gotten under way" ("Spoils"). However the introductory paragraph, like the conclusion of the novel, is in a style that blends the historical narrative and the present-day authorial perspective in a manner that is slightly jokey, as though to draw attention to the difficulty of narrating the past that James had asserted in his letter to Sarah Orne Jewett. Lodge's somewhat mannered narrator emerges out of the author's note into the opening pages of the novel, which begins "London, December 1915. In the master bedroom, (never was the estate agent's epithet more appropriate) of Flat 21, Carlyle Mansions, Cheyne Walk, Chelsea, the distinguished author is dying" (*Author*, 3). There is an echo of the opening of *Bleak House* in the first words, and the joke about a "master bedroom," which Wood objects to as anachronistic, is surely meant to be from the perspective of the twenty-first century, not from that of 1915. In any case, the self-conscious omniscient narrator soon gives way to a focus on the consciousness of Henry, and the narrator does not reappear until the end of the novel. Lodge told Jonathan Derbyshire that he had originally planned "many more authorial interventions," but in the end he confined them to the beginning and the end of the frame narrative ("Conversation").

Wood also objects that Lodge makes his fictional Henry too preoccupied with success, and that he is too prudish, when compared with the figure of historical record. In support of the latter point, Wood refers to a scene involving James and Guy de Maupassant, a scene that no less a critic than Christopher Hitchens declares "made me laugh aloud" ("Final Curtain"). In fact, Lodge's handling of tone in *Author, Author* is subtle and effective. He treats his character with a mixture of awed respect, as the Master of the English novel, and affectionate raillery as a sometimes absurd "old toff," which is how the manservant Burgess Nokes occasionally refers to him when speaking to the other servants in the novel. The complex tone of the narration of *Author, Author* derives from this mixture of respect and ironic comedy, something that few of the reviewers really discerned. It is an unusual tone for a contemporary novel, and perhaps that is the reason why Thwaite termed the novel "odd and brilliant" ("Curtains").

The crux of Wood's review is the issue of the hybrid genre of the novel, which he correctly and acutely describes. He suggests that many passages are written in what he calls "a biographer's free indirect style" and he objects to the fact that Lodge sometimes uses words like "perhaps" or "probably," arguing that "a novelist would know such a thing about his character; a biographer cannot. Lodge's style is always being contaminated in this way by its confusion of genres" ("Spoils"). It is true that *Author, Author* blends fiction and biography in a relatively unusual way; however, I would dispute Wood's contention that this vitiates the novel, and would prefer to describe it as an example of a new, but increasingly common type of literary work, which must be judged according to the standards of a different kind of writing from either the realistic novel or the classic historical novel. In terms of the theory of the novel, the most interesting part of Lodge's essay "The Year of Henry James" is the beginning, where he introduces the term "biographical novel" and speculates on some of the reasons for the popularity of fiction that is closely based on documentary records. He defines the biographical novel as "the novel which takes a real person and their real history as the subject matter for imaginative exploration, using the novel's techniques for representing subjectivity rather than the objective, evidence-based discourse of biography" (*Year*, 8). According to Lodge, this kind of fiction "makes no attempt to disguise its hybrid nature" (9). Discussions of biographical fiction often refer to this issue of the mixed or hybrid form. For example, Vanessa Guignery begins her analysis of *Author, Author* by suggesting that "its generic status is uncertain" ("David Lodge's *Author, Author*," 160). Cora Kaplan addresses the same issue in her book *Victoriana*. In the context of a discussion of both biography and biographical fiction, she invokes James on the impossibility of historical fiction and argues that there is a fundamental difference between biography and fiction: "there is something stubbornly insoluble in what separates the two genres and that prevents them from being invisibly sutured; the join will always show" (*Victoriana*, 65). Lodge uses the same metaphor from surgery or tailoring in *The Year of Henry James*, but he describes his aim in writing *Author, Author* as "to write a novel in which the joins between documented facts and imaginative speculation would be seamless and invisible" (*Year*, 52). Ironically, though, he appends a section of several pages that he calls "Acknowledgements, etc." where he itemizes his major inventions and additions to the historical record (385–9).

Lodge is aware throughout the process of writing *Author, Author* that James had suggested the impossibility of succeeding in the very task that Lodge was undertaking. However, *Author, Author* is not a historical novel in the sense that James would have understood that term. As Georg Lukács influentially explains, the classic examples of the genre such as Sir Walter Scott take as their hero "a more or less mediocre, average English gentleman" (*The Historical Novel*, 32), while the famous actors of the historical record, whom Lukács refers to with the Hegelian term "world-historical individuals," only appear onstage briefly (see *The Historical Novel*, 38–51). The biographical novel, on the other hand, focusses on a famous person, such as a writer or scientist, or in the case of Hilary Mantel's *Wolf Hall* a political figure, and it tends to draw heavily on the archival record, while inventing the consciousness of the figure and inventing incidents where the record is silent. Often the difficulty of knowing the past is signalled by metafictional devices, by drawing attention to the narration or commenting on the epistemological challenges involved in historical inquiry. John Fowles provided a repertoire of such metafictional techniques for other authors to use in his novel *The French Lieutenant's Woman* (1969). Thus through the very devices that Wood claims "contaminate" his novel, Lodge seeks to refute Henry James's argument against historical fiction.

I will further consider the nature of the biographical novel in my last chapter, when I discuss *A Man of Parts*, Lodge's second work in this emerging literary genre. In an interview in 2009, Lodge says that he has at last read *The Master* "without pain and indeed with pleasure," and with the relief of realizing how different Tóibín's characterization of James is from his own (M. Thwaite, "Interview"); however, one suspects that the true exorcism of the year of Henry James was probably the composition of a new novel about H.G. Wells, a writer who had a high-profile quarrel with James, and who differs from him in almost every way.

6

A Novelist Still at the Crossroads

All the characters are portrayals of real people, and the relationships between them were as described in these pages.
~David Lodge, Author's Note, *A Man of Parts*

I can't help it if it is like Dickens, because it happened this way. Real life is often something like books.
~Edith Nesbit, *The Treasure Seekers* (qtd. in *A Man of Parts*)

David Lodge's involvement with the novels of H.G. Wells goes back to his first major critical book, *Language of Fiction*, where he makes a case for the aesthetic value of Wells's *Tono-Bungay* (1909). Lodge locates *Tono-Bungay* within the tradition of the condition of England novel and argues that its value resides not in its characterization or formal structure but in the narrator George Ponderevo's descriptions of setting and commentary on his experiences. The major technical problem confronting the author of the social problem novel "is how to accommodate within an imaginative structure an abundance of material of a kind which is usually treated discursively." Wells solves that problem by placing at the centre of the novel "a narrator who asserts at the outset his intention of commenting, describing, and theorizing" (*Language*, 221). It is through the intensity of George Ponderevo's voice and the symbolic resonances and cumulative imagery of the descriptions of houses, parts of London, and the countryside, that Wells conveys his vision of the state of England, and Lodge notes that this makes Wells a very different kind of novelist from Henry James.

This analysis of the difference between Wells and James is echoed in the final chapter of *Language of Fiction* in the distinction – borrowed from Stephen Spender – between "modern" writers who "seek a radical transformation of conventional forms of communication" (244) and "contemporary" writers, "who engage in a direct, prosaic way with their social and political circumstances" (243). Lodge here is torn between nostalgia for the age of modernism, which he clearly regards as aesthetically superior, and an affinity for the neo-realist techniques of the young novelists who can be classed as contemporaries by reason of their style and narrative method. He discusses the work of Kingsley Amis as emblematic of the dilemma faced by the post-war British novelist: Amis is a writer who at once accepts the formalist theory that a novel is an aesthetic verbal structure and yet "remains keenly aware of the circumstances which divide him from those writers – the great moderns – who seem to have put it most whole-heartedly into practice" (250). This is what Lodge refers to on the last page of *Language of Fiction* as "the difficulty of being Amis," and he links himself implicitly to Amis when he adds "There must be few practising writers in England today who do not feel the pressure of this situation" (267).

The "situation" that Lodge refers to was foreshadowed by the quarrel between Henry James and H.G. Wells, a quarrel between a rigorously formalist view of the novel that in the hands of James produced great works with a remarkable lack of specific reference, and an "impure" view of the novel more in line with the English tradition as it goes back through the great Victorians to Defoe, in which the novel's representation of society and its connection to immediate history are as important as its formal properties. Lodge begins his chapter on *Tono-Bungay* with a brief account of this quarrel, and it becomes something of a touchstone for him, as he returns to it in numerous pieces of criticism, and eventually rehearses both sides of it by writing long novels representing the perspective of each of the two combatants. In the sense that it represents the choice between modernism and realism, or in Roman Jakobson's terms metaphor and metonymy, the dispute between James and Wells also structures one of Lodge's most influential critical books, *The Modes of Modern Writing*.

The first interaction between James and Wells, before they had met one another, was Wells's review of James's play *Guy Domville*, published in the *Pall Mall Gazette* on 7 January 1895.[1] *Author, Author* includes a vividly imagined scene where George Bernard Shaw and H.G. Wells walk home together after attending the play's first night, which is also Wells's first night on the job as a drama critic (*Author, Author*, 259–63). It seems that the personal acquaintance of James and Wells began with the celebrated visit of James and Edmund Gosse to the ailing Wells at New Romney in 1898. Gosse was staying with James at Lamb House, and they bicycled over from Rye so that Gosse could determine whether Wells required financial assistance from the Royal Literary Fund. However, Wells proudly concludes his account of the episode in *Experiment in Autobiography*, "I never had any assistance of that kind and at that time I did not want it. I was now some hundreds of pounds on the solvent side and thinking of building a house with my balance" (508). Lodge uses the episode in both *Author, Author* (342–5) and *A Man of Parts* (142–3), and it is one of numerous connections between the two books.

A literary friendship between James and Wells ensued from this initial meeting, facilitated by the fact that they lived near one another in the south of England. They professed admiration for each other's works, but as Wells confesses in the *Autobiography*, "I bothered him and he bothered me. We were at cross purposes based as I shall show later on very fundamental differences, not only of temperament but training" (410–11). Slightly later in the *Autobiography*, Wells refers to their "sincere yet troubled friendship" and adds that James "was the most consciously and elaborately artistic and refined human being I ever encountered, and I swam in the common thought and feeling of my period, with an irregular abundance of rude knowledge, aggressive judgments and a disposition to get to close quarters with Madame Fact even if it meant a scuffle with her" (452–3). Wells amusingly plays up the role of the bluff journalist, bored with the artistic talk of James, Joseph Conrad, and Ford Madox Ford, in his descriptions of various encounters with these writers: "I write as I walk because I want to get somewhere and I write as straight as I can, just as I walk as straight as I can, because that is the best way to get there ... I remain definitely on the side opposed to the aesthetic valuation of literature" (532).

James was twenty-three years older than Wells, and assumed the role of artistic mentor, but Wells was uncomfortable with being cast as disciple or pupil. He regularly sent copies of his books to James, who replied in elaborate letters of praise, characterized by what Edel and Ray nicely describe as "mandarin politeness, coupled with a cushioning of harsher criticism in fantastic metaphors and polysyllabic ponderosities" (*James and Wells*, 22). The following may serve as a representative sample; James is writing from Cambridge, Massachusetts, and commenting on Wells's latest novel, *The New Machiavelli*: "Your big feeling for life, your capacity for chewing up the thickness of the world in such enormous mouthfuls, while you fairly slobber, so to speak, with the multitudinous taste – this constitutes for me a rare and wonderful and admirable exhibition, on your part, in itself, so that one should doubtless frankly ask one's self what the devil, in the way of effect and evocation and general demonic activity, one wants more" (3 March 1911; Edel and Ray, *James and Wells*, 127–8). Despite his praise James always does want more, praising Wells for his "native wood-notes wild," yet at the same time managing to insinuate that the natural facility of his imagination needs to be disciplined by the rigours of art. And the fastidious grossness of James's metaphor itself implies that Wells's enthusiasm for life is itself a shortcoming, a kind of literary bad manners.

The differences between the two men concerning the art of fiction are highlighted by three public statements, two by Wells framing one by James. In these pronouncements they not only declare their own positions, but perhaps vent the resentments that each had built up against what he considered the mistaken aesthetics of the other. In the first, "The Contemporary Novel," which originated as a talk given to the Times Book Club in 1911, Wells rejoices at signs of a revival of what he provocatively calls "the lax freedom of form, the rambling discursiveness, the right to roam, of the earlier English novel, of 'Tristram Shandy' and of 'Tom Jones'" (Edel and Ray, *James and Wells*, 138). Far from being an aesthetic artifact that transcends its embarrassing origins, the modern novel for Wells "is the only medium through which we can discuss the great majority of the problems which are being raised in such bristling multitude by our contemporary social development" (148). In 1914, James responded by taking on the novelists of "The Younger Generation" in an article of that title published in the *Times Literary Supplement*. It is written in the obscure very late style of James's autobiographical writings and final essays, a style that makes even the three major novels of his late phase seem relatively straightforward reading. The references to Wells in "The Younger Generation" extend into a public forum the backhanded praise and subtle denigration of Wells's fiction that are found in the letters, but without the compensatory extravagance of compliment. Wells is, for James, "a novelist very much as Lord Bacon was a philosopher." He continues:

> It is literally Mr. Wells's own mind, and the experience of his own mind, incessant and extraordinarily various, extraordinarily reflective, even with all sorts of conditions made, of whatever he may expose it to, that forms the reservoir tapped by him, that suffices

> for his exhibition of grounds of interest. The more he knows and knows, or at any rate learns and learns – the more, in other words, he establishes his saturation – the greater is our impression of his holding it good enough for us, such as we are, that he shall but turn out his mind and its contents upon us by any free familiar gesture and as from a high window forever open (Mr. Wells having as many windows as an agent who has bought up the lot of the most eligible to retail for a great procession). (Edel and Ray, *James and Wells* 189–90)

In *A Man of Parts,* Lodge imagines Wells and his wife reading this passage, and Jane Wells asking, "Is he referring to slops being emptied from tenement windows, like they used to do in Scotland, calling out 'Gardy loo!'" (443). Wells does not think that this is the case, but replies to Jane in an entirely plausible piece of dialogue, "we have utterly different ideas of what novels are for. We've both been writing increasingly insincere letters to each other for years, and it's a relief in a way that it's finally over" (443). In Lodge's reading of the rivalry between the two novelists, James is jealous of Wells's commercial success, and in *A Man of Parts* Jane Wells suggests that this jealousy motivated the comments in "The Younger Generation." Lodge thus continues the analysis of the psychology of literary competitiveness that is at the heart of *Author, Author*.

In Lodge's fictional account, Wells proceeds to express his annoyance with James by taking out of a locked drawer the manuscript of the partly finished book that was published in 1915 as *Boon*, and that comprises the literary remains of a fictional author of rather conventional novels who has channelled all his subversive energies into a series of satirical fragments that Lodge compares to Swift, Sterne, and Peacock (*Man of Parts*, 443). Today *Boon* is known only for its extended and cruel caricature of Henry James, including the parodic outline of a James novel entitled "The Spoils of Mr. Blandish," featuring a butler with "the perfect name – Mutimer!" (*Boon*, 116). Some of Wells's descriptions of James's novels, themselves parodies of James's own elaborate metaphors, are justly famous, but what was probably more hurtful to James was the relentless presentation of both author and work as etiolated, excessively fastidious, and passionless: "For example, he omits opinions. In all his novels you will find no people with defined political opinions, no people with religious opinions, none with clear partisanships or with lusts or whims, none definitively up to any specific impersonal thing. There are no poor people dominated by the imperatives of Saturday night and Monday morning, no dreaming types – and don't we all more or less live dreaming? And none are ever decently forgetful. All that much of humanity he clears out before he begins his story. It's like cleaning rabbits for the table" (*Boon*, 105).

In the essay on Wells in *Language of Fiction*, Lodge suggests that "on the purely human level," James probably emerges with more credit in the quarrel with Wells, in addition to having "the best of the literary debate" (214). It would seem that Lodge has not modified this opinion more than forty years later. In *A Man of Parts*, the character H.G. Wells is interrogated by a voice "in his head" that questions him, challenges him, and sometimes says those things that "people will probably say about him in the future after he is dead" (14–15). This voice is essentially that of an interviewer, and its interventions are printed in a bold font. The interrogating voice appears repeatedly to confront Wells with the issues that his critics raise against him, asking about topics such as racism and his treatment of women. He is also questioned about the treatment of Henry James in *Boon*. The interviewing voice characterizes Wells's caricature as "incredibly cruel" and "brutal" (470; 471), while describing James's essay in the *TLS* as "mostly fair comment" (471). Wells attempts to defend himself, but concedes that he managed the inevitable break-up of their friendship tactlessly. In real life, James responded to *Boon* with a letter setting forth his own position and his reasons for being offended by Wells's satire. In *Language of Fiction*, Lodge writes that "the eloquence of [James's] *credo* in the final letter ... is overwhelming" (214–15), and he quotes the following passage from it both there and in *A Man of Parts*: "It is art that *makes* life, makes interest, makes importance, for our consideration and application of these things, and I know of no substitute whatever for the force and beauty of its process" (10 July 1915; Edel and Ray, *James and Wells*, 267; italics James's).

Lodge's modernist predilections engage his sympathy with James's final statement in the debate, but in *A Man of Parts* he does show some sympathy for Wells by putting *Boon* into its historical context. The narrator reminds the reader that at almost exactly the same time as *Boon* was published, Henry James identified with Britain's cause in the First World War by taking out British citizenship, causing the neglected author to be transformed into "a national treasure." As the narrator ruefully observes, "It was not a good moment to criticise Henry James" (472). Furthermore, Lodge's own idea of the novel has as much in common with Fielding, Dickens, or Amis as it does with James. His novels frequently satirize intellectual positions and include comedy and literary parody, and so have affinities with what Wells was undertaking, whatever his motives, in *Boon*. The difference is that Lodge's parodies are generally the product of affection, like his academic satire, which rarely has a harsh edge to it. *Boon*, on the other hand, is described in *A Man of Parts* as "a very private, almost secret work into which [Wells] periodically discharged the black bile of his feelings about English literary and intellectual life in the twentieth century: satirical, iconoclastic, fragmentary, digressive, bookish, a bit like Swift's *A Tale of a Tub*" (*Man of Parts*, 443). The phrase "black bile" suggests the attitudes of Evelyn Waugh rather than David Lodge, but the bookish, intertextual nature of *Boon* does have a kinship with the David Lodge who was an admirer of Bakhtin.

Michael Sherborne notes that it was two Roman Catholic critics who rehabilitated Wells's literary reputation in the 1960s, Bernard Bergonzi and David Lodge. He conjectures that "perhaps the interplay of faith and scepticism in his work was something they were particularly well equipped to understand" (*H.G. Wells*, 349). Bergonzi published an important monograph in 1961, *The Early H.G. Wells*, while Lodge commented on Wells's middle-period work in three influential essays: "*Tono-Bungay* and the Condition of England" in *Language of Fiction* and "Assessing H.G. Wells" and "Utopia and Criticism: The Radical Longing for Paradise," collected in *The Novelist at the Crossroads* in 1971. More recently, Lodge introduced *Kipps* (1905) for a Penguin series of Wells's fiction that was published in 2005.

The Novelist at the Crossroads was well-named: in his fictional practice as well as in his theory of the novel, Lodge found himself at the meeting place of a variety of divergent traditions and theories. I have already discussed the way in which he mediated between the modernists and the neo-realism of Amis and other novelists of the 1950s. Additionally, as a result of the time he spent in the United States and his openness to American influences, he found himself addressing the very different developments of "fabulation," typified by Thomas Pynchon, and the "non-fiction novel" exemplified by Norman Mailer. He gives a brief account of these forms of fiction in the title essay of *The Novelist at the Crossroads*, explaining that "fabulation" consists of a revival of the modes of allegory and romance. The term has since given way to the broader and generally used phrase "postmodern fiction." In contrast, the "non-fiction novel" narrates historically true events using the techniques of fiction. The term originates with Truman Capote, as Lodge points out, and was invented as a description of his 1959 book *In Cold Blood* (*Crossroads*, 9). Mailer's *The Executioner's Song* and the "new journalism" associated with Tom Wolfe are other examples of the genre.

In his fictional practice prior to *The Novelist at the Crossroads*, the neo-realist mode dominated Lodge's fiction, although *The British Museum Is Falling Down* makes extensive use of parodic and stylized discourse. But his novel of 1975, *Changing Places*, goes further in the direction of fabulation; it is a playful, carnivalesque academic novel whose plot and characterization owe at least as much to the needs of formal patterning as to the requirements of realistic representation. He describes the novel on the opening page, in a phrase very much in the spirit of American fabulation, as a "duplex chronicle" (7). "Duplex," Lodge helpfully informs the reader in an aside, "as well as having the general meaning of 'two-fold,' applies in the jargon of electrical telegraphy to 'systems in which messages are sent simultaneously in opposite directions' (OED)" (7–8). Technological allusions and analogies are characteristic of the more innovative fiction of the 1970s. *Changing Places* then continues with a fanciful description of one of the central images of postmodern culture, travel in an intercontinental jet:

> Imagine, if you will, that each of these two professors of English literature (both, as it happens, aged forty) is connected to his native land, place of employment and domestic hearth by an infinitely elastic umbilical cord of emotions, attitudes and values – a cord which stretches and stretches almost to the point of invisibility, but never quite to breaking-point, as he hurtles through the air at 600 miles per hour. Imagine further that, as they pass each other above the polar ice-cap, the pilots of their respective Boeings, in defiance of regulations and technical feasibility, begin to execute a series of playful aerobatics – criss-crossing, diving, soaring and looping, like a pair of mating bluebirds, so as thoroughly to entangle the aforesaid umbilical cords, before proceeding soberly on their way in the approved manner. (8)

Lodge is wary of the absolutism of the more fervent advocates of either fabulation or non-fiction novels, and he advances his own characteristic liberal compromise, the "problematic novel" ("Crossroads," 22). By this, he means that realistic novelists cannot continue as though the critique of realism does not exist, but must rather "hesitate at the crossroads," and by becoming more self-conscious about what they are doing, must "*build their hesitation into the novel itself*" (22; italics Lodge's). *The French Lieutenant's Woman* may be seen as an example of a "problematic novel." Malcolm Bradbury implies as much in the conclusion to a long essay on post-war fiction: "Like many British writers, Fowles is concerned to protect the concept of character, and therefore a kind of realism. His novel, poised between realism and anti-realism, a strong sense of narrative authority and a sense of its counterfeit nature, is an ending from the middle ground. And this is perhaps appropriate, for it is much the point that the debate within the British novel reached at the time – leaving the way open for the much freer sense of form and possibility that marked the spirit of the British novel in the 1970s, when another generation, far less oriented to realism, far more internationalist in perspective, began to find itself" (*No, Not Bloomsbury*, 114). Fowles is referred to frequently in Linda Hutcheon's *A Poetics of Postmodernism* (1988), an important work in defining both the concept of postmodernism and a canon of postmodern fiction. Hutcheon observes that the boundaries between the novel and genres such as history, biography, and autobiography have become fluid, and she emphasizes a form of novel that she calls "historiographic metafiction," which sounds quite similar to Lodge's "problematic novel."[2] She explains that this term refers to "those well-known and popular novels which are both intensely self-reflexive and yet paradoxically also lay claim to historical events and personages" (5). The many examples she gives of such novels include *The French Lieutenant's Woman*, along with Gabriel García Márquez's *One Hundred Years of Solitude*, Salman Rushdie's *Midnight's Children* and *Shame*, Timothy Findley's *Famous Last Words*, Graham Swift's *Waterland*, and Peter Ackroyd's *Hawksmoor*. Lodge and Hutcheon touch on many of the same issues in their criticism, with the crucial underlying difference that Lodge has never repudiated the liberal tradition, but sought to extend it with various influences from structuralism and post-structuralism. Hutcheon, on the other hand, suggests that postmodernism is contradictory in the way that it can both incorporate preceding artistic modes and at the same time radically call into question the traditions of Western humanism and bourgeois realism. However, the rhetoric of her book emphasizes the latter aspect of postmodernism, as she celebrates its power to demystify the ideology of earlier fictional forms. Hutcheon is a very wide-ranging critic, but rarely analyzes a single text for very long, whereas Lodge, who retains key aspects of his early formalism, tends to develop his theoretical positions from close readings of individual novels.

It is not surprising that Lodge was writing about Wells in the late 1960s, at the same time that he was preoccupied with fabulation, for he emphasizes the importance of popular genre fiction to fabulation, notably "science fiction, pornography and the thriller" (*Crossroads*, 20).[3] The *Crossroads* book includes two excellent assessments of Wells, one an overview of his fiction and thought, and the other situating him in the tradition of utopian literature, along with an essay on John Updike that touches on both utopian literature and pornography. (In spite of the great influence of Greene on his fiction, the thriller does not seem to be a genre that has interested Lodge very much.) In "Assessing H.G. Wells," the overview just mentioned, Lodge addresses several issues that in retrospect seem important to his own identity as a novelist. He discusses the conflict between optimism and pessimism in Wells and relates it to Lionel Trilling's contention that "most of us lead double lives; liberal, humane, civic-minded citizens in practical matters, we nevertheless seem to prefer artists and thinkers who cry havoc on the civilization we are constructing" (*Crossroads*, 213). Although he was a Fabian socialist advocate of world government, Wells was at his most powerful in imagining violent destruction, as in *The War of the Worlds*. By contrast, Lodge has consistently written novels that affirm liberal and humane values, and that offer optimistic and comic resolutions; perhaps for that reason he seems to me undervalued by the intellectual consensus that Trilling describes, and that survives today in the common critical preference for violent and apocalyptic authors (witness the high critical esteem for Cormac McCarthy and Don DeLillo, as compared with a quieter voice such as Richard Ford).[4]

A second point that Lodge makes in "Assessing H.G. Wells" is his recognition of the way that literary success takes one out of one's social class (217). Lodge and Wells both came from the lower middle class and from south London, and their success was facilitated by educational institutions that rewarded merit, though of course in Wells's time there were far fewer such opportunities, whereas Lodge's experience is typical of a whole generation. Something of Wells's impatience with the remnants of feudalism in late Victorian England can be found in Lodge's description of the survival of class privilege in the British army and elsewhere. Lodge may well be expressing views of his own when in *A Man of Parts* he describes Wells's reflections during a visit to Cambridge: "How he would have loved to study here! But it was of course an environment steeped in privilege, and its retention of archaic and obsolete terminology, of peculiar customs and shibboleths, were methods of exclusion and defences against change. If I had the power, he thought, after a morning spent asking his way from strangers in the street, I would pass laws forcing the colleges to display their names on their frontages, and forbidding the pronunciation of 'Caius' as 'Keys'" (*A Man of Parts*, 251). One is reminded of Virginia Woolf's contrast, in *A Room of One's Own*, between the comfortable world of male privilege at "Oxbridge" and the spartan earnestness of the women's college.

A third point relates obliquely to the Wells-James controversy, namely the relationship between literary merit and popular appeal. Lodge describes Wells's position during the latter part of his life as follows: "It would seem that in a complex, pluralist and specialized culture like ours, 'to be the most popular of the serious writers and the most serious of the popular' is to forsake real seriousness and with it real influence" (*Crossroads*, 213–14). This paradoxical description has some application to Lodge's own position, as a best-selling author who has considerable critical respect, but who is neither as widely popular as John le Carré nor as critically well-regarded as Ian McEwan. An example of this ambivalence towards Lodge comes in the conclusion of a largely favourable review of *Therapy* in the *New York Review of Books* by John Banville, a novelist of impeccable high-literary qualifications: "I feel curmudgeonly making these criticisms of such an entertaining and, in places, moving book, but the fact is that despite all its felicities of style, plotting, and characterization, I do not believe it succeeds. There is too much wishful thinking here. Certainly there is no reason for a novel not to have a happy ending … but the neat tying-up of knots that concludes *Therapy* casts a roseate glow backward that robs what has gone before of much of its authenticity" ("Nice Work"). I think Banville exaggerates the tone of the end of *Therapy*, and that like many writers who are more firmly in the modernist camp than Lodge he dislikes comic structures and happy endings. His grudging concession that "there is no reason for a novel not to have happy ending" is hardly a ringing endorsement of the practice.

Lodge provided another major theoretical statement concerning the poetics of the novel in his keynote address to the "Why the Novel Matters" conference in 1987. The conference, which coincided with the twentieth anniversary of the journal *Novel*, aimed to examine "the premises of the novel, its traditional sources of meaning and function," in order to investigate the possibility of "bridging the differences between old humanist approaches to fiction … and the new semiotic and poststructural approaches that have more or less taken over the field of fiction theory in the last decade" (Spilka, *Why the Novel Matters*, 122; 121). Lodge was ideally suited to provide a keynote address in this context, since as the contributor's note in the conference issue of *Novel* informs readers, he had just retired from the University of Birmingham "to become a full-time writer." The note goes on to mention that 1988 would see the publication of both a new novel, *Nice Work*, and the textbook *Modern Criticism and Theory* (Spilka, *Why the Novel Matters*, n.p.). Lodge's address, "The Novel Now: Theories and Practices," thus comes at a crucial moment in his career. He is looking back on more than a decade of intense preoccupation with the latest trends in literary theory, while looking forward to a second career as a writer outside the university, no doubt fully conscious that in making this move he is emulating Kingsley Amis, who resigned from Cambridge in 1962 to devote himself to both fiction and journalism (Leader, *Life*, 503–4).

In reflecting on the theoretical ferment of the 1980s in "The Novel Now," Lodge laments "the loss of a common language of critical discourse which used to be shared between academic critics, practicing writers, literary journalists and the educated common reader" (128). In hindsight, one can see this as a description of the type of criticism that he would write over the next two decades, criticism that unlike most academic writing was successfully marketed to the general reading public.[5] After discussing examples from Graham Greene and other writers, Lodge reaffirms the position of compromise between realism and metafiction that he called the "problematic novel" in the "Crossroads" essay. He concludes with a discussion of Mikhail Bakhtin, arguing that his poetics of the novel helps to bridge the gap between tradition and theory that the conference is concerned with. Bakhtin's theory of the novel, Lodge maintains, is illustrated in a representative range of works of recent British fiction, from *Lucky Jim* through *The French Lieutenant's Woman*, *A Clockwork Orange*, *Money*, and Lodge's own *Small World*. Lodge also quotes from two of the most celebrated theorists of the 1980s, Roland Barthes and Paul de Man, on the topics of the function of the author and the nature of literary representation. He contests their post-structuralist theories by saying that his fiction "is in some significant sense a representation of the real world," and far from being dead, the author, according to Lodge, remains at the centre of the dissemination and reception of literary texts. He adds sardonically, "Some of the most committed poststructuralists among my acquaintances are also the most determined to read my novels as *romans à clef*" ("The Novel Now," 130).

The criticism that Lodge has published since leaving academic life has been largely comprised of occasional pieces on what he calls, in the title to one of his collections, "the practice of writing." Lodge writes about the creative process, and about literary influence, production, and reception, sometimes in the form of overviews of the life and work of a particular writer. These critical pieces are contained in the collections *The Practice of Writing* (1996), *Consciousness and the Novel* (2002), and *The Year of Henry James* (2006), and they deal with a wide range of writers, including Henry Green, Anne Michaels, Philip Roth, Vladimir Nabokov, and J.M. Coetzee. In several essays, Lodge continues to reflect on "the state of the novel," notably in the two pieces that commence *The Practice of Writing*. In the first of these, "The Novelist Today: Still at the Crossroads?", Lodge revisits his "Crossroads" essay of 1971 and comments that in retrospect it is surprising to see the extent to which traditional realism "has survived the obsequies pronounced over it by [Robert] Scholes, and by a number of other writers and critics in the Sixties and Seventies" (*Practice*, 6).[6] The "aesthetic pluralism" that Lodge sought to defend in the earlier essay is now taken for granted (*Practice*, 11). However, Lodge concludes with some gloomy reflections on the way that the imperatives of the marketplace have become much more prevalent in literary publishing with the takeover of most small independent publishing houses by conglomerates, and the way that new novels are now aggressively marketed to the public in a way previously reserved for popular bestsellers.

The second essay in *The Practice of Writing*, "Fact and Fiction in the Novel," is focussed on a topic that has become increasingly central in discussions of fiction. In a striking metaphor, Lodge declares that

"Novels burn facts as engines burn fuel," which nicely captures both the necessity of realistic representation to the novel, and the paradox that this basis in the factual is not the final purpose of the genre; just as engines burn fuel to create motion, novels burn facts to create aesthetic artifacts. He goes on to explain that there are only two sources for these facts: either the personal experience of the author, or knowledge acquired by research. Usually a novelist begins by writing out of the former source, and when it is exhausted he or she is forced to rely increasingly on the second (27). Lodge gives the example of Joyce's development from *Dubliners* "to the increasingly encyclopaedic *Ulysses* and *Finnegans Wake*" (28), and then turns to a fellow midlands author for another instance: "George Eliot ... began with *Scenes of Clerical Life*, so closely based on the Nuneaton of her childhood that 'keys' to 'Janet's Repentance' were soon in circulation in the town, and ended with the massively researched *Daniel Deronda*" (28). Similarly, Lodge began by drawing on his own experiences as a Roman Catholic, a student, and a National Serviceman, but in the twenty-first century he published the massively researched *Author, Author* and *A Man of Parts*.

If one reason Lodge turned to writing biographical fiction was the need to find new material, another reason seems to be a cultural trend towards the documentary and historical modes. As he told Alistair Duncan in the *Oxford Times*, "Increasingly in society, there has been a general interest in narrative rooted in fact" (Duncan, "Interview with David Lodge"). This interest manifests itself in the popularity of biographies and of novels about historical individuals, including an example Duncan himself mentions, Hilary Mantel's best-seller *Wolf Hall*, a historical novel about Thomas Cromwell that won the 2009 Man Booker Prize. Mantel's previous fiction includes historical novels, notably *A Place of Greater Safety* (1992). *An Experiment in Love* (1995) is a realistic account of three young women from the north of England at the University of London, but it includes a dinner scene where the guest of honour is an unnamed Secretary of State for Education, who is clearly Margaret Thatcher.

Lodge spends some time in "The Year of Henry James" discussing the popularity of what he calls the biographical novel, mentioning examples such as J.M. Coetzee's *The Master of Petersburg* (1994), a novel about Dostoevsky, and Julian Barnes's *Arthur and George* (2005), in which Arthur Conan Doyle is a major character. He notes that "I would certainly not have thought of writing a book like *Author,*

Author twenty years ago ... simply because my concept of what constituted a novel, especially my own kind of novel, did not then include the possibility of writing one about a real historical person" (*Year of Henry James*, 10–11). The convergence of biography and the novel can also be illustrated by the fact that some prominent contemporary writers are known for both genres, such as A.N. Wilson, whose biographies and memoirs seem to have been more successful with the reading public than his fiction. Peter Ackroyd is an even more interesting example, as he has written major biographies of Dickens and T.S. Eliot, along with examples of what Hutcheon calls "historiographic metafiction," making use of biographical information about characters from previous centuries, as in *The Last Testament of Oscar Wilde* (1983), *Hawksmoor* (1985), and *Chatterton* (1987).

A further reason for the turn to fact – which is of course a return to the kind of fiction that Daniel Defoe wrote in the early days of the novel as a distinct genre[7] – may well be the challenge of science, and especially cognitive science, to the humanities and to literature. This is something that Lodge deals with in *Thinks...*, a novel structured as a debate between a cognitive scientist and a humanist novelist. In both *Thinks...* and in the contemporaneous critical book *Consciousness and the Novel*, Lodge asserts the importance of the novel as a means of representing consciousness, but *Thinks...* is buttressed throughout with detailed information about cognitive science, and a lengthy bibliography is contained in the acknowledgements which appear at the end of the book. Ian McEwan's novels have recently shown a similar preoccupation with science; for example, *Saturday* (2005) features extensive references to neurology, and its acknowledgements mention several medical professionals and a book about neurosurgery (*Saturday*, 280).

Another example of a humanist reflecting on science can be found in a column by Carolyn Heilbrun published in the March 2004 issue of PMLA, the most prestigious journal of literary studies in the United States. Its reception was complicated by the fact that Heilbrun had committed suicide in October of the previous year, between the final editing of her article and its appearance in print. "Guest Column: From Rereading to Reading" is a melancholy reflection on aging, and it ends with Heilbrun saying that she now spends her time reading about great scientists, and confessing to finding "strangely comforting" the way that many scientists dismiss the humanities entirely ("Rereading to Reading," 215). The first part of the essay describes the experience of rereading *The Ambassadors* as a retired person, and begins with a remembered quotation: "'So much living with so little life. Thus did Henry James, writing to Mrs. Humphry Ward, describe H.G. Wells, or so I remember it" (211).[8] It is a nice coincidence for my purposes that Heilbrun invokes the James-Wells quarrel, though she doesn't return to Wells in her discussion of her scientific reading. She does implicitly endorse some of Wells's critique of James when she problematizes the idea that *The Ambassadors* could serve as a guide for living; she suggests from her post-retirement perspective that Strether's advice to Little Bilham is "universally misread" (212). Heilbrun's column correlates in some ways with the interest in science that Lodge manifests, at least in *Thinks...*, and with the broader turn towards fact exemplified in his biographical novels. Her rejection of the James of *The Ambassadors* is in some ways repeated in Lodge's recent focus on Wells, although Lodge has been at least intermittently interested in Wells since his first book of criticism, counterbalancing the influence of James and the tradition of Jamesian aesthetics by the influence of a writer who boasted of his "disposition to get to close quarters with Madam Fact even if it meant a scuffle with her" (Wells, *Autobiography*, 452–3).

One could argue that Wells's scientific literacy, his tendencies towards utopianism and apocalypticism, and his concern for the social good, all engage with aspects of the early twenty-first century in ways that the artistic form of James's fiction does not. And while there have been numerous successful film adaptations of James's books, many of the most popular films of the last few decades are in the alien invasion genre invented by Wells. Two of Steven Spielberg's most notable recent films, *Minority Report* (2002) and *War of the Worlds* (2005), are in the tradition of Wells, the latter, of course, directly adapted from one of his best novels. Thus it should not be surprising that Wells became a compelling figure for Lodge as the first decade of the twenty-first century came to an end, for it was a time marked by the rapid development of social media, widespread fear of terrorism, and preoccupation with global warming, climate change, and the globalized economy. Furthermore, Wells represents the antimodernist pole of the novel in the dichotomy set up by Virginia Woolf in her classic essay "Modern Fiction," where she opposes the kind of fiction written by herself and James Joyce to that of Wells, Arnold Bennett, and John Galsworthy.[9] Lodge has been interested in exploring the implications of this dichotomy throughout his critical writing, and its tensions have creatively fuelled his fiction.

A Man of Parts is an exhaustively researched novel: Wells wrote more than one hundred books, and Lodge summarizes, alludes to, or mentions many of them in the course of his own 559 pages. At the end, five pages of Acknowledgements include an extensive bibliography. No one could doubt that Lodge has acquired a great deal of knowledge as fuel for his historical novel. *A Man of Parts* resembles a conventional novel less than does *Author, Author*, and a number of the early reviews struggled to classify it generically. The contemporary historical novel includes a number of distinct sub-categories, and one way of categorizing them is by their different attitudes towards the historical record. This point was made effectively in a conversation between the novelist and journalist Kate Taylor and two well-known authors of historical fiction, Philippa Gregory and Wayne Johnston. According to Johnston, "Every book of historical fiction sets its own parameters and I think mainly what should be asked of the writer is that they remain consistent to those parameters throughout the book" (K. Taylor, "Truth, Lies and Historical Fiction"). Gregory agrees with him, saying that there are no established generic rules constituting something called historical fiction, and "I'm really struck when I speak to other historical novelists how we all have privately invented the rules we all individually obey." Johnston's novels include important characters, notably Sheilagh Fielding in *The Colony of Unrequited Dreams*, who have no basis in historical fact, and he imagines scenes with a literary significance but no historical basis, whereas Lodge's self-imposed rules include fidelity to the historical record. He said in an interview about *A Man of Parts*: "I'm interested in keeping faithfully to the facts as we know them about a person's life, but imaginatively exploring the gaps in between, including the subjective life" (Kerridge, "A Page in the Life"). By imagining what is not known, and what in many cases cannot be known, Lodge believes that a work of fiction "can give a more vivid sense of a person's life as lived than the discourse of biography" and that "By putting himself imaginatively inside the consciousness of a historical individual the novelist can contribute to the understanding of biographical 'facts'" ("H.G. Wells: Prophet of Free Love"). As ever fair to the reader, Lodge explains in a brief author's note at the beginning that the characters in the novel all actually existed, and the quotations are all genuine (with the exception of a few invented fragments of letters that are scrupulously noted in the acknowledgements), "But," he concludes the note, "I have used a novelist's licence in representing what they thought, felt and said to each other, and I have imagined many circumstantial details which history omitted to record" (*A Man of Parts*, n.p.). Hilary Mantel's novels about Thomas Cromwell begin with a list of characters several pages long, giving their full titles and official positions as aids to the reader, followed by two family trees, of the Tudors and of the House of York.[10] This implies that these novels have considerable respect for historical facts, while in the author's note that follows *Bring Up the Bodies* (2012) Mantel makes a claim for the novelist's imagination analogous to Lodge's: "In this book I try to show how a few crucial weeks might have looked from Thomas Cromwell's point of view. I am not claiming authority for my version; I am making the reader a proposal, an offer" (409).

The narrative techniques employed by both biographers and biographical novelists have become more and more self-conscious as practitioners of the two genres have influenced one another. Just as Lodge alludes to Wells's 1895 novel *The Time Machine* when he imagines himself "somehow time-travelling back to that afternoon of late February 1916" to tell the dying Henry James about his posthumous reputation (*Author, Author*, 375), so Michael Sherborne begins his biography of H.G. Wells with a fantasy of Wells himself appearing via his fictional time machine in the twenty-first century (*H.G. Wells*, 19–21). When Peter Ackroyd's biography of Charles Dickens was published in 1990, amidst a cavalcade of celebrated literary biographies such as those of Hermione Lee, Lyndall Gordon, and Claire Tomalin, it was controversial for including interludes such as a conversation between Dickens and the subjects of Ackroyd's other biographies, a scene where Dickens enters the world of his novels, an account of the author's dream of Dickens, and the author's self-interview.

Both of Lodge's biographical novels incorporate similar devices. *A Man of Parts* begins as a conventional historical narration. The scene is London in the spring of 1944, near the end of Wells's life and also the time of Lodge's childhood. The invisible narrator refers to Wells, after his initial introduction as "Mr H.G. Wells," as "H.G." However, we soon enter the mind of the dying author, and are to imagine most of the narration as taking place within his head, as he reflects on his life, prompted by a voice that seems to be located in his own consciousness, and that is sometimes "friendly, sometimes challenging, sometimes neutrally enquiring" (15). As Lodge's narrator further explains, "The mind is a time machine that travels backwards in memory and forwards in prophecy, but he has done with prophecy now. His mind is at the end of its tether, he cannot bear to look forward into the chaos ahead. He looks back, at his life: has it, taken all in all, been a story of success or failure? In trying to answer this question it is useful to have a second voice. He can, for instance, interview himself about his past, lobbing easy questions and answering them expansively, as he used to do in the days when journalists were still interested" (43). Other sections of *A Man of Parts* are narrated in the third person, but from a perspective limited to that of Wells. After the questioning voice has asked about why Wells fell out with the Fabian Society, Part Two of *A Man of Parts* begins: "It is a very long story, one that began years before he ever heard the word 'Fabian', and it is another voice that tells it in his head, not an interlocutor or an interrogator, but a novelist, a novelist both like and unlike himself in earlier years when he wrote quasi-autobiographical novels" (65).

David Lodge could himself be described as a novelist both like and unlike H.G. Wells. They are alike in their social origins, in their use of comedy and interest in representing sexual relationships, and in their acute social observation. At the end of *A Man of Parts*, Rebecca West thinks of Wells as "a born teacher" (558), which is certainly the impression one has of Lodge, both from his books and from the testimony of those who know him. On the other hand, Lodge has never written science fiction, and he has had far more involvement with the Jamesian craft of writing than Wells ever did. So it is tempting to think of the voice in the fictional H.G. Wells's head as that of David Lodge, telling his story. This device may have been inspired in part by Muriel Spark's first novel *The Comforters* (1957), whose heroine Caroline Rose periodically hears the sound of typewriter keys and a voice narrating the novel in which she is a character.

In narrating the story, apart from the framing chapters set in the 1940s at the beginning and end, Lodge usually refers to Wells as "he," and occasionally as "himself" (e.g., "With James, Hueffer, Conrad and himself all living in the same area" [144]; "Edith was as prolific and work-driven as himself" [156]). Sometimes the logical grammatical reference of the third-person pronoun is not to Wells at all, as in the following example, where the reader has to pause to realize that "him" refers to Wells and not Henry James: "'*I re-write you, much, as I read – which is the highest tribute my damned impertinence can pay an author*,' James wrote after reading, rather late in the day, *The Time Machine*. But it pleased him to have this intimate connection with the most distinguished, if not the most popular, exponent of the novel as a form of art in the English language"(143; italics Lodge's). Adam Mars-Jones notes the lengths to which Lodge goes to avoid writing "Wells," commenting that the use of "himself" "is awkward and sounds almost Irish" (Rev. of *A Man of Parts*). Mars-Jones thinks that Lodge does this to avoid having his novel sound like a "straightforward biography." It is interesting that Mantel employs a similar technique in *Wolf Hall*, where the reader is often left to determine that the pronoun "he" is in fact referring to the protagonist Thomas Cromwell, rather than to Henry VIII or any other male character who is present in the scene. Cromwell is usually simply "he," a number of times "he, Cromwell," and at least once "he himself" (*Wolf Hall*, 398) and "he, Thomas Cromwell" (481). In *Bring Up the Bodies*, Mantel continues her distinctive use of the third-person pronoun, but not so insistently, and occasionally she also brings the reader into a scene by using the first-person plural. She also several times identifies the referent of "he" in a way that seems almost like a response to reviewers' comments on the narration of *Wolf Hall*, for example, "He says – he, Cromwell" (*Bring Up the Bodies*, 17), or "Riche had ... gone straight from the Tower of London to him, to Thomas Cromwell" (55).

This avoidance of the proper name must be one of the means by which novelists seek to transform an historical figure, about whom the reader will already have some preconceived ideas, into a fictional character who lives with the immediacy and intimacy of a character in Henry James or Virginia Woolf.[11] In contrast, if one looks at *The Ambassadors* one finds that the name Strether occurs regularly, even if James's practice of "elegant variation" sometimes substitutes pronouns for names; *The Ambassadors*, of course, begins "Strether's first question, when he reached the hotel" (1). *Wolf Hall* begins with the unattributed speech of Thomas Cromwell's father, followed by a graphic description of the violence inflicted on young Thomas by that father, without any identification of who the character is: "Felled, dazed, silent, he has fallen; knocked full length on the cobbles of the yard. His head turns sideways; his eyes are turned towards the gate, as if someone might arrive to help him out. One blow, properly placed, could kill him now" (3). Another comparison that might help to characterize the form of free indirect discourse used by Lodge and Mantel is with first-person narration, where by definition the narrator does not normally use his or her proper name, so that sometimes contrived or awkward means have to be used to include it in the text, for example, in Charlotte Brontë's *Villette*, Lucy's well-known declaration, early in the novel, "I, Lucy Snowe, was calm" (22).[12]

A Man of Parts does not have many sustained scenes, but is rather the kind of novel written largely as retrospective summary at which Lodge excels, as evidenced by his success with this device in *How Far Can You Go?* There is certainly nothing in *A Man of Parts* of the intensity of the opening scene of *Wolf Hall.* Nor does Wells emerge with the almost hallucinatory vividness of the figure of Dostoevsky in Coetzee's *Master of Petersburg* (1994). However, the novel as extended biographical essay is a form with its own distinct merits, and Lodge's novel provides its own unique rewards to the reader. His narrator comments that "Women, and his relationships with them, had been at the heart of his difficulties with the Fabians" (*Man of Parts*, 66); women, and Wells's relationships with them, are similarly at the heart of *A Man of Parts* itself. Most of the dramatic scenes involve Wells's complicated erotic life, so that one could alternatively entitle the novel, adapting Kingsley Amis, "Bertie and the Women." The tone is rather genial, as is usual with Lodge; Wells's own autobiographical writings have a harder edge, as he is always aware, with his scientifically informed and unsentimental view of life, that things could easily have turned out very differently. He describes himself as a young man in the Postscript to his autobiography, published by his son in 1984, "I was at war with the world and by no means sure that I should win" (*Wells in Love*, 27). If *A Man of Parts* were a Wells novel, one might expect a lot more biological imagery surrounding the descriptions of the protagonist's affairs, and the hero would probably end up as a much less attractive figure. Certainly Wells's own account of his relationship with Odette Keun in *H.G. Wells in Love* presents neither party in a very attractive light.

There are many points of connection and contrast between Lodge's two biographical novels. They both begin with a writer near to his death, and look back on a centrally important part of his life. Whereas Wells was an inveterate sexual adventurer, James was a celibate bachelor. James is referred to as "Henry" throughout *Author, Author*, which perhaps works as effectively to defamiliarize him as the use of the third-person pronoun in *A Man of Parts*. Both novels discuss the purchase or construction of a house in the south of England. James buys Lamb House, redolent with English history, even to the extent of having once given shelter to a monarch. Wells builds a house with every modern convenience, including a separate lavatory for each bedroom (a detail that "seemed to disturb" James [*Man of Parts*, 143]). But what above all unites the two novels, and their two principal characters, is of course the focus on literary life.

However different they were as men and as artists, James and Wells have in common a prodigious output of writing. Each novel includes an early scene where a character reads one of the author's works: in *Author, Author*, the housemaid Minnie Kidd is described as endeavouring to read "The Beast in the Jungle," and in *A Man of Parts* Wells's son Anthony West rereads "The Door in the Wall." Lodge also describes Wells looking through some of his early books while avoiding others. Lodge was in the fifth decade of his career as a novelist when he wrote these novels, so it is easy to imagine a personal source for their preoccupation with looking back on the accomplishments of a life of letters.

A Man of Parts, even more than *Author, Author*, can be regarded as a kind of gigantic "Life and Works" essay, and as such it has affinities with other works of fiction that are hard to categorize. For example Thomas Carlyle's *Sartor Resartus* (1836) contains elements of a Bildungsroman, but as Kerry McSweeney and Peter Sabor point out in their edition of it, more than anything else, it is a gigantic review essay of a fictional book (Carlyle, *Sartor*, xvi). Among the most critically acclaimed of the many novels about writers in recent decades is Julian Barnes's remarkable *Flaubert's Parrot* (1984), a novel described by Lodge as "highly original and idiosyncratic" ("Home Front"). He observes that it was hailed by post-structuralists as an exemplary text, and indeed Hutcheon refers to it a number of times in *A Poetics of Postmodernism*. At the same time, Lodge argues that a traditional literary scholar might characterize *Flaubert's Parrot* as a Menippean satire, a form distinguished by its use of a diversity of styles and interpolated genres, and by the centrality of ideas, rather than plot or character, to its structure.

A Man of Parts has something in common with *Sartor Resartus* and *Flaubert's Parrot* in that it could be classified as a piece of literary criticism written in the form of a historical novel. This is something that was recognized by some of the most insightful reviews. In the *Guardian*,

Blake Morrison wrote that "parts of *A Man of Parts* read like literary criticism" (Rev.). In the *Telegraph*, Claudia FitzHerbert said that Lodge's novel "is both outrageously clunky and curiously engrossing" and that "Generically, but for its length, *A Man of Parts* resembles a profile or interview in the better sort of broadsheet" (Rev.). In the alternation of accounts of sexual relationships and literary creation and in the fact that a number of Wells's lovers were themselves writers, Lodge implies a connection between sexual energy and literary productivity. Furthermore, in Wells's relationships with some of these women, Lodge imagines rivalry and envy, emotions that played a large role in the characterization of James in *Author, Author*. For example, an amusing scene represents Dorothy Richardson putting on her glasses in bed in order to berate Wells for some sloppy writing she has noted in an advance copy of *In the Days of the Comet* (220–1). Elsewhere, Wells briefly becomes a character in another Lodge novel, as he is depressed by the gloom of the British Museum Reading Room on a foggy day (312). Like James and Lodge, Wells suffers anxieties about the process of publication, "finance, publicity, sales, critical reception" (309), and he is jealous of the extraordinary publishing success of *Elizabeth and Her English Garden*, by the Countess Elizabeth von Arnim, who will shortly become another of his mistresses (381). At other points *A Man of Parts* is less anxious in tone, for example when Lodge teases the reader in a manner that recalls his earlier comic works, describing the story of Amber Reeves as one "full of drama, and emotional twists and turns that would have strained the credence of a novel reader" (342).

Wells enjoyed literary success early, and later made a great deal of money from his *Outline of History* and *Short History of the World*.[13] But he outlived his celebrity, and Lodge depicts him as conscious that after his death the latter part of his career will be regarded as a decline. He broods over an article in *Horizon* by George Orwell that both pays tribute to him and firmly puts him in his historical place, while making the accusation that "much of what Wells has imagined and worked for is physically there in Nazi Germany. The order, the planning, the State encouragement of science, the steel, the concrete, the aeroplanes are all there" (*Man of Parts*, 15). Lodge cannot offer the dying Wells the consolation of a splendid posthumous reputation, as was the case with Henry James, although there has been a revival of interest in some of his works, and Penguin published a significant selection of new editions in 2005. Michael Sherborne's biography of 2010 and *A Man of Parts* itself are further signs of interest, and some of Wells's creations, such as the time machine, the invisible man, and the Martian invaders live in the popular imagination. However, a number of the Penguin volumes did not stay in print for very long, and Wells's position in literary history may be said to remain uncertain at the present time. Lodge offers the image of a comet, taken from Wells himself, to represent the writerly hope of eventual vindication by posterity, or at least of periodic revival. *A Man of Parts* concludes with Rebecca West remembering what Wells taught her about the nature of comets, then in the last paragraph the narrative voice becomes more authoritative and authorial:

> H.G was like a comet. He appeared suddenly out of obscurity at the end of the nineteenth century and blazed in the literary firmament for decades, evoking astonishment and awe and alarm, like the comet of *In the Days of the Comet* which threatened to destroy the earth, but in fact transformed it by the beneficial effect of its gaseous tail ... As time went on his imagination and intellect dwindled in brightness, gradually people ceased to look up and stare in wonder, and now he has passed out of sight. But there are eccentric orbits in literary history. Perhaps one day he will glow in the firmament once again. (558–9)

Certainly Wells's reputation remains strong among readers and scholars of science fiction, and some of his early social novels, such as the new woman novel *Ann Veronica* (1909), speak to the concerns of the present. Two of his works, *The Time Machine* and *The War of the Worlds*, would seem to have achieved a secure place in the literary canon.

I have suggested some reasons for Lodge's interest in Wells, and for the resonance of Wells at the present time. In reading *A Man of Parts* one finds traces of Lodge's reflections on politics and public life, in addition to the more literary and personal echoes that I have mentioned. In one scene, Wells witnesses the crowds celebrating the end of the First World War and reflects, "This is the real people. This seething multitude of vague, kindly, uncritical brains is the stuff that dear old Marx counted on to exercise the dictatorship of the proletariat" (483). One cannot help thinking that Lodge was replying to the Marxist critics who wrote about him so harshly in his days as a literary theorist, and also, of course, he is writing from the perspective of a world in which

Marxism has receded in importance in relation to other global ideologies and concerns. Another perspective that often shows up in recent fiction is that of the post–September 11 world, and Lodge invokes this (whether or not consciously thinking of Spielberg's remake of *War of the Worlds*, a film saturated by imagery of September 11) in the following passage: "He could not get this vision out of his head: the proud skyscrapers of New York crumbling and collapsing under a ruthless bombardment from the air, whole blocks on fire, panic in the streets" (247). Lodge includes a description of the London terror attack of 7 July 2005 in *Deaf Sentence*. To cite some other contemporary examples, September 11 and the Iraq war form the background to Ian McEwan's novel *Saturday*, while Graham Swift's condition of England novel *Wish You Were Here* (2011) focusses on the repatriation of a soldier's body from Iraq, and his brother's attempts to deal with both his loss and with the more general state of the nation. Similarly, the religious persecution, executions, political intrigue, and the contest over the future of England that form the subject of Mantel's *Wolf Hall* and *Bring Up the Bodies* have many applications to the present. Read against this background of contemporary concerns, the gloomy Wells whose last book was called *Mind at the End of Its Tether* again emerges as a figure for our time.

Lodge's last three novels can be seen as end-of-life novels. Two are about dying novelists looking back on their life, while in *Deaf Sentence* a retired professor must deal with the death of his father. The same preoccupation can be found in the novel that won the 2011 Man Booker Prize, Julian Barnes's *The Sense of an Ending*. This novel is also about a retired person looking back on his life, and the title is taken from Frank Kermode's critical book of the same name, a book that explores the way that the Christian tradition has conditioned readers in Western societies to look for a certain kind of shape in stories, whether novels or the stories of people's lives. Thus we can see that in *A Man of Parts* Lodge is engaging with the same issues and concerns as other important contemporary novelists, as well as continuing to explore questions that have interested him since his books first appeared in the 1960s. His turn to historical fiction was initially something of a surprise, but here again he is part of a trend in British fiction.

David Lodge therefore remains in the second decade of the twenty-first century, as he described himself many years earlier, a novelist at the crossroads, a writer combining a Jamesian sense of form and a Joycean sense of the writerly vocation, and a writer who followed Graham

Greene in making Catholicism a subject of enduring fictional interest. Lodge's attention to the language and comedy of everyday life links him to Kingsley Amis, while his awareness of the social significance of the minutiae of everyday life gives him an affinity with H.G. Wells, a fellow product of the suburban London lower middle class. He continues to write highly original fiction in the twenty-first century, just as he impressed reviewers in 1960 with his first novel, *The Picturegoers*. By negotiating the diverse variety of his literary influences, shifting the balance of their influence from novel to novel, while organizing them by means of a personal vision that is humane, generous, liberal, and tolerant, Lodge has consistently surprised and delighted his readers with the new directions his work has taken over his fifty-year career, producing a wonderfully rewarding oeuvre of both fiction and criticism.

Notes

CHAPTER ONE

1 References to Lodge are common in academic periodicals such as the *Chronicle of Higher Education* and *University Affairs*. See, for example, Showalter, "*Changing Places* in Changed Times," and Overall, "Academic Conferences." A reference to *Changing Places* turned up in a 2010 article on Darwinism in *American Scientist* (Thomson, "Darwin's Literary Models," 196).

2 *Changing Places*, *Small World*, and *Nice Work*, the three novels that feature Philip Swallow and Morris Zapp, have been published together as *A David Lodge Trilogy* (1993) and as *The Campus Trilogy* (2011).

3 This information was taken from the website of *The Man Booker Prizes*.

4 For example, Hilary Mantel begins a review of Lodge's *Nice Work* and Drabble's *A Natural Curiosity* with some generalizations about "the middlebrow novelist" ("England, Whose England?", 18).

5 See Bodenheimer, "*Nice Work* of Victorian Novels" for an analysis of Lodge's use of the tradition of "condition of England" writing in *Nice Work*. Lodge reflects on the changes in British higher education since the 1960s in an interview with Richard Garner that was published in the *Independent* in 2011 under the headline "A Novelist's Lament for the Golden Age of Universities."

6 For various perspectives on Modernism, including its relationship to English Catholicism, see the essays contained in Jodock, ed., *Catholicism Contending*.

7 Lodge edited 20th *Century Literary Criticism: A Reader* in 1972 and in 1988 he edited the theory textbook, *Modern Criticism and Theory: A Reader*.

8 In a discussion of his political views in his *Autobiography*, Trollope said "I consider myself to be an advanced, but still a conservative Liberal – which I regard not only as a possible but as a rational and consistent phase of political existence" (291).

9 The word "modern" is complex and sometimes confusing. I am using it in a broad sense, to refer to literature from Henry James to the 1960s. In *The Modes of Modern Writing* Lodge uses the word in a similarly inclusive sense, though he sometimes defines it more narrowly in other works.

10 Wayne Booth discusses *Emma* in similar terms in *The Rhetoric of Fiction* (242–66). Booth analyzes the balance of sympathy and judgment in Austen's handling of Emma, and notes that Emma functions "as a kind of narrator" (245), but one who is supplemented by "the dramatized author as friend and guide" (264).

11 According to Zachary Leader, Leavis's hostility was provoked not only by his view of Amis's writing, but by his objection to the way that Peterhouse College made the appointment. At a faculty meeting, Leavis is reported to have said "Peterhouse can't be expected to be taken seriously about anything now that it's given a fellowship to a *pornographer*" (*Life of Amis*, 454; italics in original).

12 Lawrence is discussed in essays in *Write On* (188–93), *The Art of Fiction* (138–41), *After Bakhtin* (57–74), and *The Practice of Writing* (98–112). The essay in *Write On*, "D.H. Lawrence: Genius, Heretic, Classic," is a reprinting of the 1985 *Guardian* piece.

13 See Spark, *Curriculum Vitae*, 205–8. Graham Greene's *Life in Letters*, ed. Richard Greene, contains nine letters to Spark, most of them responding with praise and sometimes minor criticisms when Spark had sent him her latest book. A number of times Greene compares the book he has just received to *Memento Mori*, which he considered her best novel.

14 Lodge's column "Rereading: *Memento Mori*" was published in the *Guardian* in 2010, and his review of Martin Stannard's biography of Spark appeared in the *New York Review of Books* during the same year ("Prime of Muriel Spark").

15 The essay in *The Novelist at the Crossroads* is entitled "The Uses and Abuses of Omniscience: Method and Meaning in Muriel Spark's *The Prime of Miss Jean Brodie*" (119–44). It first appeared in *Critical Quarterly*. Lodge's original review, "Human Predicaments," was published in the *Tablet*.

16 Norbert Schürer's indispensable *Annotated Bibliography* of David Lodge is exhaustive on Lodge's publications up to 1994, including minor pieces of journalism. It is thorough on secondary sources, but selective when it comes to documenting the reviews of Lodge's books.

17 There is some discussion of Lodge in Thomas Woodman's *Faithful Fictions: The Catholic Novel in British Literature*. See also Bergonzi's "Decline and Fall of the Catholic Novel" and my "Pilgrimages of David Lodge."

18 See Daniel Ammann, *David Lodge*; Bárbara Arizti, *Textuality as Striptease*; Jean-Michel Ganteau, *David Lodge*; Roberta Mullini, *Il demone della forma*; Göran Nieragden, *Figurendarstellung im Roman*; and Ingrid Pfandl-Buchegger, *David Lodge*.

19 Forty years later, in 2010, a "Lost Booker" competition was held but, regrettably to my mind, *Out of the Shelter* failed make the shortlist (see Cooke, "Lost Booker").

20 *The Anxiety of Influence* is largely comprised of six chapters devoted to the six revisionary ratios; Bloom gives a brief synopsis of them in his introduction (14–16).

21 Jauss's theory of literary history is most fully articulated in "Literary History as a Challenge to Literary Theory" (*Toward an Aesthetic*, 3–45).

CHAPTER TWO

1 A report of the lecture was published in the newsletter of the Graham Greene Birthplace Trust. In the question and answer session, the issue of Greene's influence on Lodge came up: "When asked to elaborate on Greene's influence on his own work, Professor Lodge said that he had learned from Greene '... an obligation to take pains.' We were definitely to be the beneficiaries of this as it was clear that great 'pains' had been taken to make this a closely-worked, informative lecture which both explained and elaborated on its title and was delivered with consummate professionalism. A capacity audience demonstrated this lecture had been eagerly anticipated and we were not disappointed" (Christensen, "Graham Greene," 14). "Graham Greene

and the Anxiety of Influence" was published in 2006 in *The Year of Henry James*.

2 "The Lost Childhood" inspired the publisher Max Reinhardt to bring out a new edition of *The Viper of Milan* with The Bodley Head in 1960; Reinhardt had brought Greene into the firm as a director after taking it over in 1957. See Sherry, *Life of Graham Greene*, 3:113–14; 121–2.

3 Cates Baldridge writes in *Graham Greene's Fictions*: "Greene's affinity for extremes, his hankering after absolutes, is the prime mover of his narrative art ... if Greene's response to the era he lived through is itself full of a violence and an extremity that is both attractive and repellent, then this is only indication the more that he is the century's most representative English novelist" (2).

4 The American edition of *The British Museum Is Falling Down* was published by Holt, Rinehart and Winston in 1967. The Greene quotation appears very prominently at the top of the back panel of the dust jacket, with the slight difference of a comma following the word "funny."

5 Shirley Hazzard's account of her friendship with Greene in *Greene on Capri* is revealing on the subject of Greene's engaging but sometimes difficult personality. Lodge reviewed Hazzard's book for the *New York Review of Books* ("Friendship") and tactfully excused himself from participating in a subsequent quarrel between Hazzard and Greene's longtime companion, Yvonne Cloetta, in the "Letters" column of the *New York Review*, 30 Nov. 2000: 65.

6 Shelden's biography of Greene discusses his use of modernist techniques (see *Graham Greene*, 95–102). For Greene's use of popular genres in his early work see Diemert, *Greene's Thrillers*.

7 Lodge draws attention to the influence of Hoggart in "The Limits of the Movement," *Write On*, 106; see also his comments in the introduction to *The Picturegoers*, x–xi.

8 Thomas Woodman employs a broadly inclusive definition of the genre: "I take a Catholic novel to be one that deals with specifically Catholic themes or subject matter or indeed with any themes or subject matter from a distinctively Catholic perspective and with a sufficient degree of inwardness" (*Faithful Fictions*, xi). However, he also acknowledges the existence of a "more rigorist" definition that views the Catholic novel as "a violently pessimistic work written in reaction against the humanist values of the modern world. The mode is seen as originating in the French Catholic revival of the late nineteenth century, which had

pronounced decadent overtones, and held to continue in the works of George Bernanos, François Mauriac and in this country Graham Greene" (xi).

9 Richard Griffiths comments on this same passage and on the later description of the moment of Mark's conversion (*The Pen and the Cross*, 230–1). He sees parallels with another Catholic novel, Compton Mackenzie's *The Heavenly Ladder* (1924).

10 The quotation occurs in *Graham Greene*, 23. This brief study of Greene has its origins in Lodge's MA thesis, and it was reprinted in *The Novelist at the Crossroads*, 87–118.

11 See Hoggart, "The Force of Caricature," 47–8.

12 See the section entitled "In the Thirties," *Modes of Modern Writing*, 188–212, especially 200–1.

13 Amis was commissioned to write the book on Greene for an Argentinian press (see Leader, *Kingsley Amis*, 214–15). The affair is obliquely alluded to in *Lucky Jim*, when Jim Dixon's article on medieval shipbuilding techniques is plagiarized by another scholar, who subsequently takes up a chair in Argentina.

14 Amis's review announced *The Picturegoers* as "a Catholic novel, but written without the nose-to-the-grindstone glumness, all sin and significance, that the phrase often implies" ("Insolent Chariots").

15 I am thinking of the description of Scobie and Ali being ferried across a river during a night journey: "Then at last it was the turn of the police van. They moved down the red laterite slope on to the raft, and then edged foot by foot across the dark styx-like stream towards the woods on the other side" (*Heart*, 73–4).

16 The essay "The Lives of Graham Greene" (*Practice of Writing*, 40–84) incorporates material published in a two-part article in the *New York Review of Books* (8 and 22 June 1995) and in the *Times Literary Supplement* (12 Apr. 1991). It includes an exchange with Michael Shelden from the Correspondence section of the *New York Review* (21 Sept. 1995). See also Lodge, "End of the Affair," a discussion of the third volume of Norman Sherry's life of Greene; "Friendship," a review of Shirley Hazzard's memoir of Greene; and Lodge's review of Neil Jordan's film adaptation of *The End of the Affair*, "The God Behind Great Sex." Sherry's biography is excessively long, and often rambling; Lodge describes it as "self-indulgently and often eccentrically written" ("End of the Affair"). While Shelden provides a lucid and critically intelligent one-volume biography, the usefulness of his book is undermined by its hostility towards its subject; at one point Shelden virtually

accuses Greene of an unsolved and sensational murder. Two decades after his death, an even-handed and well-organized biography of Greene remains something to be wished for in Greene scholarship.

17 In his autobiography, *A Sort of Life*, Greene wrote that if he had to choose a single epigraph for all of his novels, it would be the passage from "Bishop Blougram's Apology" containing the lines that I have quoted (115).

18 The distinction between novels and entertainments ceases to be made with the list of Greene's works at the front of *Travels with My Aunt* (1969).

19 Robert Morace notes that the scenes involving Philip Swallow and his mistress Joy are written in a stylized discourse that takes on some of the features of popular romance (*Dialogic Novels*, 198).

20 This comment was made in a talk posted on *The Martin Amis Web*, "Amis Reading." Part of the talk is a reading from Martin Amis's essay "Graham Greene," but the comment, like several of the funnier parts of the talk, does not occur in the printed version.

21 In this, he resembles Father Cyprian in Mary Gordon's *The Company of Women*, another novel that follows a group of Roman Catholics over a long span of time (and that like *How Far Can You Go?* was published in 1980): "Father Cyprian had a real thing about English converts, Felicitas thought. He was always giving her books by 'highly educated Englishwomen.' The pictures on the back would always be of women in terrible glasses whose blouses looked four sizes too big for them. Felicitas decided there were some things she didn't have to listen to Father Cyprian about. Highly educated English converts were at the top of the list" (64). In this scene in the novel, the teenaged Felicitas is reading *Quartet in Heaven*, by Sheila Kaye-Smith.

22 The epigraph comes from a passage late in *Ways of Escape* that Greene quotes in his Preface to the same work (xiii): "Writing is a form of therapy; sometimes I wonder how all those who do not write, compose or paint can manage to escape the madness, the melancholia, the panic fear which is inherent in the human situation" (237).

23 According to its website, Rules now has both a "Graham Greene Room" and a "John Betjeman Room." The Rules website also includes a negative and characteristically curmudgeonly review by Kingsley Amis ("Where Disaster Rules").

24 I discuss the representation of the Compostela pilgrimage in *Therapy* in my article "The Pilgrimages of David Lodge."

25 In the first edition of the novel, Richard Smythe has a birthmark which miraculously disappears, making a naturalistic explanation more difficult.

26 There are a number of similarities between Henry Miles in *The End of the Affair* and Bede Harrington in *Therapy*. They are both civil servants who have received the OBE for their work, and they are both represented as fussy, sometimes absurd figures who have ceased to have sexual relations with their wives. They live comfortably in suburban London, Henry Miles in Clapham and Bede Harrington in Wimbledon.

27 David Lodge reviewed Iyer's book in the *New York Review of Books* ("Heart of the Obsession").

CHAPTER THREE

1 In a brief interview with Mark Thwaite, Lodge identifies *Ulysses* as his favourite book, listing as other contenders *Emma*, *Bleak House*, *The Ambassadors*, *Heart of Darkness*, *Vile Bodies*, *The End of the Affair*, and *Lucky Jim*.

2 In a letter to Harriet Shaw Weaver (1 May 1935), Joyce said of Newman that "nobody has ever written English prose that can be compared with that of a tiresome footling little Anglican parson who afterwards became a prince of the only true church" (*Selected Letters*, 375). In *Portrait of the Artist*, Stephen thinks of "the cloistral silver-veined prose of Newman" (147–8). For a discussion of Newman and Joyce, including the influence of the *Apologia*, see Muller, "John Henry Newman and the Education of Stephen Dedalus."

3 William York Tindall, *James Joyce*, 3. Lodge writes, "It was not surprising to me to learn – from, I think, William York Tindall – that one American reader actually claimed to have been converted to Catholicism through reading Joyce's books, so accurately, tangibly, *fairly*, did he represent the Faith in them" (*Write On*, 61; italics Lodge's). Merton is mentioned briefly in Lodge's first published work, *About Catholic Authors*, 59.

4 See Ellmann, *James Joyce*, 160. Ellmann notes that in *Ulysses*, Leopold Bloom thinks of his wife Molly's urination in the same context: "Chamber music. Could make a kind of pun on that. It is a kind of music I often thought when she" (*Ulysses*, 271).

5 The discussion of James Joyce comprises the first chapter of Part Three

of the book, "Modernists, Antimodernists and Postmodernists" (*Modes*, 125–44).

6 The paper was also partially incorporated into "Mimesis and Diegesis in Modern Fiction," *After Bakhtin*, 25–44.

7 The passage is from Bakhtin's *Problems of Dostoevsky's Poetics*, 201.

8 As Bakhtin's work became available in the west, various critical factions sought to appropriate it. In the course of a discussion about how best to use Bakhtin for a Marxist critique, both Robert Young ("Back to Bakhtin") and Allon White ("The Struggle over Bakhtin") find it a problem that a "liberal Catholic such as David Lodge" (White, 218) can make use of Bakhtin's work. A liberal critic, on the other hand, may want to comment on the irony of Marxist attempts to appropriate Bakhtin, given the persecution he endured from Soviet authorities.

9 Roland Barthes distinguishes between the "writerly text," where the reader must take an active role in the production of meaning, and the "readerly text," which accords more with the norms of classic realism. See *S/Z*, 4.

10 See for example Michael Rosenthal, "Randy Roads," and Robert Towers, "Moveable Types."

11 Andrew Motion asserts that Larkin retains Yeatsian qualities after his "conversion" to the native tradition, for example, "intermittent transcendence" (*Larkin*, 141). For a discussion of the presence of Romanticism in the work of the Movement poets generally, see Michael O'Neill, "Movement Poetry and Romanticism."

12 In *Paradise News* Bernard Walsh quotes from Larkin's "This Be the Verse" (307) and Yeats's "News from the Delphic Oracle" (333–4, 339) and "Second Coming" (353); in *Therapy* Tubby Passmore quotes Larkin's "Mr Bleaney" (112); Larkin is mentioned a number of times in *Deaf Sentence*, and Desmond Bates quotes from "Days" (246) and "Aubade" (306). Lodge discusses his admiration for Larkin in the interview with Jerzy Jarniewicz, 52–3.

13 For a useful discussion of the philosophical context of the Movement, see Colin McGinn, "Philosophy and Literature in the 1950s."

14 See Norman White's *Hopkins in Ireland* for an exploration of Hopkins's poetic output during his Irish period. See also Bergonzi, "Hopkins the Englishman."

15 See Wroe, "High Priest," for a profile of Eagleton written in 2002. Wroe notes that the Irish have not always welcomed Eagleton's discussions of Irish matters, and that he was particularly ridiculed in Ireland

for the comment, in *The Gatekeeper*, that "Nobody in Ireland is called Nigel … Hardly anyone in Ireland is called Julian or Mark" (162).

16 A useful history of the conflict over the estate of Sir Hugh Lane can be found in Kelly, "The Lane Bequest." Eventually a compromise was reached between the two sides, and in 2008 for the first time all of the paintings in the bequest were exhibited in Dublin at once (see Arnold, "After 100 Years").

17 In *Finnegans Wake*, Joyce makes the seventeenth-century Italian philosopher Giordano Bruno (Bruno of Nola) into an Irishman by fusing his name with that of the Dublin bookshop Browne and Nolan. See Dibble, "A Brunonian Reading," for Bruno's importance to Joyce.

18 In an interview with Douglas Keay for *Woman's Own*, Thatcher said "If children have a problem, it is society that is at fault. There is no such thing as society. There is living tapestry of men and women and people and the beauty of that tapestry and the quality of our lives will depend upon how much each of us is prepared to take responsibility for ourselves and each of us prepared to turn round and help by our own efforts those who are unfortunate" (Thatcher, "Interview").

CHAPTER FOUR

1 Lodge argues that Amis's *I Like It Here* is about the difficulty of being committed to aesthetic and philosophical principles that are "more reliable but drabber" than those of modernism, adding "There must be few practising writers in England today who do not feel the pressure of this situation. Amis's acute awareness of the situation, his sardonic sense of the literary tradition and of the limitations of his own stance towards it, and above all his success in finding a language which articulates very exactly the temper of his generation, make him, I think, a writer of genuine literary 'importance'" (*Language*, 267). Bernard Bergonzi published a book in 1970 entitled *The Situation of the Novel*.

2 Lodge's writing on Amis includes a review of *The Old Devils* published in the *New York Review of Books* in 1987 ("Closing Time"); an obituary notice in the *Independent*, 23 Oct. 1995 ("Obituary"); a review of Leader's edition of Amis's *Letters* and Martin Amis's *Experience*, first published in the TLS in 2000 ("Putting Down Good Words") and reprinted in *Consciousness and the Novel* (182–199); and a review of Leader's *Life of Kingsley Amis* in the *New York Review of Books* in 2007 ("'Bad Behavior'").

3 For a discussion of the way that education affected social identity, see the section entitled "Scholarship Boy" in Richard Hoggart's *Uses of Literacy*, 241–52. There were far fewer scholarship girls than boys in the 1950s. Fictional accounts of northern scholarship girls who attend university in the south include Margaret Drabble's *Jerusalem the Golden* (1967) and Hilary Mantel's *An Experiment in Love* (1995). The university scenes in the latter take place in 1970.

4 In "Philosophy and Literature," Colin McGinn writes that "Lodge is surely right" about the influence of Oxford language philosophy on Amis (131); McGinn analyzes *Lucky Jim* with reference to J.L. Austin, Ludwig Wittgenstein, and others.

5 See Cameron, "Virtues of Good Prose," 149–50; see also Lodge, *Modes*, 213–14.

6 The idea of the "educated plain man" was important in twentieth-century English philosophy as well as in literary circles. McGinn writes that in the middle of the century, "Suddenly the common man began to seem like not such a bad sort of chap, once you took the trouble to get to know him. There was something bracingly down to earth about him. His time-tested workaday language came to be admired and cited" ("Philosophy and Literature," 126).

7 Bradbury questions what he calls "a somewhat unreliable orthodoxy" about post-1945 fiction in his introduction to *The Novel Today* (17). An excellent overview of recent developments in scholarship on post-1945 literature can be gained from two collections of essays, *The Movement Reconsidered*, edited by Zachary Leader, and *British Fiction after Modernism*, edited by Marina MacKay and Lyndsey Stonebridge.

8 Allsop's *The Angry Decade* (1958) is a useful guide, written when the alleged movement was in full swing. He provides a long list of the associations of the phrase "Angry Young Man": "irreverence, stridency, impatience with tradition, vigour, vulgarity, sulky resentment against the cultivated and a hard-boiled muscling-in on culture, adventurousness, self-pity, deliberate disengagement from politics, fascist ambitions, schizophrenia, rude dislike of anything phoney or fey, a broad sense of humour but low on wit, a general intellectual nihilism, honesty, a neurotic discontent and a defeated, reconciled acquiescence that is the last flimsy shelter against complete despondency" (18). Leader has a useful summary of the creation of the idea of the Angry Young Man and of Amis's response (*Life*, 358–63).

9 In a review of *Author, Author* in the *London Review of Books* in 2004, Eagleton sardonically alludes to Lodge's "suburban reasonableness" ("Living as Little").

10 "Maureen: A Memoir" takes up pages 222–58 of *Therapy*.

11 The introduction to *Howards End* is reprinted as "Forster's Flawed Masterpiece" in *Consciousness and the Novel* (135–60).

12 The phrase "pram in the hall" still turns up in literary journalism; for example, I noticed it in the *TLS* in January, 2010 (Moore, "Bodies of Work"). Connolly may have derived the image from Katherine Mansfield's story "Bliss," first published in 1918, in which one of the artistic friends of the protagonist looks at the baby perambulator and says "'This is a sad, sad fall! ... When the perambulator comes into the hall–' and he waved the rest of the quotation away" (179). I have not been able to trace a source for this "quotation" in Mansfield's story.

13 Wilde's comic swapping of baby and manuscript is paralleled by a tragic fusion of manuscript and child in Ibsen's *Hedda Gabler*, where Eilert Lövborg's destruction of his manuscript is symbolically the destruction of a child, as is made clear by both Thea Elvsted, symbolically the child's mother, and by Hedda Gabler when she burns the manuscript (Ibsen, *Hedda*, 342, 345).

14 *Therapy* is a significant departure from this pattern, since Tubby and his wife are divorced in the course of the novel.

15 This was quoted in chapter 2. Adam says that "Literature is mostly about having sex and not much about having children. Life is the other way round" (56).

16 In "Motherhood in the Novels of Margaret Drabble," Ann Rayson argues that Drabble "ushers in a new era for the woman writer in which the relationship between a mother and her children is catalytic rather than destructive. Domesticity, instead of contributing to her depression and sapping her creativity, spurs a Drabble woman to achievement" (43).

17 Lodge reviewed Drabble's first novel, *A Summer Bird-Cage*, in *The Spectator*, objecting to a pretentious blurb about how Drabble received a first at Cambridge "even though admitting to doing nothing but act at the ADC and the Arts." Lodge comments on the novel with unusual acerbity: "Miss Drabble will have to work a bit harder if her native fluency and wit are to produce anything substantial" ("Picaresque and Gawky," 504). In 1980, he reviewed *The Middle Ground* in the *Month*, saying that in this work Drabble "shows herself to be not a

neorealist (as her early work encouraged one to think), but a postmodernist. And a very skilful, subtle literary artist" ("Novel of the Middle Years," 320).

18 In *Faculty Towers*, Elaine Showalter says that "Anthony Trollope's comic masterpiece *Barchester Towers* (1857) is the great ur-narrative of academic politics" (5).

19 Bradbury discusses his own fiction in relation to other novels about the university in "Campus Fictions," where he notes that Howard Jacobson's *Coming from Behind* features an institution called "Bradbury Lodge" (330).

20 What Gekko actually says in the film is "Greed, for lack of a better word, is good" (Scene 12 of the DVD), but the simplified version is the one that has entered the popular memory, like other "famous quotations" that were never actually said. In *Therapy*, Tubby Passmore says that his therapist is such a talented persuader that "She should be working in the City of London convincing people that Greed is good" (87).

21 Blake Morrison analyzes the extent to which the Movement's anti-Americanism was a pose in "Still Going On," 24–8.

22 Morrison argues there was always an element of posture in the Movement's antimodernism ("Still Going On," 20–2). Building on a comment about Amis's style by Lorna Sage, Zachary Leader says that "Sometimes late Amis can be as orotund and impenetrable as late James, a comparison Amis would not have welcomed" (Leader, *Life*, 790).

23 Cf. "And with that he took the bloody old towser by the scruff of the neck and, by Jesus, he near throttled him" (*Ulysses*, 284). A "towser" is a large, rough dog, and here the word refers to the Citizen's "bloody mangy mongrel, Garryowen" (*Ulysses*, 283).

24 See especially the interview with Rachel Cooke, "Nice Work." Cooke writes that "Lodge knows how lucky he has been."

CHAPTER FIVE

1 The other author was W.B. Yeats, who has been important to Lodge throughout his career.

2 See Tintner, *Henry James's Legacy*, 202–24; 332–4; 414–16.

3 Shelden, *Greene*, 341–2. Although Shelden's biography of Greene is in some ways highly problematic, he does a far better job than Norman

Sherry of documenting the importance of James for Greene, who was, Shelden asserts, "his model of excellence in fiction" (341).

4 See Amis's letters to Philip Larkin of 12 June and 30 July 1950 (*Letters*, 232; 238).

5 Beerbohm's "The Guerdon" may be found in Chatman, *Later Style*, 114–16. For Lodge's review of Chatman, see "James' Later Abstractness."

6 In *Aspects of the Novel*, E.M. Forster concedes that *The Ambassadors* "becomes, within its ordained limits, most amusing" (158); Ian Watt, in an article that Lodge cites several times in *Language of Fiction*, says that "James's tone is in the last analysis ironic, comic, or better, as I shall try to suggest, humorous" ("First Paragraph," 263).

7 In 1957, R.W. Stallman made a cogent argument for identifying the nameless object as a clock ("Time and the Unnamed Article").

8 Lodge has an essay on Hemingway's story "A Clean, Well-lighted Place" in *The Novelist at the Crossroads* (184–202), a chapter on his "Cat in the Rain" in *Working with Structuralism* (17–36), and an analysis of a passage from "In Another Country" in *The Art of Fiction* (89–93). Hemingway is also discussed in a number of places in *The Modes of Modern Writing*.

9 In *The Sun Also Rises*, Jake Barnes and his friend Bill Gorton discuss the mystery of "Henry's bicycle" in the context of references to impotence (115–16), though it should be acknowledged that Bill also describes him as "a good writer" (116). Hemingway is of course troping on the celebrated "horrid even if an obscure hurt" that James describes himself as having incurred while helping to fight a fire in Newport (*Autobiography*, 415). James's account of the event is problematic, as Leon Edel demonstrates in his biography (*Life* 1:173–83). See also Eakin, "Henry James's 'Obscure Hurt.'" Tintner discusses parallels between *The Sun Also Rises* and *The Ambassadors* (*Henry James's Legacy*, 183–4).

10 Lodge discusses James's use of the word "thing" in *The Ambassadors* in *Language of Fiction*, 196–7. See also his introduction to *The Spoils of Poynton*, 15–16.

11 Michael Sherborne offers some incisive and judicious commentary on Wells's relationship with James and on *Boon* in *H.G. Wells: Another Kind of Life*, 223–4; 228–32.

12 Greene's portrayal of Pyle and his grasp of American idiom was questioned by A.J. Liebling in a very hostile review of *The Quiet American*

("A Talkative Something-or-Other"). For a reading of *The Quiet American* in the context of the Vietnam war, including a discussion of the American reception of the novel, see Whitfield, "Limited Engagement."

13 *Austerity Britain* is the title of the first volume of Kynaston's social history of modern Britain.

14 See my article "The Pilgrimages of David Lodge" for a discussion of tourism in *Paradise News* and the Compostela pilgrimage in *Therapy*.

15 The long essay "Consciousness and the Novel" originated as the Richard Ellmann lectures at Emory University, Atlanta, October 2001.

16 James, Forster, Leavis, Booth, and Kermode are among the critics of the novel discussed in Daniel Schwarz's valuable monograph *The Humanistic Heritage*, which seeks to define a "tradition of humanistic novel criticism" (2). David Lodge is mentioned once in passing in Schwarz's book, as the author of the "important *Language of Fiction*" (88).

17 Kundera has written four books of essays on fiction, the best-known of which, at least in the English-speaking world, is *The Art of the Novel*.

18 Lodge again followed a precedent established by James when he reworked his play *Home Truths* into a novella in the hope of reaching a larger audience. James had done this with two plays of his own; one became the story "Covering End" and the other was turned into the novel *The Outcry*. The novel *Thinks...*, like James's novels *The American* and *The Other House*, underwent a transformation in the opposite direction, as Lodge transformed it into the play *Secret Thoughts* in 2011.

19 Discussions of *Author, Author* and *The Master* include my "Imagining Henry"; Daniel K. Hannah, "The Private Life"; John Harvey, "Lessons of the Master"; Cora Kaplan, *Victoriana*, 62–76; Max Saunders, "Master Narratives"; and Pamela Thurschwell, "The Typist's Remains." It is noteworthy that in *All a Novelist Needs* (2010), a book collecting various pieces about James, Colm Tóibín only mentions David Lodge in passing, as though for him there was no anxiety involved at all in the competition of 2004. Of course, this silence may also be a strategic response to Lodge's extensive narrative of the history of his relationship with Tóibín in *The Year of Henry James*.

20 Lodge summarizes the first reviews of *Author, Author* in "The Year of Henry James," 84–5.

CHAPTER SIX

1 The review is included in Edel and Ray's *Henry James and H.G. Wells*, 48–52.

2 Hutcheon refers to Lodge as someone who, like Umberto Eco, is both a postmodern artist and a theorist (14), and she cites *Modes of Modern Writing* in her bibliography, but she does not refer to the earlier "Crossroads" essay.

3 Kingsley Amis was interested in popular genres, giving a seminar on science fiction at Princeton, and writing both *The James Bond Dossier* and *Colonel Sun: A James Bond Adventure*. See Leader, *Life*, 412–18, for a discussion of the science fiction seminar.

4 In an insightful and appreciative profile of Lodge in the *Sunday Times of Malta*, Ivan Callus wrote "What makes Lodge unique … is his generosity. This may be a strange thing to point out in a satirist, but the simple truth is that Lodge is being generous even when he is being punitive. It is striking that even when he is at his sharpest, he is never caustic. He has an empathetic eye and turn of phrase even for his most unspeakable characters" ("Generous Satirist").

5 *The Practice of Writing* and *The Year of Henry James* were published in hard cover by Secker and Warburg and by Harvill Secker respectively, and in paperback by Penguin, just like Lodge's novels, and although *Consciousness and the Novel* was published by an academic press, it was widely available in bookstores alongside Lodge's other works.

6 Also relevant in this context is Lodge's 1996 review of the literary magazine *Granta*'s "Best of Young American Novelists" issue. He suggests that the selections represent a resurgence of realism in American writing: "Young American novelists today are (to judge by these samples) less idiosyncratic, less experimental, and certainly less raunchy, than not only older American writers, but also their British contemporaries" (*Year of Henry James*, 292).

7 In both "The Novel Now" (131–2) and "Fact and Fiction in the Novel" (*Practice*, 26–7), Lodge draws on Lennard Davis's account in *Factual Fictions* of the birth of the novel from the journalism of the early phase of print culture. Defoe is a key figure in this aspect of literary history.

8 Heilbrun writes of the quotation, "I should look this up, and probably will not" ("Rereading to Reading," 211). The passage that she is re-

membering reads as follows: "Strange to me – in his affair – the coexistence of so much talent with so little art, so much life with (so to speak) so little living!" (qtd. in Edel and Ray, *James and Wells*, 27).

9 Lodge includes Woolf's "Modern Fiction" in his textbook 20th *Century Literary Criticism: A Reader*. It is worth noting that Margaret Drabble is the author of *Arnold Bennett: A Biography* (1974). Like Lodge, she has consciously attached herself to the tradition of English realism. She has also written a biography of Angus Wilson (1995).

10 At the time of writing, Mantel had published the first two of a projected sequence of three novels about Cromwell, *Wolf Hall* and *Bring Up the Bodies*.

11 In a review of *Wolf Hall* in the TLS, Michael Caines nicely characterizes the effect of the insistent pronominal reference as "grammatical intimacy" ("Arrange One's Face").

12 A little earlier in the novel, there is another mention of Lucy's full name: "I, Lucy Snowe, plead guiltless of that curse, an overheated and discursive imagination" (*Villette*, 12).

13 See chapter 14 of Sherborne's *H.G. Wells* (251–64) for a succinct account of Wells's historical writing and of its phenomenal success.

Works Cited

WORKS BY DAVID LODGE

Where more than one edition of a novel by David Lodge is cited, quotations in the text are from the Penguin edition unless otherwise noted.

About Catholic Authors. London: St Paul Publications, 1957.

After Bakhtin: Essays on Fiction and Criticism. London and New York: Routledge, 1990.

Afterword. *Ginger, You're Barmy* [1962], 212–8. London: Penguin, 1984.

Afterword to the revised edition. *Out of the Shelter* [1985], 273–82. London: Penguin, 1986.

Afterword to the second edition. *Language of Fiction: Essays in Criticism and Verbal Analysis of the English Novel* [1984], 286–300. London and New York: Routledge, 2002.

The Art of Fiction: Illustrated from Classic and Modern Texts. London: Penguin, 1992.

Author, Author: A Novel [2004]. London: Penguin, 2005.

"'Bad Behavior' and Kingsley Amis." *New York Review of Books* 31 May 2007.

The British Museum Is Falling Down. New York: Holt, Rinehart and Winston, 1965.

The British Museum Is Falling Down [1965]. London: Penguin, 1983.

The Campus Trilogy. London: Vintage, 2011.

"The Catholic Church and Cultural Life." *Write On: Occasional Essays '65–'85*, 32–7. London: Secker and Warburg, 1986.

"Catholic Fiction since the Oxford Movement: Its Literary Form and Religious Content." MA Thesis, University of London, 1959.

Changing Places: A Tale of Two Campuses [1975]. Harmondsworth: Penguin, 1978.

"Closing Time." Review of *The Old Devils*, by Kingsley Amis. *New York Review of Books* 26 March 1987.

Consciousness and the Novel: Connected Essays. Cambridge, MA: Harvard University Press, 2002.

A David Lodge Trilogy: Changing Places, Small World, Nice Work. London: Penguin, 1993.

Deaf Sentence [2008]. London: Penguin, 2009.

"D.H. Lawrence: Genius, Heretic, Classic." *Write On: Occasional Essays '65–'85*, 188–93. London: Secker and Warburg, 1986.

"Double Discourses: Joyce and Bakhtin." *James Joyce Broadsheet* No. 11 (June 1983): 1–2.

"The End of the Affair." Review of *The Life of Graham Greene, Volume Three: 1955–1991*, by Norman Sherry. *New York Review of Books* 2 Dec. 2004.

Evelyn Waugh. Columbia Essays on Modern Writers 58. New York and London: Columbia University Press, 1971.

Foreword. *Dangerous Edges of Graham Greene: Journeys with Saints and Sinners*. Ed. Dermot Gilvary and Darren J.N. Middleton, xi–xiv. New York and London: Continuum, 2011.

Foreword. *No Man's Land*, by Graham Greene. Ed. James Sexton, vii–xi. London: Hesperus, 2005.

"Friendship." Review of *Greene on Capri: A Memoir*, by Shirley Hazzard. *New York Review of Books* 15 June 2000.

Ginger, You're Barmy [1962]. London: Penguin, 1984.

"The God behind Great Sex." Review of *The End of the Affair*, dir. Neil Jordan. *Times Literary Supplement* 18 Feb. 2000.

Graham Greene. Columbia Essays on Modern Writers 17. New York and London: Columbia University Press, 1966.

"Graham Greene and the Anxiety of Influence." *The Year of Henry James: The Story of a Novel* [2006], 202–23. London: Penguin, 2007.

"The Heart of the Obsession." Review of *The Man within My Head*, by Pico Iyer. *New York Review of Books* 5 Apr. 2012.

"Heretic of the Heart." *Guardian* 6 Sept. 1985.

"H.G. Wells: Prophet of Free Love." *Guardian* 11 March 2011.
"The Home Front." Review of *Staring at the Sea*, by Julian Barnes. *New York Review of Books* 7 May 1987.
Home Truths: A Novella [1999]. London: Penguin, 2000.
Home Truths: A Play. London: Secker and Warburg, 1999.
How Far Can You Go? [1980]. London: Penguin, 1981.
"Human Predicaments." Review of *The Prime of Miss Jean Brodie*, by Muriel Spark. *Tablet* 11 Nov. 1961: 1083–4.
Introduction. *Lucky Jim*, by Kingsley Amis, v–xvii. London: Penguin, 1992.
Introduction. *The Picturegoers* [1960], vii–xvi. London: Penguin, 1993.
Introduction and Note on the Text. *The Spoils of Poynton*, by Henry James, 1–20. Harmondsworth: Penguin, 1987.
"James' Later Abstractness." Review of *The Later Style of Henry James*, by Seymour Chatman. *Novel: A Forum on Fiction* 7.2 (1974): 187–9.
Language of Fiction: Essays in Criticism and Verbal Analysis of the English Novel. London: Routledge and Kegan Paul, 1966.
"The Limits of the Movement." *Write On: Occasional Essays '65–'85*, 101–8. London: Secker and Warburg, 1986.
A Man of Parts. London: Harvill Secker, 2011.
Adaptation of *Martin Chuzzlewit*, by Charles Dickens. Dir. Pedr James. 6 episodes. BBC television, 7 Nov. – 12 Dec. 1994.
"Marvels and Nasty Surprises." Review of *The Stories of Muriel Spark*. *New York Times* 20 Oct. 1985.
"Memories of a Catholic Childhood." *Write On: Occasional Essays '65–'85*, 28–31. London: Secker and Warburg, 1986.
Modern Criticism and Theory: A Reader, ed. London and New York: Longman, 1988.
Modernism, Antimodernism and Postmodernism. An Inaugural Lecture Delivered in the University of Birmingham on 2 Dec. 1976. Birmingham: University of Birmingham, 1977.
"The Modern, the Contemporary, and the Importance of Being Amis." *Critical Quarterly* 5.4 (1963): 335–54.
The Modes of Modern Writing: Metaphor, Metonymy, and the Typology of Modern Literature [1977]. Chicago: University of Chicago Press, 1988.
"My Joyce." *Write On: Occasional Essays '65–'85*, 57–69. London: Secker and Warburg, 1986.
Nice Work [1988]. London: Penguin, 1989.
"The Novelist at the Crossroads." *The Novelist at the Crossroads and*

Other Essays on Fiction and Criticism, 3–34. London: Routledge and Kegan Paul, 1971.

The Novelist at the Crossroads and Other Essays on Fiction and Criticism. London: Routledge and Kegan Paul, 1971.

"The Novel Now: Theories and Practices." *Why the Novel Matters: A Postmodern Perplex Conference Issue*. Ed. Mark Spilka et al. *Novel: A Forum on Fiction* 21.2/3 (1988): 125–38.

"Novel of the Middle Years." Review of *The Middle Ground*, by Margaret Drabble. *Month* 2nd new ser. 13.9 (Sept. 1980): 319–20.

"Obituary: Sir Kingsley Amis." *Independent* 23 Oct. 1995.

Out of the Shelter. London: Macmillan, 1970.

Out of the Shelter [Revised edition 1985]. London: Penguin, 1986.

Paradise News: A Novel [1991]. London: Penguin, 1992.

"Picaresque and Gawky." Review of *A Summer Bird-Cage*, by Margaret Drabble. *Spectator* 19 Apr. 1963: 504.

The Picturegoers [1960]. London: Pan, 1962.

The Picturegoers [1960]. London: Penguin, 1993.

The Practice of Writing [1996]. New York: Penguin, 1997.

"The Prime of Muriel Spark." Review of *Muriel Spark: The Biography*, by Martin Stannard. *New York Review of Books* 19 Aug. 2010.

"Prime Spark." Review of *The Abbess of Crewe*, by Muriel Spark. *Tablet* 7 Dec. 1974: 1185.

"Putting Down Good Words." Review of *The Letters of Kingsley Amis*, by Zachary Leader, and *Experience*, by Martin Amis. *Times Literary Supplement* 26 May 2000.

"Rereading: *Memento Mori* by Muriel Spark." *Guardian* 5 June 2010.

Review of *Henry James and His Cult*, by Maxwell Geismar. *Modern Language Review* 60.1 (1965): 101–2.

Secret Thoughts: A Play for Two Actors Based on the Novel Thinks.... London: Harvill Secker, 2011.

Small World: An Academic Romance [1984]. Harmondsworth: Penguin, 1985.

"Strangers and Pilgrims." Review of *Exiles and Emigrés: Studies in Modern Literature*, by Terry Eagleton. *Tablet* 24 Oct. 1970: 1028.

Therapy: A Novel [1995]. London: Penguin, 1996.

Thinks... [2001]. New York: Penguin, 2002.

20th Century Literary Criticism: A Reader, ed. London and New York: Longman, 1972.

"The Uses and Abuses of Omniscience: Method and Meaning in Muriel

Spark's *The Prime of Miss Jean Brodie.*" *Critical Quarterly* 12.3 (1970): 235–57.

"Various Vocations." Review of *The Bachelors*, by Muriel Spark. *Tablet* 17 Dec. 1960: 1175–76.

Working with Structuralism: Essays and Reviews on Nineteenth- and Twentieth-Century Literature. Boston, London and Henley: Routledge and Kegan Paul, 1981.

Write On: Occasional Essays '65–'85. London: Secker and Warburg, 1986.

The Writing Game: A Comedy. London: Secker and Warburg, 199[illegible].

"The Year of Henry James; or, Timing is All: The Story of a Novel." *The Year of Henry James: The Story of a Novel* [2006], 3–103. London: Penguin, 2007.

The Year of Henry James: The Story of a Novel [2006]. London: Penguin, 2007.

OTHER SOURCES

Ackroyd, Peter. *Chatterton.* London: Hamish Hamilton, 1987.

– *Dickens* [1990]. Toronto: Stewart House, 1991.

– *Hawksmoor.* London: Hamish Hamilton, 1985.

– *The Last Testament of Oscar Wilde.* London: Hamish Hamilton, 1983.

Ali, Monica. "Afterword: Reading Graham Greene in the Twenty-First Century." *Dangerous Edges of Graham Greene: Journeys with Saints and Sinners.* Ed. Dermot Gilvary and Darren J.N. Middleton, 277–9. New York and London: Continuum, 2011.

– Introduction. *The End of the Affair*, by Graham Greene, vii–xvi. London: Vintage, 2004.

Allsop, Kenneth. *The Angry Decade: A Survey of the Cultural Revolt of the Nineteen-Fifties.* London: Peter Owen, 1958.

Alvarez, A. "A Joke's a Joke." Review of *A Case of Samples*, by Kingsley Amis. *Observer* 18 Nov. 1956.

Amis, Kingsley. [As Robert Markham]. *Colonel Sun: A James Bond Adventure.* New York: Harper and Row, 1968.

– "Fresh Winds from the West." *Spectator* 2 May 1958: 565–6.

– *I Like It Here.* London: Gollancz, 1958.

– "The Insolent Chariots." Review of *The Picturegoers*, by David Lodge. *Observer* 14 Aug. 1960.

– *The James Bond Dossier.* London: Jonathan Cape, 1965.

– *The Letters of Kingsley Amis*. Ed. Zachary Leader. London: HarperCollins, 2000.
– *Lucky Jim* [1954]. Intro. David Lodge. London: Penguin, 1992.
– *Memoirs*. London: Hutchinson, 1991.
– *The Old Devils*. London: Hutchinson, 1986.
– *Stanley and the Women*. London: Hutchinson, 1984.
– *That Uncertain Feeling* [1955]. New York: Harcourt, Brace, 1956.
– "Where Disaster Rules." *Rules: London's Oldest Restaurant*. Web. 9 Sept. 2011.
– "Why Lucky Jim Turned Right." *What Became of Jane Austen? And Other Questions*, 200–11. London: Jonathan Cape, 1970.
Amis, Martin. "Amis Reading His Essay 'Graham Greene.'" 27 April 2006. MP3 File. *The Martin Amis Web*. Web. 15 May 2011.
– "Graham Greene." *Visiting Mrs Nabokov and Other Excursions*, 1–7. London: Jonathan Cape, 1993.
– *Yellow Dog*. London: Jonathan Cape, 2003.
Ammann, Daniel. *David Lodge and the Art-and-Reality Novel*. Anglistische Forschungen, H. 216. Heidelberg: Universitätsverlag C. Winter, 1991.
Aristotle. *Poetics*. Trans. S.H. Butcher. *Critical Theory Since Plato*. Ed. Hazard Adams. Revised edn., 49–66. Fort Worth: Harcourt Brace Jovanovich, 1992.
Arizti, Bárbara. *Textuality as Striptease: The Discourses of Intimacy in David Lodge's* Changing Places *and* Small World. Anglo-American Studies, Vol. 20. Frankfurt: Peter Lang, 2002.
Arnold, Bruce. "After 100 Years, Lane's Collection Comes Home." *Irish Independent* 28 June 2008.
Augustine. *Confessions*. Trans. Henry Chadwick. Oxford: Oxford University Press, 1991.
Austen, Jane. *Emma*. Ed. James Kinsley and David Lodge. Oxford: Oxford University Press, 1971.
Bakhtin, Mikhail M. *Problems of Dostoevsky's Poetics*. Ed. and trans. Caryl Emerson. Theory and History of Literature, Vol. 8. Minneapolis: University of Minnesota Press, 1984.
Baldridge, Cates. *Graham Greene's Fictions: The Virtues of Extremity*. Columbia and London: University of Missouri Press, 2000.
Banville, John. "Nice Work." Review of *Therapy* and *Small World: An Academic Romance*, by David Lodge. *New York Review of Books* 10 Aug. 1995.
Barnes, Julian. *Arthur and George* [2005]. Toronto: Vintage, 2006.

– *Flaubert's Parrot* [1984]. New York: Vintage, 1990.
– *The Sense of an Ending*. Toronto: Vintage, 2011.
Barthes, Roland. *S/Z*. Trans. Richard Miller. New York: Farrar, Straus and Giroux, 1974.
Beerbohm, Max. "The Guerdon." *The Later Style of Henry James, by* Seymour Chatman. [1972], 114–16. Westport, CT: Greenwood, 1986.
– "The Mote in the Middle Distance." *A Christmas Garland*, 1–10. London: Heinemann, 1912.
Bergonzi, Bernard. "A Conversation with David Lodge." *War Poets and Other Subjects*, 201–5. Aldershot: Ashgate, 1999.
– *David Lodge*. Plymouth: Northcote, 1995.
– "The Decline and Fall of the Catholic Novel." *The Myth of Modernism and Twentieth Century Literature*, 172–87. New York: St Martins, 1986.
– *The Early H.G. Wells: A Study of the Scientific Romances*. Toronto: University of Toronto Press, 1961.
– "Hopkins the Englishman." *War Poets and Other Subjects*, 131–48. Aldershot: Ashgate, 1999.
– *Reading the Thirties: Texts and Contexts*. Pittsburgh: University of Pittsburgh Press, 1978.
– *The Situation of the Novel*. London and Basingstoke: Macmillan, 1970.
"Bibliofile" [Interview with David Lodge]. *Sunday Times* 24 May 1998.
Blair, Tony. *A Journey: My Political Life*. New York and Toronto: Knopf, 2010.
Bloom, Harold. *The Anxiety of Influence: A Theory of Poetry*. 2nd edn. New York and Oxford: Oxford University Press, 1997.
– Introduction. *Graham Greene*. Ed. Harold Bloom, 1–8. Modern Critical Views. New York: Chelsea House, 1987.
– *A Map of Misreading* [1975]. Oxford: Oxford University Press, 2003.
Bodenheimer, Rosemarie. "The *Nice Work* of Victorian Novels in Thatcher's Britain." *Victorian Turns, NeoVictorian Returns: Essays on Fiction and Culture*. Ed. Penny Gay, Judith Johnson, and Catherine Waters, 171–81. Newcastle: Cambridge Scholars, 2008.
Booth, Wayne C. *The Rhetoric of Fiction*. Chicago and London: University of Chicago Press, 1961.
Bowen, Marjorie. *The Viper of Milan: A Romance of Lombardy* [1906]. Intro. note by Graham Greene. London: Bodley Head, 1960.
Bradbury, Malcolm. "Campus Fictions." *No, Not Bloomsbury*, 329–35. New York: Columbia University Press, 1988.
– *The History Man* [1975]. London: Picador, 2000.

– Introduction. *The Novel Today: Contemporary Writers on Modern Fiction*. Ed. Malcolm Bradbury, 7–21. Manchester: Manchester University Press, 1977.
– *No, Not Bloomsbury*. New York: Columbia University Press, 1988.
– *Rates of Exchange*. London: Secker and Warburg, 1983.
– *Stepping Westward* [1965]. Harmondsworth: Penguin, 1968.
Brontë, Charlotte. *Villette* [1853]. Ed. Margaret Smith and Herbert Rosengarten. Oxford: Oxford University Press, 2000.
Brookner, Anita. "Rising Far Above Failure." Review of *Author, Author*, by David Lodge. *Spectator* 11 Sept. 2004: 45.
Burgess, Anthony. "Coketown in the 80s." Review of *Nice Work*, by David Lodge. *Observer* 18 Sept. 1988.
Caines, Michael. "Arrange One's Face." Review of *Wolf Hall*, by Hilary Mantel. *Times Literary Supplement* 15 May 2009.
Callus, Ivan. "The Generous Satirist." *Sunday Times of Malta* 7 Aug. 2011.
Cameron, Deborah. "'The Virtues of Good Prose': Verbal Hygiene and the Movement." *The Movement Reconsidered: Essays on Larkin, Amis, Gunn, Davie, and Their Contemporaries*. Ed. Zachary Leader, 139–54. Oxford: Oxford University Press, 2009.
Carlyle, Thomas. *Sartor Resartus* [1836]. Ed. Kerry McSweeney and Peter Sabor. Oxford: Oxford University Press, 1987.
Chatman, Seymour. *The Later Style of Henry James* [1972]. Westport, CT: Greenwood, 1986.
Christensen, Yan. "Graham Greene and the Anxiety of Influence: '... An Obligation to Take Pains.'" *A Sort of Newsletter: The Newsletter of the Graham Greene Birthplace Trust* (Autumn 2004): 14.
Coetzee, J.M. *The Master of Petersburg*. 1994. London: Vintage, 1999.
Connolly, Cyril. *Enemies of Promise*. 1938. Harmondsworth: Penguin, 1961.
"A Conversation with David Lodge." "*Author, Author*" *Reading Guide*. Penguin Group USA Website. 7 May 2011.
Cooke, Rachel. "The Lost Booker: A Judge Tells All." *Observer* 28 March 2010.
– "Nice Work." *Observer* 20 Apr. 2008.
Crowe, Marian E. *Aiming at Heaven, Getting the Earth: The English Catholic Novel Today*. Lanham, MD: Lexington, 2007.
Culler, Jonathan. *On Deconstruction: Theory and Criticism After Structuralism*. Ithaca: Cornell University Press, 1982.
Cunningham, Valentine. "How Tubby Got the Grail." Review of *Therapy*, by David Lodge. *Observer* 30 Apr. 1995.

Dante Alighieri. *Vita Nuova*. Trans. and ed. Mark Musa. Oxford: Oxford University Press, 1992.

Davis, Lennard J. *Factual Fictions: The Origins of the English Novel*. New York: Columbia University Press, 1983.

Derbyshire, Jonathan. "A Conversation with David Lodge." *Jonathan Derbyshire: Politics, Philosophy, Culture*. Web. 15 Oct. 2004.

Dibble, Brian. "A Brunonian Reading of Joyce's *A Portrait of the Artist*." *James Joyce Quarterly* 4.4 (1967): 280–5.

Diemert, Brian. *Graham Greene's Thrillers and the 1930s*. Montreal and Kingston: McGill-Queen's University Press, 1996.

Drabble, Margaret. *Angus Wilson: A Biography*. London: Secker and Warburg, 1995.

– *Arnold Bennett: A Biography*. London: Weidenfeld and Nicolson, 1974.

– *The Garrick Year* [1964]. Harmondsworth: Penguin, 1966.

– *The Ice Age* [1977]. Harmondsworth: Penguin, 1978.

– "I Loathe America, and What It Has Done to the Rest of the World." *Telegraph* 8 May 2003.

– *Jerusalem the Golden* [1967]. Harmondsworth: Penguin, 1969.

– *The Millstone* [1965]. Harmondsworth: Penguin, 1968.

– ed. *The Oxford Companion to English Literature*. 5th edn. revised. Oxford: Oxford University Press, 1995.

– *The Pattern in the Carpet: A Personal History with Jigsaws*. London: Atlantic, 2009.

– *The Radiant Way: A Novel*. Toronto: McClelland and Stewart, 1987.

– *The Realms of Gold* [1975]. Harmondsworth: Penguin, 1977.

– *The Waterfall* [1969]. London: Penguin, 1971.

– *A Writer's Britain* [1979]. New York: Thames and Hudson, 2009.

Duncan, Alistair. "Interview with David Lodge." *Oxford Times* 24 March 2011.

Eagleton, Terry. *The Gatekeeper: A Memoir* [2001]. New York: St Martin's, 2002.

– *Literary Theory: An Introduction*. Oxford: Blackwell, 1983.

– "Living as Little as Possible." Review of *Author, Author*, by David Lodge. *London Review of Books* 23 Sept. 2004.

– "The Silences of David Lodge." *New Left Review* 172 (Nov.–Dec. 1988): 93–102.

Eakin, John Paul. "Henry James's 'Obscure Hurt': Can Autobiography Serve Biography?" *New Literary History* 19.3 (1988): 675–92.

Edel, Leon. *The Life of Henry James*. 5 vols. 1953–72. New York: Avon, 1978.

Edel, Leon and Gordon N. Ray, eds. *Henry James and H.G. Wells: A Record of Their Friendship, Their Debate on the Art of Fiction, and Their Quarrel*. Urbana: University of Illinois Press, 1958.

Eliot, T.S. "*Ulysses*, Order, and Myth" [1923]. *Selected Prose of T.S. Eliot*. Ed. Frank Kermode, 175–8. London: Faber and Faber, 1975.

Ellmann, Richard. *James Joyce*. Oxford: Oxford University Press, 1959.

FitzHerbert, Claudia. Review of *A Man of Parts*, by David Lodge. *Telegraph* 25 March 2011.

Forster, E.M. *Aspects of the Novel* [1927]. Harmondsworth: Penguin, 1962.

– *Howards End* [1910]. Introduction and Notes by David Lodge. New York: Penguin, 2000.

Fowles, John. *The French Lieutenant's Woman*. London: Jonathan Cape, 1969.

Fussell, Edwin Sill. *The Catholic Side of Henry James*. Cambridge: Cambridge University Press, 1993.

Ganteau, Jean-Michel. *David Lodge: Le Choix de l'Éloquence*. Pessac: Presses Universitaires de Bordeaux, 2001.

Garner, Richard. "David Lodge: A Novelist's Lament for the Golden Age of Universities." *Independent* 28 March 2011.

Geismar, Maxwell. *Henry James and the Jacobites*. Boston: Houghton Mifflin, 1963.

Gordon, Mary. *The Company of Women*. New York: Random House, 1980.

Greene, Graham. *Brighton Rock* [1938]. Harmondsworth: Penguin, 1970.

– *A Burnt-Out Case* [1960]. Harmondsworth: Penguin, 1963.

– *Collected Essays*. London: Bodley Head, 1969.

– *The Comedians* [1966]. London: Vintage, 1999.

– *The Confidential Agent* [1939]. Harmondsworth: Penguin, 1963.

– *The End of the Affair* [1951]. London: Vintage, 2004.

– *Graham Greene: A Life in Letters*. Ed. Richard Greene. Toronto: Knopf, 2007.

– *A Gun for Sale* [1936]. London: Heinemann, 1947.

– *The Heart of the Matter* [1948]. London: Vintage, 2004.

– *Monsignor Quixote* [1982]. London: Vintage, 2000.

– *The Name of Action*. London: Heinemann, 1930.

– *No Man's Land*. Ed. James Sexton. London: Hesperus, 2005.

– *Our Man in Havana: An Entertainment* [1958]. Harmondsworth: Penguin, 1962.

– *The Power and the Glory* [1940]. London: Vintage, 2001.
– *The Quiet American* [1955]. London: Penguin, 1974.
– *Rumour at Nightfall*. London: Heinemann, 1931.
– *A Sort of Life*. London: Bodley Head, 1971.
– *Travels with My Aunt*. London: Bodley Head, 1969.
– *Ways of Escape*. Toronto: Lester and Orpen Dennys, 1980.
Griffiths, Richard. *The Pen and the Cross: Catholicism and English Literature, 1850–2000*. London: Continuum, 2010.
Guignery, Vanessa. "David Lodge's *Author, Author* and the Genre of the Biographical Novel." *Études Anglaises* 60.2 (2007): 160–72.
Haffenden, John. Interview with David Lodge. *Novelists in Interview*, 145–67. London and New York: Methuen, 1985.
Hannah, Daniel K. "The Private Life, The Public Stage: Henry James in Recent Fiction." *jml: Journal of Modern Literature* 30.3 (2007): 70–94.
Harvey, John. "Lessons of the Master: The Henry James Novel." *Yearbook of English Studies* 37.1 (2007): 75–88.
Hazzard, Shirley. *Greene on Capri: A Memoir*. New York: Farrar, Straus and Giroux, 2000.
Hebert, Hugh. "The Signs of Love and Laughter." *Guardian* 19 March 1984.
Heilbrun, Carolyn G. "Guest Column: From Rereading to Reading." *PMLA* 119.2 (2004): 211–17.
Hemingway, Ernest. *The Sun Also Rises*. New York: Scribner's, 1926.
Hitchens, Christopher. "The Final Curtain." Review of *Author, Author*, by David Lodge. *Washington Post* 7 Nov. 2004.
Hoggart, Richard. "The Force of Caricature: Aspects of the Art of Graham Greene" [1953]. *About Literature*, 40–55. Vol. 2 of *Speaking to Each Other: Essays*. London: Chatto and Windus, 1970.
– *The Uses of Literacy: Aspects of Working Class Life with Special Reference to Publications and Entertainments* [1957]. Harmondsworth: Penguin, 1958.
Hopkins, Gerard Manley. *Further Letters of Gerard Manley Hopkins, Including His Correspondence with Coventry Patmore*. Ed. Claude Colleer Abbott. London: Oxford University Press, 1938.
– *A Hopkins Reader*. Ed. John Pick. London: Oxford University Press, 1953.
Howard, Philip. Review of *Changing Places*, by David Lodge. *Times* 13 Feb. 1975.
Hutcheon, Linda. *A Poetics of Postmodernism: History, Theory, Fiction*. New York and London: Routledge, 1988.

Ibsen, Henrik. *Hedda Gabler and Other Plays*. Trans. Una Ellis-Fermor. Harmondsworth: Penguin, 1961.

Iyer, Pico. *The Man within My Head*. Toronto: Knopf, 2012.

James, Henry. *The Ambassadors* [1903]. Ed. Christopher Butler. Oxford: Oxford University Press, 1985.

– "The Art of Fiction." *Literary Criticism: Essays on Literature, American Writers, English Writers*, 44–65. New York: Library of America, 1984.

– "The Aspern Papers." *Complete Stories 1884–1891*, 228–320. New York: Library of America, 1999.

– *Autobiography*. Ed. Frederick W. Dupee. New York: Criterion, 1956.

– "Crapy Cornelia." *Complete Stories 1898–1910*, 818–46. New York: Library of America, 1996.

– *Daisy Miller: A Study* [1879]. Ed. David Lodge. London: Penguin, 2007.

– *The Europeans* [1878]. Ed. Ian Campbell Ross. Oxford: Oxford University Press, 1985.

– *The Golden Bowl* [1904]. Ed. Virginia Llewellyn Smith. Oxford: Oxford University Press, 1983.

– A London Life *and* The Reverberator [1888]. Ed. Philip Horne. Oxford: Oxford University Press, 1989.

– *The Portrait of a Lady* [1881]. Ed. Geoffrey Moore. Harmondsworth: Penguin, 1984.

– Preface to *Roderick Hudson*. *Literary Criticism: French Writers, Other European Writers, The Prefaces to the New York Edition*, 1039–52. New York: Library of America, 1984.

– *The Spoils of Poynton* [1897]. Ed. David Lodge. Harmondsworth: Penguin, 1987.

– *What Maisie Knew* [1897]. Ed. Paul Theroux. Harmondsworth: Penguin, 1985.

– *The Wings of the Dove* [1902]. Ed. Peter Brooks. Oxford: Oxford University Press, 1984.

Jameson, Fredric. *The Political Unconscious: Narrative as a Socially Symbolic Act*. Ithaca: Cornell University Press, 1981.

Jarniewicz, Jerzy [and Craig Raine]. "An Interview with David Lodge." *Areté: The Arts Tri-Quarterly* 5 (Spring/Summer 2001): 47–64.

Jauss, Hans Robert. *Toward an Aesthetic of Reception*. Trans. Timothy Bahti. Theory and History of Literature, Vol. 2. Minneapolis: University of Minnesota Press, 1982.

Jennings, Elizabeth. "New Novels." Review of *The Picturegoers*, by David Lodge. *Listener* 18 Aug. 1960: 273.

Jodock, Darrell, ed. *Catholicism Contending with Modernity: Roman Catholic Modernism and Anti-Modernism in Historical Context*. Cambridge and New York: Cambridge University Press, 2000.

Johnson, Samuel. From "Preface to Shakespeare." *Critical Theory since Plato*. Ed. Hazard Adams. Revised edn., 320–7. Fort Worth: Harcourt Brace Jovanovich, 1992.

Johnston, Wayne. *The Colony of Unrequited Dreams*. Toronto: Knopf, 1998.

Joyce, James. *Dubliners* [1914]. Ed. Jeri Johnson. Oxford: Oxford University Press, 2000.

– *Finnegans Wake*. London: Faber and Faber, 1939.

– *A Portrait of the Artist as a Young Man* [1916]. Ed. Jeri Johnson. Oxford: Oxford University Press, 2000.

– *Selected Letters of James Joyce*. Ed. Richard Ellmann. London: Faber and Faber, 1975.

– *Ulysses* [1922]. Ed. Jeri Johnson. Oxford: Oxford University Press, 1993.

Kaplan, Cora. *Victoriana: Histories, Fictions, Criticism*. Edinburgh: Edinburgh University Press, 2007.

Kelly, Anne. "The Lane Bequest: A British-Irish Cultural Conflict Revisited." *Journal of the History of Collections* 16.1 (2004): 89–110.

Kermode, Frank. *The Sense of an Ending: Studies in the Theory of Fiction*. New York: Oxford University Press, 1967.

Kerridge, Jake. "A Page in the Life: David Lodge." *Telegraph* 21 Apr. 2011.

Kundera, Milan. *The Art of the Novel*. Trans. Linda Asher. New York: Harper and Row, 1988.

Kynaston, David. *Austerity Britain, 1945–1951*. London: Bloomsbury, 2007.

Lane, Anthony. "Hack Work." *New Yorker* 1 Aug. 2011: 24–30.

Larkin, Philip. *Collected Poems*. Ed. Anthony Thwaite. London: Marvell Press and Faber and Faber, 2003.

– *The Less Deceived: Poems*. Hessle, East Yorkshire: Marvell Press, 1955.

– *Letters to Monica*. Ed. Anthony Thwaite. London: Faber and Faber, 2010.

– *The North Ship* [1945]. London: Faber and Faber, 1966.

– ed. *The Oxford Book of Twentieth-Century English Verse*. Oxford: Clarendon, 1973.

– *Selected Letters of Philip Larkin, 1940–1985*. Ed. Anthony Thwaite. London: Faber and Faber, 1992.

Lawson, Mark. "Always Connect." *Guardian*. 19 May 1995.
– Introduction. *The British Museum Is Falling Down*, v–x. Penguin Decades Edition. London: Penguin, 2010.
Leader, Zachary. *The Life of Kingsley Amis*. New York: Pantheon, 2006.
– ed. *The Movement Reconsidered: Essays on Larkin, Amis, Gunn, Davie, and Their Contemporaries*. Oxford: Oxford University Press, 2009.
Leavis, F.R. *D.H. Lawrence: Novelist* [1955]. Harmondsworth: Penguin, 1964.
– *The Great Tradition: George Eliot, Henry James, Joseph Conrad* [1948]. Harmondsworth: Penguin, 1962.
Leavis, Q.D. *Fiction and the Reading Public* [1932]. London: Chatto and Windus, 1965.
Le Carré, John. *Our Kind of Traitor*. London: Penguin, 2010.
Lenoski, Daniel S. "*How Far Can You Go?* to *Therapy*: Catholicism and Postmodernism in the Novels of David Lodge." *Between Human and Divine: The Catholic Vision in Contemporary Literature*. Ed. Mary R. Reichardt, 32–49. Washington, DC: Catholic University of America Press, 2010.
Liebling, A.J. "A Talkative Something-or-Other." Review of *The Quiet American*, by Graham Greene. *New Yorker* 7 Apr. 1956: 136–42.
"Literary Titan Gained Popularity and Acclaim." Obituary for Graham Greene. *Globe and Mail*, 4 Apr. 1991.
Llewellyn, Julia. "Bad Reviews Spoil My Lunch." *Telegraph*, 23 Aug. 2004.
Londe, Greg. "Reconsidering *Lucky Jim*: Kingsley Amis and the Condition of England." *British Fiction after Modernism: The Novel at Mid-Century*. Ed. Marina MacKay and Lyndsey Stonebridge, 131–44. Houndmills, Basingstoke: Palgrave Macmillan, 2007.
Lubbock, Percy. *The Craft of Fiction* [1921]. London: Jonathan Cape, 1954.
Lukács, Georg. *The Historical Novel*. Trans. Hannah and Stanley Mitchell [1962]. Harmondsworth: Penguin, 1969.
MacKay, Marina, and Lyndsey Stonebridge, eds. *British Fiction after Modernism: The Novel at Mid-Century*. Houndmills, Basingstoke: Palgrave Macmillan, 2007.
MacMonagle, Niall, ed. *Lifelines: An Anthology of Poems Chosen by Famous People*. London: Penguin, 1993.
The Man Booker Prizes. Web. 5 Jan. 2012.
Mansfield, Katherine. "Bliss." *Selected Stories*. Ed. Angela Smith, 174–85. Oxford: Oxford University Press, 2002.

Mantel, Hilary. *Bring Up the Bodies*. Toronto: HarperCollins, 2012.
– "England, Whose England?" Review of *A Natural Curiosity*, by Margaret Drabble and *Nice Work*, by David Lodge. *New York Review of Books* 23 Nov. 1989.
– *An Experiment in Love* [1995]. New York: Henry Holt, 1996.
– *A Place of Greater Safety*. New York: Henry Holt, 1992.
– *Wolf Hall*. Toronto: HarperCollins, 2009.
Mars-Jones, Adam. "James the Second." Review of *Author, Author*, by Henry James. *Observer* 12 Sept. 2004.
– Review of *A Man of Parts*, by David Lodge. *Observer* 17 Apr. 2011.
Martin, Bruce K. *David Lodge*. Twayne's English Authors 553. New York: Twayne, 1999.
Maschler, Tom, ed. *Declaration*. London: MacGibbon and Kee, 1957.
McEwan, Ian. *Saturday*. London: Jonathan Cape, 2005.
McGinn, Colin. "Philosophy and Literature in the 1950s: The Rise of the 'Ordinary Bloke.'" *The Movement Reconsidered: Essays on Larkin, Amis, Gunn, Davie, and Their Contemporaries*. Ed. Zachary Leader, 123–38. Oxford: Oxford University Press, 2009.
Merton, Thomas. *The Seven Storey Mountain* [1948]. New York and London: Harcourt Brace Jovanovich, 1978.
Moore, Wendy. "Bodies of Work." Review of *The Life and Poems of Anne Hunter*, by Caroline Grigson. *Times Literary Supplement* 15 Jan. 2010.
Morace, Robert A. *The Dialogic Novels of Malcolm Bradbury and David Lodge*. Carbondale and Edwardsville: Southern Illinois University Press, 1989.
Morrison, Blake. Review of *A Man of Parts*, by David Lodge. *Guardian* 9 Apr. 2011.
– "'Still Going On, All of It,': The Movement in the 1950s and the Movement Today." *The Movement Reconsidered: Essays on Larkin, Amis, Gunn, Davie, and Their Contemporaries*. Ed. Zachary Leader, 16–33. Oxford: Oxford University Press, 2009.
Moseley, Merritt. *David Lodge: How Far Can You Go?* San Bernardino, CA: Borgo, 1991.
Motion, Andrew. *Philip Larkin: A Writer's Life*. London: Faber and Faber, 1993.
Muller, Jill. "John Henry Newman and the Education of Stephen Dedalus." *James Joyce Quarterly* 33.4 (1996): 593–603.
Mullini, Roberta. *Il demone della forma: Intorno ai romanzi di David Lodge*. Imola: Mandragora, 2001.

Newman, John Henry. *Apologia Pro Vita Sua* [1864]. Ed. Ian Ker. London: Penguin, 1994.
Nieragden, Göran. *Figurendarstellung im Roman: Eine narratologische Systematik am Beispiel von David Lodges* Changing Places *und Ian McEwans* The Child in Time. Horizonte: Studien zu Texten der europäischen Moderne, Bd. 18. Trier: WVT Wissenschaftliche Verlag, 1995.
Oates, Joyce Carol. "Hot-Blooded Brits." Rev. of *Thinks…*, by David Lodge. *Times Literary Supplement* 23 Feb. 2001.
O'Neill, Michael. "'Fond of What He's Crapping On': Movement Poetry and Romanticism." *The Movement Reconsidered: Essays on Larkin, Amis, Gunn, Davie, and Their Contemporaries*. Ed. Zachary Leader, 270–91. Oxford: Oxford University Press, 2009.
Osborne, John. *Look Back in Anger* [1957]. London: Penguin, 1982.
Overall, Christine. "Academic Conferences, Hate'em or Love'em." *University Affairs* March 2011: 40.
Perkin, J. Russell. "Imagining Henry: Henry James as a Fictional Character in Colm Tóibín's *The Master* and David Lodge's *Author, Author*." *jml: Journal of Modern Literature* 33.2 (2010): 114–30.
– "The Pilgrimages of David Lodge." *Christianity and Literature* 57.3 (2008): 419–42.
Pfandl-Buchegger, Ingrid. *David Lodge als Literaturkritiker, Theoretiker und Romanautor*. Anglistische Forschungen, H. 222. Heidelberg: Universitätsverlag C. Winter, 1993.
Pritchard, William H. "Appreciating Kingsley Amis." *Critical Essays on Kingsley Amis*. Ed. Robert H. Bell, 103–10. New York: G.K. Hall, 1998.
Rayson, Ann. "Motherhood in the Novels of Margaret Drabble." *Frontiers: A Journal of Women Studies* 3.2 (1978): 43–6.
Ricks, Christopher. *The Force of Poetry*. Oxford: Clarendon, 1984.
Rosenthal, Michael. "Randy Roads of the Professoriat." Review of *Small World*, by David Lodge. *New York Times Book Review* 17 March 1985.
Roth, Philip. *Letting Go* [1962]. *Novels and Stories 1959–62*, 227–894. New York: Library of America, 2005.
Rules: London's Oldest Restaurant. Web. 9 Sept. 2011.
Saunders, Max. "Master Narratives." *Cambridge Quarterly* 37.1 (2008): 121–31.
Schürer, Norbert. *David Lodge: An Annotated Primary and Secondary Bibliography*. Frankfurt: Peter Lang, 1995.
Schwarz, Daniel R. *The Humanistic Heritage: Critical Theories of the English Novel from James to Hillis Miller*. Houndmills, Basingstoke: Macmillan, 1986.

Shaffer, Brian W., ed. *A Companion to the British and Irish Novel 1945–2000*. Malden, MA and Oxford: Blackwell, 2005.
Shelden, Michael. *Graham Greene: The Man Within*. London: Heinemann, 1994.
Sherborne, Michael. *H.G. Wells: Another Kind of Life*. London and Chester Springs, PA: Peter Owen, 2010.
Sherry, Norman. *The Life of Graham Greene*. 3 vols. London: Jonathan Cape, 1989–2004.
Showalter, Elaine. "*Changing Places* in Changed Times." *Chronicle of Higher Education* 55.3 (2008): B4-5.
– *Faculty Towers: The Academic Novel and Its Discontents*. Philadelphia: University of Pennsylvania Press, 2005.
– *A Literature of Their Own: British Women Novelists from Brontë to Lessing*. Princeton: Princeton University Press, 1977.
Smith, Zadie. Introduction to *The Quiet American*, by Graham Greene, vii–xiii. London: Vintage, 2004.
Snow, C.P. *The Masters* [1951]. Harmondsworth: Penguin, 1956.
– *The Two Cultures*. London and New York: Cambridge University Press, 1993.
Spark, Muriel. *The Ballad of Peckham Rye* [1960]. London: Penguin, 1999.
– *The Comforters* [1957]. London: Penguin, 1963.
– *Curriculum Vitae: Autobiography*. Boston and New York: Houghton Mifflin, 1993.
– *The Prime of Miss Jean Brodie* [1961]. London: Penguin, 2000.
Spielberg, Steven, dir. *Minority Report* [2002]. Dreamworks, 2003. DVD.
– *War of the Worlds* [2005]. Dreamworks, 2005. DVD.
Spilka, Mark et al., eds. *Why the Novel Matters: A Postmodern Perplex Conference Issue. Novel: A Forum on Fiction* 21.2/3 (1988).
Stallman, R.W. "Time and the Unnamed Article in *The Ambassadors*." *Modern Language Notes* 72.1 (1957): 27–32.
Stovel, Bruce. "Traditional Comedy and the Comic Mask in Kingsley Amis's *Lucky Jim*." *Critical Essays on Kingsley Amis*. Ed. Robert H. Bell, 158–69. New York: G.K. Hall, 1998.
Strout, Cushing. "Border Country: Novelist or Biographer?" *Sewanee Review* 113.2 (2005): xxxii–xxxiv, xxxvi.
Swift, Graham. *Wish You Were Here*. Toronto: Vintage, 2011.
Taylor, D.J. *After the War: The Novel and English Society since 1945*. London: Chatto and Windus, 1993.
Taylor, Kate. "Truth, Lies and Historical Fiction: How Far Can an Author Go?" *Globe and Mail* 12 Nov. 2011.

Tennyson, Alfred. *In Memoriam*. Ed. Susan Shatto and Marion Shaw. Oxford: Clarendon, 1982.

Thatcher, Margaret. "Interview for *Woman's Own* ('No Such Thing as Society')." 23 Sept. 1987. *Margaret Thatcher Foundation*. Web. 14 June 2011.

The Third Man. Screenplay by Graham Greene. Dir. Carol Reed [1949]. Criterion Collection, 1999. DVD.

Thompson, E.P. *The Making of the English Working Class*. London: Victor Gollancz, 1963.

Thomson, Keith. "Darwin's Literary Models." *American Scientist* (May–June 2010): 196–9.

Thurber, James. "The Beast in the Dingle." *The Beast in Me and Other Animals: A New Collection of Pieces and Drawings about Human Beings and Less Alarming Creatures*, 128–48. New York: Harcourt Brace, 1948.

Thurschwell, Pamela. "The Typist's Remains: Theodora Bosanquet in Recent Fiction." *Henry James Review* 32 (2011): 1–11.

Thwaite, Anthony. "Curtains for a Dramatist." Review of *Author, Author*, by David Lodge. *Daily Telegraph* 6 Sept. 2004.

Thwaite, Mark. "Interview with David Lodge." 19 June 2009. *The Book Depository*. Web. 27 Jan. 2010.

Tindall, William York. *James Joyce: His Way of Interpreting the Modern World* [1950]. Westport, CT: Greenwood, 1979.

Tintner, Adeline R. *Henry James's Legacy: The Afterlife of His Figure and Fiction*. Baton Rouge: Louisiana State University Press, 1998.

Tóibín, Colm. *All a Novelist Needs: Colm Tóibín on Henry James*. Ed. Susan M. Griffin. Baltimore: Johns Hopkins University Press, 2010.

– *The Master*. Toronto: McClelland and Stewart, 2004.

Tonkin, Boyd. "David Lodge: Artist in the Goldfish Bowl." *Independent* 27 Aug. 2004.

Towers, Robert. "Moveable Types." Review of *Small World*, by David Lodge, *Later the Same Day*, by Grace Paley, and *Self-Help*, by Lorrie Moore. *New York Review of Books* 15 Aug. 1985.

Trollope, Anthony. *An Autobiography*. Ed. Michael Sadleir and Frederick Page. Oxford: Oxford University Press, 1980.

Turner, Jenny. "Words Never Fail Him." *Guardian* 29 Apr. 1995.

Updike, John. "Jake and Lolly Opt Out." *Critical Essays on Kingsley Amis*. Ed. Robert H. Bell, 293–5. New York: G.K. Hall, 1998.

Vianu, Lidia. "Interview with David Lodge" [2001]. *Desperado Literature*. Web. 15 May 2011.

Wall Street. Dir. Oliver Stone [1987]. Twentieth Century Fox. 2000. DVD.
Watt, Ian. "The First Paragraph of *The Ambassadors*: An Explication." *Essays in Criticism* 10.3 (1960): 250–74.
Waugh, Evelyn. *Brideshead Revisited: The Sacred and Profane Memories of Captain Charles Ryder* [1945]. Harmondsworth: Penguin, 1962.
Wells, H.G. *Ann Veronica* [1909]. Ed. Sita Schütt. London: Penguin, 2005.
– *Boon, The Mind of the Race, The Wild Asses of the Devil, and The Last Trump*. London: Fisher Unwin, 1915.
– *Experiment in Autobiography: Discoveries and Conclusions of a Very Ordinary Brain (Since 1866)*. New York: Macmillan, 1934.
– *H.G. Wells in Love: Postscript to an Experiment in Autobiography*. Ed. G.P. Wells [1984]. London: Faber and Faber, 2008.
– *Kipps: The Story of a Simple Soul* [1905]. Ed. Simon James. Intro. David Lodge. London: Penguin, 2005.
– *The Time Machine* [1895]. Ed. Patrick Parrinder. London: Penguin, 2005.
– *Tono-Bungay* [1909]. Ed. Patrick Parrinder. London: Penguin, 2005.
– *The War of the Worlds* [1898]. Ed. Patrick Parrinder. London: Penguin, 2005.
White, Allon. "The Struggle over Bakhtin: Fraternal Reply to Robert Young." *Cultural Critique* 8 (1987–8): 217–41.
White, Norman. *Hopkins in Ireland*. Dublin: University College Dublin Press, 2002.
Whitfield, Stephen J. "Limited Engagement: *The Quiet American* as History." *Journal of American Studies* 30 (1996): 65–86.
Wicker, Brian. "Sex, an Academic Question." Review of *The British Museum Is Falling Down*, by David Lodge. *Guardian* 9 Dec. 1965.
Widdowson, Peter. "The Anti-History Men: Malcolm Bradbury and David Lodge." *Critical Quarterly* 26.4 (1984): 5–32.
Wilde, Oscar. *The Importance of Being Earnest and Other Plays*. Ed. Peter Raby. Oxford: Oxford University Press, 1995.
Wilson, Colin. *The Outsider*. London: Victor Gollancz, 1956.
"The Windup Session: Discussion." *Why the Novel Matters: A Postmodern Perplex Conference Issue*. Ed. Mark Spilka et al. *Novel: A Forum on Fiction* 21.2/3 (1988): 345–59.
Womack, Kenneth. "Academic Satire: The Campus Novel in Context." *A Companion to the British and Irish Novel 1945–2000*. Ed. Brian W. Shaffer, 326–39. Malden, MA and Oxford: Blackwell, 2005.
Wood, James. *How Fiction Works*. New York: Farrar, Straus and Giroux, 2008.

– "The Spoils." Review of *Author, Author*, by David Lodge. *New Republic* 18 Oct. 2004.
Woodman, Thomas. *Faithful Fictions: The Catholic Novel in British Literature*. Milton Keynes: Open University Press, 1991.
Woolf, Virginia. "Modern Fiction." *Collected Essays*. Vol. 2, 103–10. London: Hogarth Press, 1966.
– *A Room of One's Own; Three Guineas*. Ed. Morag Schiach. Oxford: Oxford University Press, 1992.
Wroe, Nicholas. "High Priest of Lit Crit." *Guardian* 2 Feb. 2002.
– "Seriously Funny." *Guardian* 24 Feb. 2001.
Yeats, W.B. "Easter 1916." *The Collected Poems of W.B. Yeats*. 2nd edn., 202–5. London: Macmillan, 1950.
– *A Vision* [1925]. New York: Macmillan, 1961.
Young, Robert. "Back to Bakhtin." *Cultural Critique* 2 (1985–6): 71–92.

Index